Education and Training 14–19: Continuity and Diversity in the Curriculum

Editor: Harry Tomlinson

LONGMAN

in association with the
British Educational Management and
Administration Society

Longman Group UK Limited
Westgate House, The High, Harlow, Essex, CM20 1YR
Telephone Harlow (0279) 442601
Telex 81491 Padlog
Facsimile (0279) 444501

ISBN 0-582-09105-5

A catalogue record for this publication is available from the
British Library

Typeset in Plantin 10 on 11pt by
The Midlands Book Typesetting Company

Printed and bound in Great Britain by
Dotesios Ltd, Trowbridge, Wiltshire.

Contents

Contributors

After leaving St Catherine's College, Oxford with a degree in English **John Braithwaite** took up a teaching career. This he pursued in Birmingham, Wilmslow and Stockport, where he was Deputy Headteacher at Marple Ridge High School. From there he went into the Education Advisory Service in Stockport as Secondary Schools Adviser, and at the time of writing he had just retired from the post of Senior Tertiary Adviser.

Jenny Cronin is Head of Curriculum Development Agency at Stockport College. She has previously been involved in post-16 curriculum development initiatives in FE Colleges and across Avon LEA, particularly in relation to modularisation, credit accumulation and credit transfer, and assessment and accreditation of prior learning spanning FE and HE curricula.

Malcolm Deere was successively Vice Principal and then Principal of two large Colleges of Further Education. He joined the TVEI Unit of the Manpower Services Commission at the outset as Education Adviser. Initially he worked regionally, and then exclusively and nationally on post-16 matters. Since 1988 he has been Secretary of the Standing Conference on University Entrance at the Committee of Vice Chancellors and Principals, and since 1989 Joint Secretary of the CNAA/CVCP Access Courses Recognition Group. He was a member of the SEAC Working Party on Principles for GCE Advanced Level. He is currently concerned with a range of developments in the 16–19 curriculum.

John Dunford is Head of Durham Johnston Comprehensive School, an 11–18 school with 250 students in the sixth form. He is chair of the 16–19 Forum in County Durham, a body through which school Heads and college Principals work together. He is an executive member of the Secondary Heads' Association and chair of its 16–19 Education Committee. He is on the Board of the Information Centre for State Schools and is a member of the Council of Durham University. He has written on a wide range of curriculum and education management issues and has a particular interest in school inspection from Matthew Arnold to Ofsted.

Dr Joseph Dunning, CBE, MSc, MEd, DEd, was Principal of Cleveland Technical College from 1956–63 when he came to Edinburgh to open Napier College (now Napier University). He was Principal there until retiring in 1981. He chaired the Committee on Assessment which produced the Dunning Report, and many other committees.

Dick Evans is Principal, Stockport College. He has a wide range of interests in education and training. He is chair of ASE post-16 Science Committee and served on the Royal Society's 'Beyond GCSE' and 'HE' study groups and the Technology Education Project chaired by Monty Finniston.

After a career in teaching, teacher-training and educational administration in Scotland, **Professor Duncan G. Graham**, CBE, MA, FRSA, became County Education Officer for Suffolk in 1979. While there he was responsible for the developments which put the County in the forefront of curriculum development and quality assurance. He served on the Burnham Committee as a Chairman of two National Working Parties — Mathematics and Teacher Appraisal, and as an Adviser to the Association of County Councils. From 1987–88 he was Chief Executive of Humberside County Council, and from 1988–91 Chairman and Chief Executive of the National Curriculum Council. He is now an author and consultant in education and management, lecturing widely in his field. He is a visiting Professor to the School of Education, University of Manchester.

Dr Denis Lawton, Professor of Education at the Institute of Education, University of London, is a specialist in education planning and curriculum studies. After some years teaching English and history in secondary schools, he joined the Institute of Education, University of London, as a researcher in 1963 and became its Director in 1983. He returned to curriculum studies in 1989 to concentrate on writing and research. His recent publications include *Education, Culture and the National Curriculum* (1989) and *Education and Politics in the 1990s Conflict or Consensus?* (Falmer 1992).

Lindsay Martin has worked in the further education sector for fifteen years, initially with two Regional Advisory Councils for Further Education (London and the South-East, and East Anglia) and latterly for three local education authorities. The first of these was in the North-East of England, the second in outer London and the third was the City of Westminster. Lindsay now works for a London Training and Enterprise Council as Director of Education.

He is also a long-standing member of the British Educational Management and Administration Society, having served on its Council since 1986 and been Honorary Secretary since 1989. Lindsay is a Fellow of the Royal Society of Arts and a member of the British Institute of Management.

Eileen Murdoch, OBE, MA, FScotvec, FRSE, was Headteacher of St Augustine's RC High School in Edinburgh from 1977 to 1992. She was President of the Headteachers' Association of Scotland in 1990–91 and has served on many educational committees. Now Mrs Eileen Dunning, she lives in Cumbria.

Dr Albert J. Pautler is Professor, Graduate School of Education at the State University of New York at Buffalo. Prior to this position he was a member of the faculty of the Graduate School of Education at Rutgers University. He is also owner of Instructional Systems Design and a national lecturer for the Center for the Advancement of Education of Nova University. As owner of Instructional Systems Design he is involved in consulting activities with business, industry, and educational organisations. As a National Lecturer for Nova University he presents seminars on the topic of curriculum and program planning for community college administrators and teachers. He is the author of some 50 articles and 12 books on topics related to education, training, and professional development. His most recent books are, *Vocational Education in the 1990s: Major Issues, Teaching Technical Subjects in Business and Industry, Designing Vocational Instruction, Job Seeking Guide,* and *The Future of Vocational Education.*

Richard Pring has been Professor of Educational Studies and Director of the Department of Educational Studies at the University of Oxford since 1989. Prior to this he was for 11 years Professor of Education and Dean of the Faculty of Education at the University of Exeter. He has published three books *Knowledge and Schooling, Personal and Social Education,* and most recently *The New Curriculum.* His major areas of interest are the changing policies and practice in education and training against the background of competing philosophies. He has been editor of the *British Journal of Educational Studies* since 1985.

Stewart Ranson is Professor of Education at the School of Education at the University of Birmingham. His research and teaching interests focus on the governance, politics and management of education. He is completing a three year research project on the changing governance of education following the 1988 Education Reform Act.

Robert Stradling has been working in educational research and curriculum evaluation since the mid-1970s and joined the National Foundation for Educational Research in 1987, where he is a Principal Research Officer. In recent years he has been concerned with the evaluation of the European Commission's PETRA pre-vocational education programme; he has recently completed a report on the teaching of history in western, central and eastern Europe and is the editor of a forthcoming book on educational research into secondary education in Europe.

Angus Taylor has been TVEI and now Education Adviser with the Training Enterprise and Education Directorate of the Employment Department since 1988, on secondment from Northumberland County Council. Since graduating in 1958, he has followed a career in education — as an administrator with the London County Council, a teacher of Economics (in Northumberland and Chicago), Head of Sixth Form and Deputy Head at Wyndham School, Cumbria, and Headteacher of Cramlington Community High School, Northumberland from April 1976 until 1990. He has had various roles with educational organisations including the Economics Association, Secondary Heads Association, Schools Council, Secondary Examinations Council and SEAC.

Harry Tomlinson is Principal of Margaret Danyers College, Stockport. After working abroad and in Lincolnshire, Essex and Walsall he has been headteacher and principal of three other institutions in Manchester and Stockport all of which have closed due to reorganisations. He is Treasurer of the Secondary Heads Association (SHA) and Chair of their Equal Opportunities Working Party, Chair of the Manchester Branch of the Institute of Management (IM), and National Chair of the British Educational Management and Administration Society (BEMAS). He has recently edited *The Search for Standards*.

Penelope Weston has been engaged in research on curriculum practice, management and change since the mid-seventies and since 1984 at the National Foundation for Educational Research, where she is a Principal Research Officer. She has undertaken national and local evaluations and worked on EC studies in curriculum and assessment. She is currently director of the Cohort Study of TVEI Extension Students.

Preface

This book brings together a number of major national figures to consider the issues relating to the curriculum, education and training in the 14–19 age group.

Part I: The international context

Penelope Weston and Robert Stradling place development in England and Wales in a European context. The problems are similar but the solutions are very different and varied within Europe. There is certainly no ready-made solution to our problems which can be immediately transferred from a particular country. There are however differences in the quality of the debate from which we might learn. In Spain, for example, ownership of the national curriculum by the professionals was recognised as crucial. There is a European movement away from detailed programmes of study. Common issues such as those relating to value for money and progression into appropriate education and particularly training provide an opportunity for broadening an understanding of our problems.

Joseph Dunning and Eileen Murdoch examine the particular case of Scotland. There has been an acceptance that Scotland has achieved better solutions than England and Wales. This detailed analysis of the historical development of curriculum reform in Scotland is constructively critical, partly because it is written by one of those who created the reforms and a leading headteacher who has been involved in the implementation process throughout the last twenty years. The chapter concludes with a consideration of the Howie Report, the latest set of proposals in Scotland, which is now being consulted upon.

Albert Pautler's analysis of the decentralised American education system shows how any description of the curriculum experience requires an understanding of the control of public education within the United States. The high school system means that the relationship between academic and vocational education is different to that in Britain. The various government initiatives and efforts from pressure groups result in a system which demonstrates considerable responsiveness to the market. The title of the report 'America's Choice; High Skills or Low Wages' discussed here shows how we share issues of common concern.

Part II: The theoretical context

It is almost appropriate to describe the contributions in this section as theoretical in that the contributors all have had distinguished careers in higher education departments where they have had the opportunity to research and reflect upon the changes that they discuss here. They are however firmly grounded in a detailed knowledge and understanding of the education system.

Denis Lawton examines the processes of curriculum development since the Great Debate. The movement towards an apparently arbitrary central control was largely the result of ideological contradictions within the Conservative Party. The failures in policy planning are clearly demonstrated. An example of this is the historical analysis of the various proposals for the reform of A level, all of which have largely ignored the 5–16 curriculum, and produced no significant reform. The proposals of the National Commission on Education are seen as another significant opportunity for rational curriculum planning.

Stewart Ranson concentrates his political analysis on the recent White Papers, *Education and Training for the 21st Century* and *Choice and Diversity* and the subsequent Acts. He suggests that there are real discontinuities between the Education Reform Act and more recent Acts which are related to an attack on local democracy. He challenges the assertion that schools cannot be successful if they are local education authority schools. The real challenge is to create the conditions for a learning society. Ranson develops a curriculum which is about learning for empowerment and can only be achieved in a local, democratically accountable context.

Richard Pring, the third of the education professors, concentrates on a philosophical perspective. Pring accepts that there are legitimate criticisms of the education system. He examines the economic argument, the issue of standards, and the social and personal relevance of the curriculum. It is important that educational values and the purposes of education are constantly reconsidered. There is a danger, with all the pressures to implement the latest policy changes, that educational priorities may be forgotten.

Part III: The practical context

The theoretical context allows detachment from the pragmatism of those needing to implement decisions, even if these are hopefully often underpinned by the educational values demonstrated as central in Part II.

John Braithwaite examines the practicalities of the reorganisation of 11–18 schools into 11–16 schools and sixth form colleges in one local education authority. This case study shows how the commitment to ensure coherent provision across the town faded under the pressures of the market forces recently encouraged. The local education authority had carried out its role in the interests of the students and the community in a way which will no longer be possible.

Duncan Graham was the major figure in the development of the National Curriculum. He makes it clear that he was as aware of its weaknesses as anyone, but there was a coherence which was beginning to emerge which is now being undermined. Assessment and examinations have become too much the issue and as a consequence the opportunity presented to create a curriculum which might provide a worthwhile educational experience is being thrown away. There is nevertheless still the possibility that the vision can be regenerated if all those involved are prepared to work together.

John Dunford presents a thorough analysis of the strengths and weaknesses of A level, and the implications of the developments of AS examinations. The vocational alternatives are examined in the context of the divided system. Dunford welcomes the growing consensus about the need for parity of esteem, a single system of qualifications, breadth and balance in the curriculum and core skills which he sees as shared by many groups within the education service. There is however no certainty that this will lead to appropriate change.

Dick Evans and Jenny Cronin consider the particular contribution of the FE sector to education and training, a contribution until recently largely unrecognised in public debate. They show how a quality curriculum involves breadth, balance, differentiation, entitlement and progression. Quality means fitness for purpose for all. The GNVQ and NVQ frameworks are genuinely learner centred, and offer real opportunities for a creative way forward. Their vision of the opportunities that can be provided by challenging curriculum frameworks and appropriate institutional management demonstrates an energetic commitment to meeting student needs.

Lindsay Martin establishes the place of training credits as a means of delivering National Vocational Qualifications. The relationship between youth training and the new training credits which are replacing it, is analysed. The chapter concentrates on the management opportunities and provision within the new system.

The evaluation of the first round pilots is encouraging, though improvements are necessary if high quality training for young people is to become the norm. The relationship between TECs and LEAs is seen as crucial, as is the need for government to demonstrate that it takes training seriously.

Angus Taylor shows how TVEI has developed powerfully over the decade since it was established. This has been the most significant attempt to build in coherence across the curriculum 14–18 with which this book is concerned. The emphasis on work related learning as opposed to curriculum content which characterises TVEI suggests that if the National Curriculum worked in harmony with TVEI the potential for improvement is considerable. Individual action planning, records of achievement and common learning outcomes could be planned across the divide at 16 despite the problems caused by qualification structures. There is a serious problem about how many of these gains will be lost as TVEI funding fades away.

Malcolm Deere examines many of the changes that are occurring in higher education which have clear implications for the 16–19 curriculum. Higher education is already responding positively to developments in the 16–19 phase. In practice changes in the higher education curriculum are occurring more rapidly at degree level than they are in the 16–19 phase. Credit accumulation, credit transfer and modularity are developing very effectively, particularly in subjects like physics and engineering when the curriculum must be made more student friendly. Mass higher education will require a very different curriculum and much greater responsiveness to student needs.

Part IV: On to the next millennium?

Harry Tomlinson attempts to bring together the arguments which have been advanced in the earlier chapters. It would seem that the A level issue is central to any major improvement in the curriculum 14–18. Unless there is a comprehensive co-ordinated curriculum throughout these crucial four years, and one linked into higher education and training, then any attempt to raise education and training standards will be seriously compromised. The problem may be that the CBI targets are not sufficiently ambitious. There is a need for a new comprehensive curriculum for all before the millennium arrives.

PART I: THE INTERNATIONAL CONTEXT

1 Vers l'Europe des compétences?

Setting the 14–19 curriculum in a European perspective

Penelope Weston and Robert Stradling

The educational initiatives and reforms of the last decade in the UK can be seen as part of a much larger pattern of change that has been moving across Europe. During this period Spain, Portugal, France and the Netherlands have introduced national curriculum reform programmes; there are reviews and reforms taking place in the Scandinavian countries; Luxembourg is about to introduce new curricula and Italy is reforming post-14 provision. Since 1988 the countries of central Europe have been catapulted into even more sweeping changes, transforming the very fabric of the educational system. Over the same period the member states of the EC have committed themselves more explicitly to the modernisation of their education and training systems in order to meet the needs of the single market — to build 'L'Europe des compétences'. If there is one thing all these very different education systems have in common it is the pressure to improve, to satisfy the needs of the economy and the demands of parents and students.

What lessons can we learn from our European neighbours?

One advantage of focusing on the 14–19 age-range is that it embraces, throughout Europe, the end of compulsory schooling and the beginning of differentiated provision for further education and training, even if the institutional arrangements, resources and priorities for managing this transition are enormously diverse. European countries also share, with each other and no doubt most of the world, the aim of harnessing education and training for this age group in order to meet the demand for a skilled and flexible workforce for the next century. However hollow the discussion of 'skill shortages' sounds in a period of recession and rising unemployment, it provides the rationale for many of the EC education and development programmes.

The nature of specific programmes depends, of course, on national context and history and there is therefore probably more consensus about the issues and problems than there is about solutions. For this very reason, developments in other European countries provide a testbed for evaluating the assumptions underlying the actual and proposed changes in the UK curriculum. The aim of this chapter, therefore, is not to set out nostrums borrowed from here and there, but to discuss common priorities and questions which face most European countries in the area of curriculum policy and practice for the 14–19 age group, and hopefully to learn something by understanding more about their response in their context. This involves getting some feel for that context – economic, social and political as well as educational, since the 14–19 curriculum does not exist in a vacuum.

Contexts for the curriculum

The strength of curriculum tradition

Behind the superficial similarities in the way schooling used to be organised throughout Europe before the Second World War — elementary schools for the majority, grammar schools for the elite — lie fundamental and differing curriculum philosophies which have continued to influence more recent developments. These apply mainly to secondary education and concern the purpose and scope of the curriculum. Holmes and Maclean (1989) set out four distinct traditions. The most influential, encyclopaedism, spread during the last century across much of the continent, and can be traced back 400 years to Comenius. Starting from an examination of nature and its laws, he argued that the curriculum should embrace all human knowledge. This view was developed and disseminated by the French after the Revolution; the 'encyclopaedic' curriculum was also a curriculum for all the people, since, as Condorcet proposed, all men are capable of reason. The practical outcome was a broad curriculum. Under Marxism, this approach was given a new 'applied' perspective, every element in the curriculum being related to the wider economic and social goals of the communist state; even if, in practice, this 'polytechnicalism' was never fully implemented. A third curriculum philosophy, looking to Dewey as well as to European thinkers, stressed real life problems and concerns as the starting point for curriculum planning and highlighted the potential of the school as an educative community. This kind of approach was particularly influential in shaping Danish curriculum thinking. Holmes and Maclean saw the English curriculum tradition as standing apart from these three, in its stress on the value of the academic tradition in itself, which could be equally validly pursued through differing subjects within the canon of theory-based disciplines, and which was of intrinsically greater worth than technical/practical knowledge or skill. The importance of these broadly defined traditions lies in their deep roots which have influenced generations of teachers, parents and children with very practical consequences for schooling.

Lastly, it should be recognised that the term 'curriculum' itself is problematic in the European context. There may be no equivalent word, and those in use may refer only to lists of subjects or prescribed content. Curriculum studies may be restricted to subject work closely focused on the classroom. The problems increase when discussion turns to the meaning of 'core curriculum' (van den Brink and Hooghoff 1990). Conflicting assumptions about the nature of the curriculum and how it should be managed may prove more significant obstacles to international dialogue than any linguistic or technical problems in appreciating the niceties of curriculum provision.

Political and administrative background

In England we have been accustomed to thinking we have a single national education system, although this is to forget, as we frequently do, the rather different tradition in Wales and the totally separate systems in Scotland and Northern Ireland. It is therefore important to bear in mind the diversity of political and historical frameworks for the curriculum across Europe. It is, for example, difficult to overestimate the power of the revolutionary settlement in France, in engraving in the national consciousness curriculum principles which are only now under threat. A standard curriculum, within a national system of schooling was both a means of offering equality of opportunity (through a neutral meritocracy), and building up the nation state at the expense of local, feudal ties. By contrast in Germany the curriculum is a matter for each of the *Länder* who would not take kindly to any central direction and may differ markedly in their political priorities, even if there is a broad consensus about the shape of the curriculum.

Some interesting political trends are now emerging in Europe regarding the administration of education. 'Decentralisation' is the current buzzword. In Spain, for example, the central government in Madrid has set out a broad national framework for reform within which the 17 'autonomous regional authorities' can develop more detailed programmes. In Belgium there have, for a long time been two Ministries of Education, one for the Flemish-speaking community and one for the French and German communities but education was still under the statutory control of the Central State. However, since January 1989, responsibility has been transferred to three Language Community Councils, each with its own legislative and executive powers. Equally important in some countries is the role played by the churches in managing schools and defining curriculum goals; while in Denmark the local community has played a key part in running its own schools for at least a century. The French also talk of decentralisation, set in train by the reforms of 1982, where some administrative responsibilities were transferred to the 27 Academies (or administrative districts). But, compared with developments in Spain and Belgium, it would be more appropriate to describe changes in France as devolution rather than decentralisation. An increasing number of European states, including some of the former communist states in the east, are now taking steps to give more financial and administrative autonomy to the individual school. But perhaps the most radical changes now taking place are in the former communist countries as they endeavour to reform the curriculum and reorganise their schools. Already there are signs of tensions emerging between the liberals (often former communist officials) who favour devolution of powers to schools and a pluralism of educational values; the conservative radicals, who want more educational centralisation on the grounds that the potential pace of change will be too slow and not necessarily in the desired direction if left to pluralism; and the smallest group (the new democrats), who are seeking to give more power to local government with the teaching profession being responsible for developing the curriculum.

14–19 curriculum trends

The English 14–19 curriculum debate reflects a number of assumptions about how education is, or should be developing. As we have suggested, these underlying trends are in no way unique to this country.

Expansion? Higher participation rates, a better qualified workforce

Expansion of education and training was identified as an explicit goal by the Commission of the EC in 1989: 'a steady increase in the volume of education and training will be needed at all levels, from basic through to third level training' (Commission of the EC 1989). More specifically, at the end of 1987 member states were set the objective of offering all young people at least two years of post-compulsory training or education (*ibid*). But, as national governments have made clear, what is needed is not merely an expansion of provision and participation but also of educational output, in the form of qualified personnel. Both these pressures have immediate and wide-ranging implications for the curriculum.

The numbers game — progress and prospects

The dual emphasis on quantity and quality is evident in governments' policy statements and targets, which have become notably more ambitious in recent years. The focus differs in accordance with the current stage of development in each country, but the tone is similar. Portugal wants to raise the proportion of the age group in post-compulsory education and training from 11 per cent (1988) to 25 per cent by 1993, and double this by 2000; by the same year Spain aims to have 80 per cent of 18 year olds in full-time education and France has set the target of 80 per cent reaching *Baccalauréat* level. The UK has set the more modest — but challenging — target of 50 per cent getting NVQ Level 3 (two A levels) by the same date.

In some northern European countries expansion goals have virtually been achieved, with over 80 per cent of the age group in full-time education, either through legislation (for example, in Belgium where all young people remain in full or part-time education) or by a mixture of state provision and encouragement of client demand (Sweden, Norway). In these countries the numbers question is a more subtle one, which is also relevant to other countries as they expand their provision: how much wastage is there within the high participation rates? This wastage includes those who drop out of school, often after one or more repeated years, and those who leave without qualifying. In former communist countries of central Europe the numbers question may be seen rather differently. In Hungary, for example, there has been pressure to reduce the numbers staying in full-time general schooling to 18 because the courses are too theoretical and inappropriate for many students. In other words, an over-rigid common curriculum on the academic model has been reinforcing failure for some rather than promoting success.

Improving educational output

Raising the school leaving age and/or increasing post-compulsory participation rates often involves developing new curricula seen as appropriate to the needs and capabilities of the 'new' students. Thus the French *Baccalauréat Professionel*, introduced in 1985, was introduced as a third (vocational) 'bac' option, formally of equal status with the general and technological awards but very different in content and structure (for example, it includes work placements). It was intended for those who had already entered vocational education (in the *Lyceé Professionel*), at 16 or younger, and was aimed to create the new breed of skilled technicians who, according to the economic planners, would be needed for the next century. In practice the numbers have been disappointing: only 32,000 were taking it in 1990, rather than the projected 90,000. During the last few years there has, however, been a rise in the numbers taking the most traditional 'general' *bac* course. This suggests there may be a tension between the priorities of the central planners, who see the need to increase the availability of certain types of skill; and the clients, who recognise the long-term vocational value of the general or academic qualification. Follow-up of the *Bac Professionel* graduates suggests this may be a rational response: the qualification does not provide an effective route to higher education and is viewed with suspicion by employers, particularly in stereotypical male jobs. It is still seen by many as 'a diploma in search of its identity' (Watson 1991).

In countries with major curriculum reform programmes for compulsory schooling, the drive to improve vocational education and qualifications goes hand in hand with an effort to promote general/academic education both as a separate track and as an integral part of vocational schooling. In Italy, for example, where all pupils stay in general education in common lower secondary schools until 14, the reform strategy aims to simplify the complex structure of vocational schooling and at the same time to change the balance of general and vocational elements in the curriculum from 14 to 18. The Spanish national reform programme is perhaps the most ambitious. Discussion, research and planning began in

1980, and the Reform Act was passed in 1990. The reforms will be phased in gradually through the nineties, starting with pre-school education. The most obvious and dramatic expansion comes from the decision to raise the school leaving age from 14 to 16, which will be completed in 1996–7. But it is also intended to increase participation after 16 by simplifying access to a flexible post-compulsory phase with a single certificate (the *Bachillerato*) which has real 'terminal value' as well as being a route to other studies (Eurydice 1991).

A very different set of problems and priorities has confronted policy makers in the Netherlands. Participation rates in post-compulsory education and training have been high, but the system is complex and many young people have emerged into the labour market without qualifications. The challenge has therefore been to find a way of reforming the system so that it improves its 'output' for all individuals within the age group. As we shall see, this is leading to radical solutions which directly address the outcomes issue, bypassing the complex organisational structure of 16–19 provision. Since it involves defining attainment targets and certificate units it will, however, have a profound effect on curricula in all types of schools.

The issue of 'wastage' affects almost every system and raises important questions about the feasibility of an expansion policy. In particular it is a practical test of the perceived value of the curriculum and qualifications system, and its 'fit' with economic realities. If young people are voting with their feet by declining the offer of education and training, this should be a powerful incentive for all those with an interest in the 'products' of the system to reconsider what is being offered.

Equality of opportunity? The framework of schooling and the evolution of the comprehensive curriculum

The move to offer all young citizens statutory access to full secondary education through a common curriculum (or curricula of equal worth) has passed through several stages in most countries.

Secondary schooling as a stage rather than a type of education for some while the rest made do with primary or elementary schooling

While this change took place in many countries before 1940, it is only with the recent (1987) reforms that Portugal has established universal junior secondary education (12–15). In France, the ideal of a common school (*école unique*) also went back to about 1900, but the old tradition of primary as a type rather than a stage of schooling was not finally abandoned until the Fifth Republic (1958) (Derouet 1991).

A lower secondary school for all? The organisational dilemma

Almost every country has retained some vestige of the classic bipartite or tripartite system, with secondary modern or vocational schools/classes striving for 'parity of esteem' alongside the grammar or academic stream; but in some the structural divisions have been gradually pushed back into the post-compulsory phase. In Scandinavian countries, for instance, where the decision to consolidate a 6–16 'basic school' had been taken before 1960, there has been much public debate about the effectiveness of the common school in offering equal opportunities to all. In West Germany, by contrast, attempts to introduce comprehensive schooling have had very limited success and were restricted to certain *Länder*. Derouet (1991) shows how, in France, the Haby reform of 1975, which created the 11–16 '*collège unique*', tried to bring about, at a stroke, the ideal of a single, undifferentiated school, offering equality of opportunity to all via a common curriculum, throughout the nation. But the ideal quickly turned sour; streaming persisted, morale was low and public doubts grew. By contrast, in Denmark 6 to 16 schooling is treated as a single, unified experience, provided in a single institution (*grundskola*) by a single body of teachers for a stable class group. Portugal could perhaps have adopted this pattern in the change from 6–12 basic education; instead they went for a primary/secondary divide within general education.

Upper secondary for all?

Meanwhile, the frontier for 'comprehensivisation' has moved forward to upper secondary education, with Scandinavia again leading the way. At this level of schooling, however, while the broad democratic goals are the same — securing greater educational opportunities for all the citizens — the focus has changed. Is it more important to provide a common institutional framework (a common school) or to secure common access to (differentiated) education or training? Belgium effectively raised the school-leaving age to 18, but offered a wide variety of formats and modes; general or vocational education, full or part-time, school or 'alternance' (school and work) based. Norway is now making a further attempt to integrate general (academic) and vocational courses within the single upper secondary school framework which has existed since 1974. But doubts remain about whether the aim of the reform — 'to make the twain meet' — can be realised (Mjelde 1992). In Germany, such a goal could be seen as irrelevant or misguided. There the co-existence of traditional upper secondary 'general' and technical school-based education with the (employer led) Dual System based on apprenticeship has ensured high participation, high standards and indications that 'parity of esteem' is more than a pious hope. Whatever the structure, however, a common feature of these established upper secondary systems in Europe is that they retain the majority of students to about 18, usually on a curriculum track which lasts for two years (sometimes more) and leads to a nationally recognised qualification.

Adopting curricular solutions

There are signs that the struggle for the comprehensive ideal may now be shifting from the institutional framework of schooling to the curriculum itself. In Austria, for example, the bipartite school system has been retained but a common curriculum has now been introduced for all schools in the first four years of secondary schooling. There is no formal selection for grammar school and, as a result of parental pressure, the grammar schools have expanded and the modern schools have contracted. Introducing the common curriculum has accelerated this trend. Luxembourg, too has opted for a common curriculum across its school types. The Netherlands has the most highly differentiated secondary school structure in the EC, with four sectors, three of them leading mainly to (different) types of vocational education or training. Attempts to change this structure, over a period of more than twenty years, in order to make it more 'comprehensive' or flexible, have come up against continuing political and ideological impasses and the staunchly defended interests of the four national education organisations. Two of these are denominational, and three of the four represent the 'private' (but publicly funded) schools: in all about three-quarters of the schools are private. Earlier attempts to legislate for a new (common) national curriculum were equally unsuccessful, but agreement has now been reached on a common secondary curriculum framework to 16, based on core objectives (a form of attainment targets). This reform is a 'package deal of conflicting interests, lobby groups for certain subjects or topics, power conflicts between the central government and the free schools and associations' (van Bruggen 1992). The reformers hope that this will provide a new consensus, a 'moderate comprehensive education', within the existing differentiated school structure. It remains to be seen whether common curricular requirements will prove stronger than the traditions of each school type.

Modernisation? A curriculum for the 21st century

Efforts to modernise the 14–19 curriculum, in almost all countries, have been targeted principally at vocational education. There have also been innovations in the general curriculum for the end of lower secondary education but, up till now, the form and structure of 'traditional' university preparatory programmes of the upper secondary school have been left largely untouched although there are moves afoot in some countries to introduce major reforms.

The aspects of modernisation stressed in EC documents, in particular in the medium term plan of the Commission's Task Force for Human Resources, include greater flexibility in learning approaches and in assessment options, including modular programmes and credit accumulation, active partnerships between education providers and employers and more effective careers guidance and action planning. All these goals are in keeping with the demands of larger companies for a more flexible and highly skilled workforce. But it should be recognised that some of the most highly developed vocational education and training (VET) systems, particularly the German 'Dual System', are only very slowly (if at all) recognising the need for such changes. In the Dual System, for example, apprentices who spend one or two days a week at vocational school during their three year apprenticeship qualify (and 90 per cent do so) by completing conventional courses on a fairly specific vocational area, with final written examinations and formal practical tests.

Education/industry partnerships

Providing a more work-related curriculum, with closer partnerships between education and industry, is a major challenge in many countries where there has been little contact hitherto between the two worlds of general education and employment. Work experience, which may be included in some form at the end of lower secondary education, and in junior pre-vocational courses, is by no means common in general or academic upper secondary courses. On the other hand, the vocational schools — which are usually the responsibility of the ministry of education — are often closely integrated with the world of work, drawing their instructors from relevant industries rather than from education. In Italy, the education and employment ministries have collaborated in a scheme to set up national-level working parties on curricular questions, to improve the exchange of information between the school system and employers and unions (Meijer 1991). In Portugal new vocational schools, which will provide a new form of VET for 16–18 year olds, are the joint responsibility of the education and employment ministries. More radically, local authorities are encouraged to form public–private partnerships, including employers, unions and voluntary bodies in order to set up vocational schools, in line with local training needs.

More flexible curriculum and assessment structures

As Alison Wolf has pointed out, 'only in England is assessment being used as a major instrument to change post-compulsory education and training' (Wolf 1991). However, several countries including Sweden, France and the Netherlands are experimenting with modular courses incorporating continuous assessment, especially in vocational education; and recently the Netherlands has moved towards a single system of competence-based vocational qualifications, built up from units designed with close employer collaboration (Liebrand 1991). It is hoped that this new system, which has parallels with the English NVQ framework, will help to rationalise what has hitherto been a fragmented system, and thus improve success rates and ease transition from one sector of the complex school and training system to another. In France the *Bac Professionel* is usually conventionally organised by subject, and although the vocational part of the course follows a detailed objectives format, assessment is generally by final examination. However, in recent years there have been some pilot projects in which the course has been divided into modules with continuous assessment and no final exam (Barrier and Robin 1990). The initial evaluation showed that students following the modular scheme did at least as well as those on the more conventional course, and, in the lecturers' view, had become more independent and mature in the process.

A broader curriculum?

Compared with English post-16 curricula, most other countries already offer a fairly broad curriculum. Even apprenticeship training often includes a core of continuing general education.

Where upper secondary provision has been expanded to offer a wider range of courses to a larger proportion of the age group, the pattern of core subjects established for the university preparation track has often been carried over into the new courses. The French reform plan for the *lycées*, to be implemented from September 1993 (Colomb 1992), is radical in proposing a new basis and rationale for the general and technological *Baccalauréat* curriculum. Driven by the need to respond to the actual and proposed expansion of student numbers, the planners propose to introduce a study skills/personal study element, in which students can negotiate learning targets with their teachers, based on diagnostic information. More dramatically, the traditional hierarchy of curriculum tracks is to be replaced with broad and easily understood groupings. The new scheme will be accompanied by a more coherent and flexible approach to learning strategies and assessment across the curriculum. These initiatives suggest that the effort to provide a broad curriculum is related as much to ideas about employers' priorities as to traditional liberal concerns with what it means to be an educated person. The pressure to expand the content of lower and upper secondary courses, for example to include more language teaching, information technology and careers guidance, is a familiar theme throughout the EC and beyond. The trend to a more holistic approach to curriculum design is reflected in some lower secondary reform programmes, notably in Spain, where the curriculum is to be organised within broad areas rather than conventional subjects, and in current French plans for reshaping the French 11–16 curriculum (Colomb 1992).

Within vocational courses there have been moves in a number of countries towards a broader, more pre-vocational curriculum for the 16–18 age group, with reductions in the number of industry-specific programmes and an expansion of generic skill training and education. This trend is in keeping with the priorities set out by employer groups across Europe. It has also to be said that there is often a yawning gap between such statements and the priorities that emerge in recruiting for apprenticeships and jobs.

Effectiveness? Identifying a curriculum that provides value for money

Expanding education and training, modernising curricula and raising levels of achievement can all be justified, in principle, as investments in human resources necessary for a rapidly changing economy which demands the 'intangible capital' of a skilled and enterprising workforce to match the more traditional physical capital of machines and equipment (CEC Task Force 1991). The French education budget is larger than the defence budget and has just been boosted by 7.2 per cent; it has risen by 42 per cent since being declared a priority in 1988 (Follain 1992). But even before recession took hold, questions were being asked in a number of countries about the enormous cost of reform, and whether the system was providing value for money. Widespread moves towards a performance-based evaluation model for education were signalled by the publication of the first stage of a major OECD initiative to develop performance indicators for national systems (OECD 1992).

Increasingly, however, the issue of 'value for money' is being accompanied, if not overtaken, by the more basic issue of inadequate resources, as a result of financial cutbacks which threaten existing provision as well as new programmes. In Italy, for example, teachers' salaries (which take up 98 per cent of the education budget) have been frozen until the end of 1993 and all in-service training has been suspended (Newbold 1992).

'Early leaving' and its implications for the curriculum

Early leavers do not represent educational value for money and in a number of countries value is also reduced because of the numbers of pupils repeating a year.

It is only when the problem is seen, in part, as school-induced rather than a consequence only of individual shortcomings, that it may lead to reform of the mainstream curriculum (as well as the introduction of compensatory programmes). One curricular response to the problem of early leaving has been to offer pre-vocational options within compulsory schooling which provide progression to (post-compulsory) vocational training, a solution adopted for the Portuguese reform programme. Spain has gone for a single pattern of general education, but even here there are signs of a pre-vocational option in the last two years.

16–19: criteria for a cost-effective curriculum

It is in the 16–19 arena that the debate about cost-effectiveness and its implications for the curriculum are most sharply focused. There are a number of common issues. For example, what is the most effective balance between general and specialised curriculum goals? How can the different — and often changing — demands of all young people be met? Should control be exercised through curriculum (input) or accreditation (output)? We have seen that there are moves in a number of countries to build on the 'encyclopaedic' tradition of general education by extending this principle from academic upper secondary courses to vocational education and training. There are also a few signs of a move in some systems towards more generic, less subject-bound definitions for the general curriculum component of 16–19 education, although the grip of subject disciplines is strong. But in former communist countries there are countervailing trends, rejecting the uniformity of an academically-based curriculum in favour of greater diversity. Two continental initiatives which may offer a way forward are the Dutch move towards an 'output-control' model of attainment targets, although this only applies to vocational education; and the Finnish system of modular courses which are 'non-graded', that is progression is not restricted by age and students can take from two to four years to complete the programme. These principles are now being extended to vocational schools; though once again economic problems may delay the programme (Kangasniemi and Tynjälä 1992).

What seems to be emerging is that provision needs to combine diversity (for example of content, institutional setting, classroom/ placement balance) with flexibility (allowing students to change tack and to progress at differing rates) within one coherent framework, based perhaps on one assessment and review system and embodying a common core of skills. At present, no one country has moved very far along this road.

Common issues and alternative solutions

It should be clear from the foregoing discussion of trends that although the nature and pace of reform can vary markedly from one European system to another they seem to be facing some common issues and problems. Before looking at the alternative solutions to these problems we shall briefly summarise the main issues which have emerged so far.

State administrations have become increasingly concerned about whether existing provision for 14–19 year olds is giving value for money. In some respects the problem is most apparent in central European states where they lack the skilled adaptable workforces necessary if their economies are to be regenerated but until they can regenerate their economies they do not have the resources to modernise and reform their educational systems. But some western European states are also looking for economies and ways of ensuring that provision for 14–19 gives value for money. This reflects widespread concern about the numbers of 14–16 year-olds dropping out of compulsory education or leaving school with few or no qualifications, or with qualifications which have little exchange value on the labour market. It also reflects concern about the high unit costs of schooling in the last two years of compulsory education and in post-compulsory education and training compared with primary and lower secondary schooling.

Employers and higher education institutions in most European states are concerned that the education and training offered to 14–19 year-olds is not meeting their needs. There appear to be three main dimensions to this issue. First, there is a growing concern that the time lag is too great between changes in employers' recruitment and training needs and changes in educational provision. Second there is concern about how to improve the transition from lower secondary to upper secondary education and from both to further and higher education. Third, there is the question of how to ensure students are effectively allocated to appropriate forms of post-sixteen education and training.

Parents' and students' perceptions of the value of academic and vocational qualifications are also changing and this has implications for resource allocation and government planning, links between lower secondary and upper secondary phases and institutions and the status of some vocational and pre-vocational courses and routes.

Although these are widespread concerns it is clear that the different systems between them are opting for a range of different solutions and, while many of these solutions have emerged from a particular context and tradition and may not therefore transfer effectively to another system, it is still worth examining them to see if they shed light on some of the assumptions and expectations underpinning decisions in our own system. They have been grouped under three broad headings which, it should be emphasised, are not mutually exclusive.

Systemic changes

There is growing evidence from both centralised and devolved educational systems that the impact of many of these reforms on the institution is fairly limited. In particular, the impact of reforms on classroom teaching does not seem to match the massive investment in curriculum development and publishing, or in the establishment of new administrative institutions and new procedures for monitoring, evaluation and assessment. There are a number of reasons why this should be so.

First, it has become apparent that in introducing extensive and wide-ranging reforms governments come under pressure from a plurality of different social and political interests (even within the ruling party or coalition). The resulting innovation or reform is often a political compromise which does not satisfy anyone and increases the possibility of contradictions emerging between the different elements of the reform package or between those elements of the old system which are retained and the new. It was observed earlier that in the Netherlands they have been attempting to introduce a common secondary curriculum for over twenty years. They have not been able to translate the consensus on general aims for reform into concrete measures that could be supported by a political majority. Now, rather than change the differentiated school system they have introduced the notion of core objectives which could be applied in all types of school. It is early days but there is already concern amongst curriculum planners that the system will reject this 'antibody' or severely constrain its potential impact (Diephuis 1990).

Second, in education it seems to be easier to bring about organisational changes rather than to change institutional norms. That is, the government may wish to introduce new educational goals and values, such as the entitlement curriculum or a more pupil-centred style of teaching and learning, and to do this they seek to reorganise the school through legislation, regulations, curriculum guidelines or different funding procedures. But these changes will not be internalised and become the 'norm' within each school unless they can persuade school managers, governing bodies, teaching staff, parents and students to jettison the old ones. Sweden provides an interesting case study. Since the war the bipartite secondary school system has been replaced by the comprehensive school, but in order to bring about greater equality of opportunity it was also recognised that the comprehensive school required a common curriculum and a more progressive, pupil-centred, active learning pedagogy. The evidence from curriculum research is that the latter has not happened to any great degree and a didactic, class-centred approach to teaching is still dominant. As one Swedish researcher puts it, 'The main problem in the implementation of the comprehensive-school reform was that the state left it to an institution that was built up around values which were completely different from those which formed the basis of the reform' (Berg 1992).

Third, there is some evidence that where educational systems which were relatively decentralised seek to become more centralised and prescriptive, particularly about the curriculum, there is a greater risk that the resulting curriculum specifications will bear little resemblance to the classroom practice of most teachers. In the Netherlands curriculum planners are concerned that the new core curriculum objectives may be far removed from existing practice in many secondary schools and that to bridge the gap between rhetoric and reality will require more resources (in-service training, new teaching materials, adaptations of school facilities) than the government will be prepared to make available (Diephuis 1990). Already in England Professor Paul Black, former chair of the Curriculum Review Committee of the National Curriculum Council, has observed that, in his opinion, the Statutory Orders for core curriculum subjects 'have set out specifications of the subjects which are closer to those being pursued by leading innovators than to those of the average school teacher' (Black 1991).

Fourth, and most important of all, it seems that a basic principle of curriculum development and planning, formulated and reiterated in countless evaluation reports throughout western Europe, the United States and most of the English-speaking world in the 1970s, has been ignored by several governments in the late 1980s and early 1990s. That is, that time, resources and appropriate in-service training need to be given to build a consensus in support of the proposed changes; that teachers need to be actively involved in the curriculum development process and encouraged to 'own' the innovation; that changes need to be piloted, evaluated and revised where necessary and that the innovations need to be adequately resourced (see, for example, the account by Van den Berg *et al.* 1989, of the factors essential for effective implementation of the educational reforms in Flemish-speaking Belgium).

In this respect is is worth comparing how the National Curriculum was introduced in the United Kingdom with the approach adopted in Spain. The main features of the Spanish educational reforms were outlined earlier. They were formally published in a White Paper in June 1987, but they arose out of experimental piloting in several hundred EGB (General Basic Education) schools and upper secondary schools accompanied by extensive evaluation by the Ministry of Education in Madrid. The pilot schools were volunteers but a basic requirement of participation was that each school should be prepared to implement whole-school, whole-curriculum change. The piloting identified a range of additional measures which needed to be taken to support the reform process and these are now being introduced to facilitate national implementation. It should also be noted that the Madrid government, following publication of the White Paper, allowed three years for consultation and public debate before putting the Reform Act before Parliament.

Changes in curriculum structures and frameworks

There is now broad support across western Europe for the notion of a common curriculum. Sometimes this is synonymous with the core curriculum as in Portugal, Spain, the Scandinavian countries and a number of German *Länder*. In other cases the concept of 'core curriculum' is reserved for those subjects or curriculum areas which are held to be central to or at the heart of the common curriculum. In some countries legislation or official guidelines specify the subjects which must be taught to all pupils but are not particularly specific about the content which must be taught under those subject headings. This may be because considerable autonomy is given to individual teachers and schools, as in Denmark, or because those countries still retain selective school systems (e.g. Belgium, most German *Länder*, Ireland, and Luxembourg) which offer differentiated curriculum content within each subject. In spite of the variations some key points about curriculum frameworks are emerging which have potential implications for the implementation of the National Curriculum in England and Wales.

First, most European systems are moving in the opposite direction to the one taken by England and Wales. The trend is away from detailed national programmes of study towards less specific syllabus structures which identify the broad topics to be covered but not the detailed content; towards extending the scope for curriculum diversity and the introduction of optional content and, in some systems, towards specifying the knowledge, understanding and skills which all students should learn but not the subjects and courses through which it should be delivered.

Second, as noted earlier, there is a growing recognition that effective curriculum change tends to be incremental and builds on existing practice on the grounds that minimal disturbance minimises the risk of 'tissue rejection'. So, in countries where the traditional, dominant framework has been 10–15 discrete subjects or disciplines then the practice has been to introduce change through those subjects by specifying additional content. In countries where curriculum diversity has been the norm the trend has been towards identifying core knowledge and skills which could be delivered through a variety of curriculum structures and frameworks: subjects, integrated courses, inter-disciplinary courses and cross-curricular themes and topics. The Dutch core objectives reflect the essential elements of different disciplines but do not necessarily have to be taught through a subject-based curriculum; the Scots have opted for modes of learning rather than curriculum content; others, including some central European states, are moving towards identifying core skills and processes that could be delivered through a variety of curriculum frameworks, while the Flemish-speaking authorities in Belgium are going a stage further to identify a minimal core.

Third, educationalists in most European countries are expressing concern about the problem of curriculum overload — a tension between the desire to include new areas of learning and the need to contain the curriculum within a manageable workload for both student and teacher. There is pressure to modernise the curriculum but the introduction of new subjects such as information technology into curriculum structures and prevailing pedagogies is often inhibited by insufficient organisational flexibility and by a lack of trained staff. Eastern European states are experiencing similar problems as they try to replace Russian as the compulsory second language. Pressure to take account of demands for consumer education, environmental studies, development education, the European dimension, health education, and so on is widely responded to by curriculum infusion or permeation. But the message coming from curriculum developers and researchers is that cross-curricular co-ordination is poorly developed (van Bruggen 1992). This is partly because in most European systems the school managers see themselves as administrators rather than curricular leaders. It is also partly because the cross-curricular elements and dimensions are frequently perceived to be a low priority compared with those which are specified in curriculum regulations and guidelines.

Fourth, there is growing evidence of contradictions emerging between the different aims and objectives set for the 14–19 curriculum (e.g. a common entitlement with scope for some differentiation, specialisation and choice; and breadth and balance combined with relevance) and between those aims and some of the others which underpin the educational reforms that have been initiated (e.g. raising standards, greater accountability, organisational rationalisation, reduced drop-out and failure rates and increased staying-on rates in post-compulsory education and training). There is not the space here for exploring in any depth the range of contradictions that are now beginning to emerge but it is worth drawing attention to two particularly common concerns. For example, no-one seems to have come up with a satisfactory solution to the paradox that alternative curricula and routes for low achievers seem to demotivate them leading to increased truancy and drop-out rates but a common curriculum for all can heighten their sense of failure thereby also demotivating them. By way of a second illustration, it is interesting to note that a growing number of educational systems in Europe have been attracted to the idea of a common core curriculum not so much out of an overriding commitment to social justice but because it facilitates comparison of performance and the judgement of standards, quality and progress across the system as a whole. In practice, however, governments are finding it easier to compare the performance of schools in terms of student outcomes than to assess the quality of provision and, to the best of the authors' knowledge, only the Belgians have made any serious attempt at introducing a cost benefit analysis into the equation to see if the output matches the resources put into the system and, above all, to see if educational institutions are 'competing with each other on a level playing field'.

Finally, it has become increasingly apparent in most European educational systems that the transition from compulsory to post-compulsory education and training needs to be improved. Apart from the Scandinavian countries, most post-sixteen education and training systems are still highly differentiated. Although such systems can be very stable, with their structures clearly defined and well understood by all parties, they do not necessarily provide coherence at a systemic level, or to the young persons who are making their way through the system. The prevailing view appears to be, therefore, that post-sixteen provision needs to be rationalised into a much more coherent system that links up clearly with the last two to three years of compulsory schooling. Nevertheless, a number of European countries (particularly in eastern and central Europe) have chosen to follow the pattern of the German Dual System for post-compulsory education and training, and some would argue that policy makers only become concerned about post-sixteen progression and continuity and the incoherence of the traditional system when vocational training lacks public credibility and support.

Changes in curriculum process

At present it is possible to say more about the impact of the educational reforms on the system and on curriculum structures and frameworks than about their impact on curriculum processes (curriculum content, teaching and learning styles and assessment), mostly because the reforms will not be fully implemented until the end of the decade. Consequently, as yet little is known about what is actually happening in classrooms. Nevertheless, we can draw attention very briefly to two points of comparison which may have implications for developments in the United Kingdom.

First, although only a limited amount of comparative research has been conducted on curriculum processes it is apparent that the National Curriculum for England and Wales rests on a number of assumptions (e.g. about the sequence of learning in specific subjects in order to ensure progression and continuity; about the number of levels of attainment that would be appropriate; about the specificity of attainment targets; about the relative weight to be given to teacher assessment and external assessment) which are not substantiated by practices in other countries.

Second, although most European educational systems now promote active learning, practical learning, enquiry-based learning, open learning and self-supported study, the employment of these approaches is widely constrained by poor access to audio-visual equipment and computer technology, lack of financial resources to purchase equipment and materials, and initial and in-service training which largely perpetuates more traditional pedagogies. There are grounds for believing that only the more innovative teachers in some European countries actively make use of the more flexible teaching and learning styles. In this respect in the UK, it may well emerge in the long run that TVEI has had a major impact on teaching and learning styles even if this was not originally perceived as its main purpose.

For two curriculum evaluators who have been working in this field for over twenty years, very familiar messages emerge from this review of European trends in curriculum reform. Above all these relate to the problems of implementation which go back to the Schools Council evaluations. Many of these are messages for managers and policy makers about the limitations of centrally planned reform in changing the taught curriculum. The particular context here — the 14–19 curriculum across the European spectrum — highlights the role of teachers and learners in shaping and changing the curriculum. The focus is increasingly on change in the process of learning, the most difficult kind to implement. This will require a sustained input of professional development. Perhaps the message then should be that we need to put more effort into making teachers and learners more competent in developing and structuring the learning process in order to achieve common and individual curriculum goals within a complex and constrained system.

References

Barrier, E., and Robin, D. (1990) 'Assessment and purposeful learning in France. Case studies one and two' in Weston, P. B.

(Ed) *Assessment, Progression and Purposeful Learning in Europe: a Study for the Commission of the European Communities* Slough: NFER.

Berg, G. (1992) 'Changes in the steering of Swedish schools' *Journal of Curriculum Studies* 24, 4, 327–44.

van den Berg, R., Hameyer, U. and Stokking, K. (Eds) (1989) *Dissemination Reconsidered: The Demands of Implementation* Leuven: ACCO.

Bjerg, J. (1991) 'Reflections on Danish comprehensive education 1903–1990' *European Journal of Education* 22, 2, 132–41.

Black, P. (1991) 'New Studies of a New Curriculum' Paper presented at a seminar at NFER, Slough, February.

van den Brink, G. and Hooghoff, H. (Eds) (1990) *Core Curricula for Basic Education in Western Europe: Perspectives and Implications* (Volume 1) Enschede: National Institute for Curriculum Development, for CIDREE (Consortium of Institutes for Development and Research in Education in Europe).

van Bruggen, J. C. (1992) 'The curriculum for (junior) secondary education and its basis in educational research: a critical review. From Dutch experience; with a European outlook. . .' Paper presented at the Council for Cultural Co-operation European Educational Research Workshop on 'Research into secondary school curricula', Valletta, Malta, 6–9 October.

Commission of the European Communities (1989) *Education and Training in the European Community. Guidelines for the Medium Term: 1989–1992* (Communication from the Commission to the Council) Brussels: Commission of the European Communities.

Commission of the European Communities. Task Force Human Resources, Education, Training and Youth (1991) *Commission Memorandum on Vocational Training in the European Community in the 1990s.* Brussels: Commission of the European Communities.

Colomb, J. (1992) '*Programmes de l'enseignement secondaire et recherche pedagogique en France.*' Paper presented at the Council for Cultural Co-operation European Educational Research Workshop on 'Research into secondary school curricula', Valletta, Malta, 6–9 October.

Derouet, J-L. (1991) 'Lower secondary education in France: from uniformity to institutional autonomy' *European Journal of Education* 22, 2, 119–32.

Diephuis, R. (1990) 'The meaning of a core curriculum for basic education in the Netherlands' in van den Brink, G. and Hooghoff, H. (Eds) Ibid.

Eurydice and Cedefop (1991) *Structures of the Education and Initial Training Systems in the Member States of the European Community 1990.* Brussels: Eurydice European Unit.

Follain, M. (1992) 'A franc approach to their problems' *Times Educ. Suppl.* 3982, 23 October, p. 16.
Holmes, B. and MacLean, M. (1989) *The Curriculum: a Comparative Perspective.* London: Unwin Hyman.
Kangasniemi, E. and Tynjälä, P. (1992) 'Research into secondary school curricula Finland.' Paper presented at the Council for Cultural Co-operation European Educational Research Workshop on 'Research into secondary school curricula', Valletta, Malta, 6–9 October.
Liebrand, C. G. M. (1991) 'Recent developments in the Dutch system of vocational qualifications' *European Journal of Education* 26, 1, 55–61.
Meijer, K. (1991) 'Reforms in vocational education and training in Italy, Spain and Portugal: similar objectives, different strategies' *European Journal of Education* 26, 1, 13–27.
Mjelde, L. (1992) 'Will the twain meet? The relationship between the world of work and the world of schools in Norwegian upper secondary educational reforms.' Paper presented at the Council for Cultural Co-operation European Educational Research Workshop on 'Research into secondary school curricula', Valletta, Malta, 6–9 October.
Newbold, D. (1992) 'Budgetary axe falls on schools' *Times Educ. Suppl.* 3982, 23 October, p. 16.
Organisation for Economic Co-operation and Development (1992) *Education at a glance.* OECD Indicators. Paris: OECD.
Watson, J. (1991) *The French Baccalauréat Professionel* (Post-16 Education Centre Working Paper Number 9). London: University of London, Institute of Education.
Wolf, A. (1991) 'Assessment in European vocational education and training: current concerns and trends'. *Journal of Curriculum Studies,* 23, 6, 552–57.

2 Curriculum change in Scotland 1972–1992

Eileen Murdoch and Joseph Dunning

Over the past twenty years Scottish education has been the subject of many reports, consultative exercises and subsequent changes. Many of these changes have affected the curriculum and organisation of the Secondary school.

The Munn and Dunning Reports

In 1974, two important Reports were commissioned by Government. These were the Munn Report 'The Structure of the Curriculum in the Third and Fourth Years of Scottish Secondary Schools' and the Dunning Report 'Assessment for All'.

The reasons for establishing these committees were the raising of the School Leaving Age in 1972 and the changed circumstances in which the Ordinary Grade examination operated; circumstances markedly different from those envisaged at its inception. These changed circumstances had their origins in demographic, educational, social and organisational changes which had occurred in schools in Scotland. The increasing number of births in the years 1950 to 1964 had its repercussion on the secondary school population over the period 1962 to 1980. It reached its maximum in 1978. (By 1990 the age cohort had fallen from 40,000 to 30,000.) The two factors which affected the fourth year number were the vogue to stay on at school beyond the statutory leaving age and the 1972 decision to raise the leaving age from 15 to 16. Figure 2.1 shows the growth in the number of fourth year pupils between 1962 and 1971 (this is from the introduction of the Ordinary grade examination to RSLA). The general increase in fourth year and fifth year (though not so markedly in sixth year) had meant that more pupils sought 'O' grade. It meant that there were significantly more pupils in the schools for whom 'O' grade was not suitable.

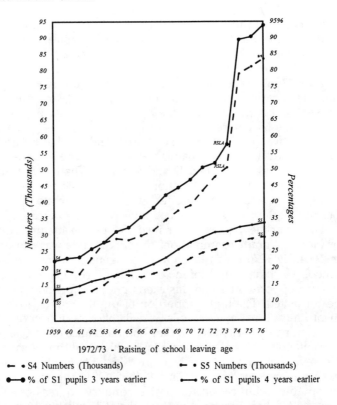

1972/73 - Raising of school leaving age

●─ ● S4 Numbers (Thousands)   ●─ ● S5 Numbers (Thousands)
●─● % of S1 pupils 3 years earlier   ●─● % of S1 pupils 4 years earlier

Notes: Figures refer to pupils in education authority, grant-aided and independent schools but exclude those in special schools.

Although the great majority of S4 pupils up to 1972 were staying on voluntarily, the above totals for S4 pupils at January include pupils who left on attaining school leaving age in the second term (and therefore before the time of the O grade examination). The S5 pupils are those staying on voluntarily in S5 and thus exclude pupils who left on attaining school leaving age in the second term.

Figure 2.1: All S4 pupils and voluntary S5 pupils at January Numbers (thousands) and percentages of corresponding S1 pupils 3 or 4 years earlier (*Source:* Dunning 1977)

By 1975 almost all secondary pupils were receiving comprehensive school education and this, in turn, led to more pupils following certificate courses. The increase in opportunities for pupils in school has led to a greater number of leavers holding qualifications for certain jobs. The resulting competition imposed a further premium on qualifications. Further reinforcement stemmed from the demand for continuing education and indeed the development of higher education. By 1992 there were four new universities in Scotland.

From 1964 the number of presentations for SCE 'O' grade had risen rapidly. About 25 per cent of the year group were presented for three or more 'O' grades in 1964. By 1976 the figure was 65 per cent. The need for change was given fresh impetus by the effect of RSLA (1972) and the banding of 'O' grade awards (1973). Five bands A–E were awarded with A, B and C representing passes and D and E failure. The trend in passes followed the trend in presentations. In 1964 21 per cent of the year group gained three or more 'O' grade passes while in 1976 40 per cent of the year group gained three or more awards.

However the 'pass rate' declined. For pupils attempting three or more 'O' grade examinations the success rate was 82 per cent in 1964. By 1976 it had fallen to 62 per cent. In a comprehensive school which has pupils of mixed abilities, people are sensitive to uneven opportunities and this exerts pressure for more pupils to be presented. The high proportion of pupils gaining low or no award meant that many pupils were the victims of over optimism in pursuing courses in which they had no chance of success. Over presentation is not a situation about which one can be sanguine. However not doing so may be more difficult to justify because for example, parents and pupils felt that 'O' grade was the only acceptable qualification for post secondary courses or jobs or because teachers preferred to teach the SCE syllabus with which they were familiar.

While RSLA in 1972/73 gave an excellent opportunity for innovative courses which motivated the less able pupils, 'O' grade presentation had become so well established that few of the curricular initiatives came to fruition. Something of a paradox existed. While teachers supported the right to give as many pupils as possible the opportunity to take SCE examinations, they had reservations about the suitability of the SCE courses for many of the pupils. The inflexibility of the SCE examination caused Scottish teachers to turn to the English CSE examinations. In 1976/77 some 22 schools were involved with Mode III courses in which both the syllabus and the method of assessment were devised by the school and moderated externally.

In the case of able pupils it was doubtful whether the 'O' grade was fulfilling its original intention. For these pupils it was recommended that 'by-passing' would mean that pupils could make significant in-roads into 'H' grade before fifth year. The idea of by-passing was not popular and involved only a small per centage of the group. The Report of an SCEEB Subcommittee noted that, 'The increased demand for University and Higher Education in Scotland in general has made entrance a matter of selection rather than qualification. In consequence, the 'O' grade plays a diminishing part in general university entrance...' (Dunning 1977).

Pupils drawn from a group somewhat lower down the ability range who sought a career in industry and wished to gain a diploma qualification needed not only a minimum of three 'O' grade passes but the right combination of subjects. Statistics show that in 1973/74 when 9 per cent of the year group left school from the fourth year with three or more 'O' grade passes, just under 3 per cent were qualified to enter any SCOTEC ONC course and only 1 per cent to enter a specific ONC course in engineering, building or science. The implications of these statistics speak for themselves!

By 1974 the 'O' grade had become a victim of its own popularity. It had been designed to be of service to a minority of pupils and by and large it could be considered to have had a fair measure of success. It was against this background that the Munn and Dunning Reports were set to provide a new framework for the education of pupils in Scottish Secondary Schools.

In 1979, under the aegis of the Scottish Education Department a study team consisting of Officers of the Department and HM Inspectors of Schools was given the task, 'To examine the problems which would arise from the implementation of the Munn and Dunning Reports, jointly and separately; to report on the feasibility of effecting the proposals in these reports, with particular reference to resources, organisation and assessment procedures'. Both Munn and Dunning supported the proposal that there should be a core and elective structure to provide a balanced curriculum with the provision of three levels of syllabus and that the corresponding certificate awards should have internally and externally assessed components. The three levels of syllabus which the reports named as Foundation, General and Credit should overlap so that transfer from one level to another would be possible. The inclusion of internal assessment in a course was designed to exploit the teacher's knowledge of the pupils across a wide range of activities. Also it was seen as necessary to provide National guidelines for both syllabus and assessment so that schools could devise their own schemes of work.

Munn's recommendation, briefly stated, was that pupils should undertake study in each of seven areas: English, mathematical studies, physical education, moral and religious education, science and technology, social studies, and the creative arts. Two-thirds of a pupil's time was to be spent in study of these areas with the remaining third being allocated to a choice of two

or three additional subjects. Table 2.1 shows the Munn proposals
with the choices available. By 1987, the guidelines for headteachers
on curriculum design for the secondary stages had increased the
core to 86 per cent of the pupil's time by including a foreign language and a distinct technological element.

Table 2.1

	Core Area			Elective Area
Pupils take all subjects	Pupils choose one subject	Pupils choose one subject	Pupils choose one subject	
English	Economics	Biology	Art	French
+	or	or	or	German
Mathematical	History	Chemistry	Music	Spanish
Studies	or	or	or	Latin
+	Geography	Physics	Drama	Biology
Physical	or	or	or	Chemistry
Education	Modern	General	Dance	Physics
+	Studies (All	Science	or	Geography
Religious	to include a	or	Creative	History
and moral	module or	Engineering	Craft	Modern Studies
Education	modules based	Science		Engineering
	on a study of	or		Drawing
	contemporary	Food Science		Metalwork
	society)			Woodwork
				Catering
				Fabrics and
				Fashion
				Food and
				Nutrition
				Accounting
				Secretarial
				Studies
				Art
				Physical
				Education
				Religious
				Education
				Integrated
				Courses
				etc.

Source: Munn 1977

The feasibility study

The feasibility study took account of the present practices and
trends in curriculum development and the consequences of
implementing the Munn and Dunning Reports.

A theoretical 'baseline' for staffing (baseline B) was
introduced by updating the 'Red Book' basic staffing standards

of 1973. The period for evaluating staffing and accommodation needs was from 1976–1990 since school populations could be calculated from known birthrates and because it had been ascertained that a long period would be needed for development and implementation. In establishing baseline B and post Munn–Dunning variants a number of assumptions were made — the Red Book allowances for administration time and pupil contact, accepted school practices such as the common first year course period allocations (School Census Returns), class sizes and teaching load. Figure 2.2 portrays the staffing levels required to support baseline B and post Munn–Dunning variants over the period 1976–1990. It can be seen that up to the early and mid-eighties all post

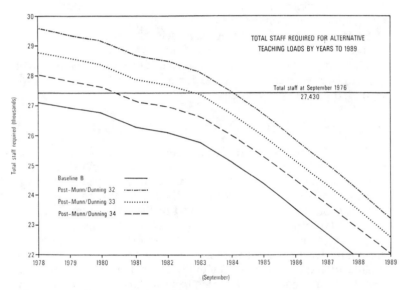

Figure 2.2: (*Source:* SED 1979)

Munn–Dunning staffing demands are above the total staff for 1976/77 so that additional staff would be required for early implementation. In the event Foundation courses in English, Mathematics and Science were piloted in 200 schools in 1983 and 1984 and the candidates for the first phase of Standard grade were examined in 1986. As Standard grade was phased in Ordinary grade was phased out but it was not until 1989 that 'S' grade presentations overtook 'O' grade presentations to become the Certificate gained by the majority of fourth year pupils.

Although the Munn Report had proposed the need for a 'more

unified' system the two major influences CCC and SCEEB
continued to function as separate entities. Although there is a great
deal of collaboration and good will on both sides, the role of the
CCC (now named the SCCC — Scottish Consultative Council on the
Curriculum) is to provide advice to the Secretary of State on the
Curriculum, it also provides guidance to headteachers on the
balance of the curriculum and the implementation of new
developments. The role of SCEEB (now renamed SEB — Scottish
Examination Board) is to provide the framework for individual
subject examinations.

It would seem to be too early to appraise fully the success or
failure of Standard grade or to consider the debate concluded. It
has certainly brought a new approach to the learning process, for
pupils, certification for all and for teachers, more skill in the
application of assessment techniques.

So far, Munn and Dunning have been the main thrust of this
chapter. Two other developments of no less significance have also
had a major impact on Scottish secondary education. These are, first
the SED's response to the need for a new post-16 system and
second, the 5–14 development.

The Action Plan

In 1983 SED published *16–18s in Scotland: An Action Plan.* The
background to the initiative was the publication of a discussion
document *16–18s in Scotland: the first two years of post-compulsory
education* (SED 1979). Traditionally there has been a clear
demarcation line between school and further education. The 16+
Action Plan aimed to close that gap. This was reflected in the
existence of separate teaching qualifications and conditions of
service for teachers in the two sectors. Teachers holding a teaching
qualification (FE) can teach only in FE. Teachers holding a teaching
qualification (secondary) can teach in secondary school or in an FE
college. This discrepancy arises because, by statute, it is necessary
to hold an appropriate teaching qualification to teach in a school
but this does not apply to the FE sector.

The Action Plan represented a new approach to vocational
education in that it resorted to criterion referencing on an extensive
scale. The unit of learning is a forty hour module with the
opportunity to develop half, double, triple or quadruple modules.
Four broad classifications were designated for these modules:
business and administration, science, technology and inter-
disciplinary. SCOTEC and SCOTBEC provided the modules. From
the start of the session 1984/85 some 742 modules were introduced
and more than half of the secondary schools in Scotland were

offering two or more modules while all FE colleges were actively contributing to the scheme. In 1985 SCOTEC and SCOTBEC merged into SCOTVEC — the Scottish Vocational Education Council — and this body is now responsible for the National Certificate. The new National Certificate was of particular benefit to YTS students and trainees.

The modular system shifts the curriculum towards a student centred approach. However, to be assured of quality, criterion referencing will be a feature of each module and this will be subject to a system of external moderation by a team of assessors. This has been an important issue in convincing employers that they should accept the new National Certificate. Two major problems are still being addressed. First the question of credit transfers between such bodies as SCOTVEC and CGLI in order to give Scottish students credibility in the UK market. Second the need for students to select modules that will satisfy the requirements of professional bodies. The development of the SVQ programme in tandem with the NVQ programme is addressing both of these matters.

Arising from the Action Plan, not only was there a desire to bring secondary and further education closer together but, in a consultative paper — *A Single Examining Body?* (SED 1984), a concern was expressed to bring the Scottish Examination Board and the Scottish Vocational Education Council into a single body so that all forms of academic and vocational awards are certified by one authority. A working group under the auspices of the Convention of Scottish Local Authorities is being established at present to explore the possibility of a merger.

As Standard grade has become established and the National Certificate grows, the nature of the fifth year cohort is changing. More pupils are choosing to stay on at school and the traditional Higher grade examination is no longer appropriate for a majority of the year group. To address the problem, in 1990 the Scottish Education Department established a Committee 'to review the aims and purposes of courses and of assessment and certification in the fifth and sixth years of secondary school education in Scotland'. The Howie Report was issued, for consultation, in 1992.

The Howie Report

At present 'highers' are taken only one year after Standard grade — in effect after little more than two terms' teaching. This means that students are under great pressure when they arrive at University. By contrast the pace of learning in the first two years of Secondary school seems to be rather leisurely. If the pace could be stepped up some students could achieve more by the end of secondary schooling. The level reached tends to be lower than in other European countries and in other parts of the United Kingdom. There has always been a belief in Scotland that breadth compensated for depth. This is not necessarily reflected in student attainment. A third of fifth year students pass no higher grade examinations and more than half get no more than one Higher. If four or five Higher passes in fifth year is regarded as a broad attainment, it is reached by only 20 per cent. It is found that many students do not develop good study skills at school and are poorly prepared for the rigours of a degree course.

Howie's proposals recommend a new Scottish Upper Secondary Award (SUSA) replacing Highers and the Certificate of Sixth Year Studies (CSYS). There would be two new but distinct qualifications — the Scottish Certificate (SCOTCERT) and the Scottish Baccalaureate (SCOTBAC). The suggestion is that this arrangement will ensure more worthwhile qualifications after a modified standard grade. Figure 2.3 illustrates the way the Howie arrangements will operate.

The proposed SCOTCERT awards are intended to prepare students for entry to employment and progression to further training or more advanced educational opportunities. They are intended not only for the 15–18 age group but also for adults. They may be offered by schools, FE colleges and school-college partnerships. It is recommended that SCOTCERT would offer a range of opportunities for the majority of the fourth year population, e.g. 60–70 per cent. The normal duration of study would be one year for Part I and a further year for Part II. The award of Part I will be made on the successful completion of 16 modules and Part II will normally be awarded on the completion of a further 16 modules. The curriculum would embrace the broad aspects of core skills, general and vocational education.

Under SCOTBAC proposals students will follow a broad curriculum to a high level and with reasonable prospects of success because of a more measured pace of study. It will be based on a systematic grouping of subjects which ensures key aims are met. It is proposed that there be a Science and an Arts line. There will be a core of subjects common to both lines (English, Modern Languages, Mathematics, Science, Social Subjects, Music, History of Art and Information Technology) although the weighting of a subject would vary with its importance in the line. It is proposed that major subjects would be taught to a level well above the present Higher level. There would be a mix of internal and external assessment with emphasis on the latter in the final year. Assessment results would contribute to a profile of the student at the end of each

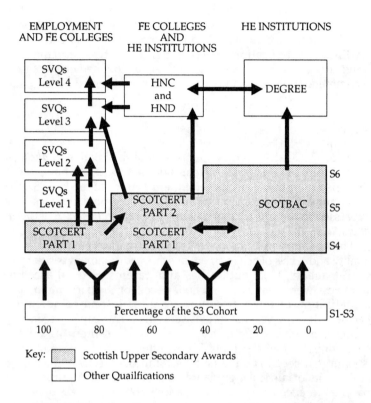

Note: The above chart shows the conventional modes of taking SCOTCERT and SCOTBAC. There are other possibilities, for example: some students may wish to extend their SCOTCERT studies into a third year; adults may wish to take SCOTBAC AR, which involves alternative modes of study.

Figure 2.3: (*Source:* The Howie Report 1992)

year as well as the overall assessment. A student need not pass every assessment to qualify for the award of SCOTBAC. Better performance in one subject can compensate for a poorer perform-ance in another. This would be regulated by a points system based on the grade of pass, weighting of subject and stage of assessment. The total points would lead to an overall banding of SCOTBAC on a performance scale of A–D.

Whether through the SCOTCERT or SCOTBAC route, parents

may be assured that whatever pathway is taken within the Scottish Upper Secondary Award system young people will benefit from a broad education, complemented by a more vocational curriculum leading to qualifications of standing. It must be remembered, however, that as yet there is no decision as to whether any of the recommendations in this Report will be implemented.

5–14

In 1986, a CCC discussion paper was published entitled *Education 10–14 in Scotland*. Many of the tenets of that document have found their usage in the '5–14 Development Programme'. In 1987 the Government's concern on national and regional policies was expressed in the consultation document *Curriculum and Assessment in Scotland: A Policy for the 90s*.

The government's main aim is to secure improvements in the quality and levels of achievement of school education in partnership with teachers, local authorities and parents. Several areas of weakness were identified — school policy for the curriculum, lack of definition of the curriculum, progress in and co-operation between the later years of primary and the early years of secondary school, inconsistency of approach to assessment and poor communication with parents. Thus in this area of education there is an urgent need to address matters of inconsistency in the nature and quality of curricular guidance, to clarify curricular purposes for parents, to encourage schools to adopt coherent assessment and testing criteria. Although no major changes in the structure of education or educational administration is envisaged, the importance of school boards is acknowledged.

The curriculum proposals are concerned with the definition of curriculum and consistency of its application, accountability and information. It is proposed through a nationally agreed set of guidelines to set out the aims of study, the content and the objectives to be achieved. There will be a need for a systematic check on the application of the national guidelines. Schools will be required to prepare statements of curricular policies for the school boards and HM Inspectorate and a statement for parents indicating the coverage and aims of curricular areas as part of the monitoring process.

The assessment proposals recommend a parallel programme of quality assessment in both primary and secondary schools. It includes testing of certain key aspects of the curriculum in Primary 4 and Primary 7, i.e. in aspects of language and mathematics, based on nationally standardised test items. Much of the development programme is now in place and its use is being phased into the primary school. Working papers exist in language, mathematics, expressive arts, environmental studies, and religious and moral education. Guidance has also been produced on assessment and reporting. National testing is also being introduced.

Conclusion

In 1984/85 TVEI was introduced to Scotland. This UK initiative made a major contribution to the Scottish system by funding the development of new courses and classroom methodology. Both Standard grade and the National Certificate benefited from this scheme.

In looking back over the last twenty years and attempting to summarise the stream of activities, no attempt has been made to criticise but rather to present the myriad of developments currently forming the Scottish system of education. They represent a search for a quality approach to education which will serve the population, enlist more fully the role of parents and meet the needs of society into the next century.

The Scots have a traditional curse — 'May you live in interesting times' (in other words — life is going to be tough!). We do!

Chronology

1972   RSLA — Raising of the school leaving age
1973   Banding of 'O' grade
1974   Establishment of Munn and Dunning Committees
1977   Munn and Dunning Reports issued for consultation
1979   *Curriculum and Assessment in the Third and Fourth Years of Secondary Education in Scotland — A Feasibility Study*
1979   *16–18s in Scotland: The first two years of post-compulsory education*
1983   Piloting of first Foundation courses
1983   *16–18s in Scotland: An Action Plan*
1984   *Consultation paper — A Single Examining Body?*
1984   TVEI introduced
1984   *16–18s in Scotland: Guidelines on Curriculum and Assessment*
1985   Merger of SCOTEC and SCOTBEC into SCOTVEC

1986   First Standard grade examinations
1986   *Education 10–14 in Scotland*
1987   *Curriculum and Assessment in Scotland: A Policy for the 90s*
1989   Establishment of Howie Committee
1989   5–14 Development Programme started
1992   Howie Report issued for consultation

References

CCC (1986) *Education 10–14 in Scotland* Discussion Paper.
The Dunning Report (1977) *Assessment for All* SED.
Gartside, P. (1990) The National Certificate in Scotland: Five Years On *Coombe Lodge Report* Vol 22, No. 4.
The Howie Report (1992) *Upper Secondary Education in Scotland* SED.
The Munn Report (1977) *The Structure of the Curriculum in the Third and Fourth Years of the Scottish Secondary School* SED/CCC.
Roebuck, M. (1985) The 16+ Action Plan in Scotland *Coombe Lodge Report* Vol 18, No. 2.
SED (1979) *Curriculum and Assessment in the Third and Fourth Years of Secondary Education in Scotland — A Feasibility Study* SED.
SED (1983) *16–18s in Scotland: An Action Plan* SED.

3 The American curriculum experience

Albert J. Pautler

Introduction

This chapter represents an attempt to describe the American curriculum by someone who experienced it as an elementary and secondary school student. That student went on to college and eventually taught technical education at the high school level for ten years. He then pursued a twenty-five year career at the university level professing the theory and practice of curriculum development, curriculum management, and curriculum evaluation. In essence, this chapter is an attempt to blend the micro testimony of that personal, lived experience with the macro reality of a complex, educational enterprise. It is a verbal concoction of memory, theory, practice, with a dash of insight and frustration.

The objective of this chapter is to offer an encapsulated summary of the curriculum that is presented in public and private schools in the United States. More specifically, attention focuses on the high school curriculum which serves the needs of those students aged 14 to 18, with some mention of the community colleges which offer technical education programmes. The perspective used in discussing these topics is based on my personal research and development of 'transition theory': the individual student's transition from school to school; school to work; or school to unemployment. Included in this large area of concern is a discussion about current 'bridging' attempts to tie secondary education with community college programmes. The intention of these programmes — variously called '2 plus 2' or 'Tech–Prep' — is to create a better prepared student for his/her transition from the academic environment to the workplace.

An underlying theme of this chapter speaks to the decentralised nature of the American educational system which, consequently, yields a diversity of curricular approaches. That is to say, the 'American curriculum experience' exists more in theory than in actuality, as there is no National Curriculum. . .and I doubt that we ever will have one in the United States due to the increasing trend of decentralisation.

Consider these facts: there are approximately 110,000 schools in the United States governed by 15,000 school districts operating under 50 different sets of state laws. The federal government offers little direction for the formal curriculum presented in the individual states. Each state and territorial possession of the United States is responsible for the policies that guide educational practices within their boundaries. In fact, it may be said that professional associations and textbook publishers have more control over the curriculum than does the Federal Government.

All the evidence indicates that the American curriculum is a very different experience for the high school student in New York compared to that of a student in California due to individualised State control of the educational program. Nevertheless, this chapter makes every attempt to describe the generic consistencies and uniform policies that transcend these differences to create the American curriculum experience.

Control of education

Following the Revolution, Americans mainly advocated a state supported system of public education. This has remained the major control function for public education in the United States. New York State has over 700 school districts which have an average size of about 1,500 students. These districts are headed by a superintendent of schools who is responsible to a 'nonpolitical' school board who are elected by the residents of the district. These are 'lay' boards of education who are responsible for policy, budget, and selection of school administrators and teachers.

Federal control

The United States Secretary of Education is a cabinet level position reporting directly to the President. The Secretary is the head of United States Department of Education (US/DOE). The United States Congress makes laws and policy concerning educational issues and the US/DOE is responsible for implementing, monitoring, and evaluating such policies.

Congress may enact legislation dealing with vocational education, special education, or other areas of national concern. Most of this federal legislation includes funding from the National Government. Individual states are usually required to write State plans to implement the legislation and tell how federal money would be spent, if obtained. If the state accepts the federal money it is held accountable for the proper use of the funds — which may well influence the curriculum in the schools.

Federal control of education is much like the rabbit and the carrot story. The carrot is money (dollars) and the rabbit is the state. If the state accepts the money it must abide by the federal policies included in the rules and regulations written by the US/DOE.

State control

Each state and territorial possession of the United States is responsible for the education of its citizens. Each state has a Commissioner of Education who is either appointed by the Governor of the state or elected by the citizens of the state. This individual is responsible for a department of education which suggests policy to a state board of one sort or another and then implements and monitors the policies.

These state departments of education have a great deal of control over curriculum requirements for the state. The departments co-ordinate committees made up of teachers and other interested parties in making decisions regarding the content of curriculum guides which would be distributed to the schools in the state.

Local control

The major control of education in the United States rests with local boards of education which are responsible for operating the public school systems. Some 15,000 plus school districts exist in the United States. New York State alone has over 700 school districts.

In some states the local boards of education exist at the county level. The county system of control exists in Florida, Maryland, and Virginia and other states. Other states use the model that is used in New Jersey, New York and Ohio of control at a level smaller than the county base.

Local boards of education may be referred to as local educational agencies (LEAs). These boards of education are controlled by elected or appointed board members who for the most part are 'lay' citizens and 'nonpolitical' in decision making.

The actual process of schooling takes place in these LEAs and this is where the 'teaching–learning process' takes place. This is where the written curriculum becomes the taught curriculum and finally the tested curriculum.

Curriculum can be influenced by the federal government, but, it is structured and controlled by the various state governments, however, it is implemented in the local school systems.

The American curriculum experience is not very easy to describe to non-American readers. I like to say that where you live determines the quality of education your children will experience. We live near Buffalo, New York. We could choose to live within some forty school districts and still not have to commute more than one hour to work. The educational experience could vary within these districts, but, the curriculum would show the influence of state control of education.

Organisation of schools

Just as control of education varies among the states so does the organisational structure differ among the local educational agencies. The most common organisational structures will include elementary, middle or junior high, and high school.

Normal school starting age is 5 and normal graduation or school completion age is 18. Education is compulsory in most states usually to age 16. Students needing more time to complete their high school may stay in school to age 20 or 21.

Elementary schooling would begin with kindergarten and continue to grades 5, 6, or 7 depending upon district structure and what is to follow. Middle school or junior high school would follow and continue to grades 8 or 9 depending upon district structure. High school would begin at grade 9 or 10 in most cases and end with grade 12. In some rural areas you may find K-12 schools in one building. Structures will vary depending upon size of the district and number of students to be educated.

Most American students will experience 13 years of public school experience, kindergarten to grade 12. At the usual exit point of grade 12 students will in general transition to:

1 more schooling (2 year college, college, private);
2 employment (including military service);
3 unemployment (or underemployment).

Most attention in the school transition experience seems to centre on those students planning to attend some form of post-secondary education programme. Students majoring in vocational education programmes in high school may receive some help in finding suitable employment in the areas they were educated for in school. General high school graduates will receive little, if any, help in their transition to employment. This is a very serious problem at the present time.

One must understand that school districts' size and therefore organisational structures vary in the United States. Problems of equality of educational opportunity also vary greatly in the United States. Jonathan Kozol (1991) in his most recent book, *Savage Inequalities*, deplores the inequalities that he believes exist in various school districts. He reports that it is not uncommon for some public school districts to spend $11,000 per student while a neighbouring district may spend $5,900 per student. He argues for equality of opportunity for all children.

High school completion

According to *The Condition of Education* (1991) one important measure of the United States' success in educating youth is the proportion completing high school. This report presents the following data:

- In 1989, the high school completion rate was 80.1 per cent. for 19 year olds, 86.5 per cent. for 24 year-olds, and 86.9 per cent. for 29 year-olds.

- Among racial/ethnic groups, whites have the highest rates of completion, and hispanics the lowest. Completion rates for blacks have been rising.

- Between 1974 and 1989, the difference between black and white completion rates for 24–25 year-olds had been narrowed from about 14 to approximately 5 per cent (p. 28).

Possession of a high school diploma, or its equivalent, signifies that an individual should have sufficient knowledge and skills to function productively in society. Monitoring high school completion rates at various age groups between 19 and 29 takes into account those who have taken longer to complete their high school education.

The data presented is taken from United States Census Data for the population in general. Actual rates vary from state to state and school district to school district. My own research shows that few local educational agencies have follow-up data on their own graduates. Most districts inquire about future plans of students upon graduation, but do not have data one or more years after school completion though school districts are not required to maintain any long term follow-up data about graduates.

United States Census Data as reported in *The Condition of Education* (1991) indicates that in 1990 27.1 per cent. of high school graduates ages 25–29 had completed four years of college. Based upon this data it is safe to say that about 27 per cent of the US population, ages 25–29, have completed four years of college. The other 73 per cent have less than a four year college degree.

High school graduation requirements

Since the major purpose of this manuscript is to describe **the American curriculum experience** for the age 14–19 group of children the high school becomes the major item of concern. By age 14 most children will be in the first year of high school (grade 9) which we refer to as the freshman/woman year. By age 18 most will be in the fourth year of high school (grade 12) which we refer to as the senior year. Grade 12 is the last year of free public school education for most children in the United States.

At the completion of high school the transition process to more schooling, employment, or unemployment takes place. Some children may exit as early as age 17, others perhaps may be 20 or 21 years of age. Normal age of completion would be about age 18.

Since the reform movement began in the United States the various states have made modifications to the graduation requirements. These requirements vary among the states and no attempt will be made to describe all such requirements in this chapter. Two examples will be described in this section.

The New York State Education Department (1991) has recently drafted *A New Compact for Learning* which includes eight strategic objectives. These are goals for the year 2000. I would like to mention three goals which are as follows:

- At least 90 per cent of all young people will earn a high school diploma by age 21.

- All high school graduates will be prepared for college, work or both.

- All students will acquire the skills and knowledge needed for employment and effective citizenship.

The reader will note that these are goals set for the year 2000 for New York State school districts and their high school graduates. Time will tell if these goals are in fact met by the various school districts and graduates.

State graduation requirements

Each state sets the minimum graduation requirements for the schools that are under its control. Local school districts may establish standards higher than those set by the State Education Department. Examples from two schools located near Buffalo, New York follow. Both are high schools, one comprehensive in nature and the other a vocational high school.

New York State requires 18½ credits to graduate from high school. The basic requirements are as follows:

English	4 credits
social studies	4 credits
mathematics	2 credits
science	2 credits
health	½ credit
art or music	1 credit
physical education	2 credits
electives	3 credits
total credits	18½ credits

These credits would be taken normally during a four year high school experience and represent the minimum requirements established by the State Education Department.

Comprehensive high school

The following graduation requirements are for a comprehensive high school which is in a suburban district near Buffalo, New York. The requirements represent the minimum credits required for students during the 1992–1996 time frame.

English	4 credits
social studies	4 credits
mathematics	2 credits
science	2 credits
health	½ credit
art and music	1 credit
physical education	2 credits
electives	5 credits
total credits	20½ credits

Vocational high school

The following graduation requirements are for a vocational high school which is one of several such schools in the city of Buffalo, New York. It offers vocational instruction in the following areas: automobile mechanics, aviation mechanics, air traffic communications, and electronic recordkeeping and inventory control.

English	4 credits
social studies	4 credits
mathematics	2 credits
science	2 credits
introduction to occupations	1 credit
technical drawing	1 credit
health	½ credit
sequence	
(shops or business courses)	5 credits
physical education (4 years)	0 credits
minimum credits	19½ credits

You will note that in this programme physical education is required for four years, but, does not carry any credit.

The first example represents the requirements currently in operation in New York State. The State has the right to set minimum requirements for all public schools in the State. Local school districts, with Board of Education approval, may require higher standards than does the State.

The other two examples are taken directly from materials supplied by two school districts in New York State. One from a comprehensive type of district and the other from a city vocational high school.

The requirements in other states may vary, but, it would be too difficult to review all others for the purposes of this chapter.

High school transition

The American curriculum experience will end for most students with graduation from high school. At the conclusion of high school, students will begin the passage or transition from school to school, school to employment, or school to unemployment. The difficulty or ease of passage depends upon many circumstances including: (1) how well prepared the student is for college or work; (2) the competition for college level programs; (3) the competition for jobs which is influenced by (4) the percentage of unemployment at that moment; and (5) the attitude of the student toward life in general.

In the United States it seems safe to say that the major purpose of education is to prepare students for life and post-secondary education. Those students completing high school and planning transition to employment without additional education/training are going to have a difficult time in making the passage. One exception would be that group of students who majored in a vocational education programme in high school. In theory, they should be prepared for both more education as well as employment. In practice only about $1/3$ of those majoring in vocational programmes will enter the area that they majored in during high school. This is a major problem and one that needs more research to be fully understood.

The 1988 report of the William T. Grant Foundation, *The Forgotten Half; Non-college Youth in America* has directed attention to non-college youth in America. This report has labelled the approximately 20 million 16–24 year-olds not likely to embark upon undergraduate education as the 'forgotten half'. This label can be applied to that group of students who finish their formal education when they leave high school, with or without, a diploma. Their passage or transition to employment and success may be a rocky road.

The Grant Foundation has correctly called attention to a serious problem for the forgotten half. The implication is that a college degree is not the only way to success for all people. However, the education system must pay more attention to people not planning on a formal programme of education beyond high school graduation.

In the United States it appears most attention to the curriculum is focused on helping students prepare for college rather than employment. Non-college bound youth may need much more help in making their transition than do college bound youth. School to employment assistance is not often available in United States schools.

I have come to the conclusion that every high school graduate should be handed over to some agency as the next step in the transition process. (The student and parents would need to agree to this process.) It might be as follows:

- Those seeking and finding employment are handed over to the employer.

- Those seeking and accepted into college/training are handed over to such a provider.

- Those seeking but not finding employment are handed over to the government sponsored employment service for more help.

- Those not seeking college/training or employment remain the responsibility of the school for at least the short term.

Please think about this model — it may make too much sense to even be considered by most people.

Community colleges

Many high school graduates will make a transition to a local and state supported community college within their general geographic area. Most such colleges are funded by means of some support from the state government, local government (county) and tuition.

Community colleges offer diploma and associate degree programmes in a variety of areas including liberal studies, business studies, medical studies, and vocational studies. These colleges provide a grade 13 and 14 level education following high school. The degrees most commonly awarded are the associate of applied science or associate of occupational science.

Many such colleges will have articulation agreements in place that will allow transfer to a four year college upon programme completion. The student would spend two years at the community college and then complete his/her studies at a college or university.

Many such community colleges have 'open door' admission policies and remedial education programmes to assist all in completing or furthering their formal education. These policies and colleges help those in the 18 year and above category to further their education.

Some general trends

To this point I have attempted to describe the American school system and the control of the curriculum. As indicated earlier the United States has some 110,000 schools in some 15,000 school districts operating under 50 sets of state laws. The system of education is complex and there is no National Curriculum — some are pushing for it — but, I doubt whether it will ever occur.

The education for those in the 14–19 year age group takes place in high schools and community colleges. The normal age of high school completion is 18. Those students desiring to continue their formal education then may move on to a two year community college, four year college, four year university, or some type of private liberal, trade, or technical school.

In the section, high school transition, I tried to explain the normal transition process for high school graduates. In this section I will attempt to give examples of trends that are developing that may improve the transition process for high school students seeking employment after high school completion.

Tech prep

Hull and Parnell (1991) in *Tech Prep Associate Degree* explain the 2+2 idea which began in about 1984 with a series of workshops at the American Vocational Association and American Association of Community and Junior Colleges' annual meetings.

The 2+2 concept represents tieing together the last two years of high school (grades 11 and 12) with the two years of community college (grades 13 and 14), though we do not refer to the community college levels as grades 13 and 14. I show it this way only to demonstrate the normal path for students in the system.

The idea is to develop articulated curriculum paths starting in high school for those planning to continue on to a community college for technical studies. The normal age group in this type of programme would be from 16 to 20.

Tech prep requires local school districts and community colleges to work closely together to develop such programmes. Some community colleges may have to work with 20 or more school districts which have high schools.

For those interested in this type of programme I would suggest a careful reading of the Hull and Parnell (1991) book.

Integrating of academic and vocational education

The United States Department of Education has been pushing for integration of academic and vocational education in the public schools of the United States. The National Center for Research in Vocational Education located at the University of California (Berkeley) has been very active in participating at conferences and institutes dealing with this topic.

The basic idea is to encourage schools to integrate academic and vocational studies. Vocational instructors are expected to integrate academic content into the vocational curriculum. In addition to teaching the technical content vocational instructors would also teach reading, mathematics, science, etc.

The idea is that technology can be used as the vehicle to encourage students to work harder at the academic subjects which are most certainly needed for success in high tech careers. Most good vocational instructors would have been doing this in past years.

This is really not a new concept, but rather one that perhaps needed attention in education. My point is that in 1917 the Smith-Hughes Act was passed in the United States and did address the idea of a connection between things academic and things vocational. Mathematics, English, and science were to be taught as related vocational subjects.

Those interested in more information on this topic should contact the National Center for Research in Vocational Education (NCRVE) at the University of California in Berkeley, California.

Cheektowaga Transition Project

In the United States graduates yearly leave high schools for the transition to the next phase of their lives. The high schools usually do a survey of those graduating and report those percentages going to college, the military, and employment. Most such data seems to be collected before the students leave school and represent plans rather than success rates of graduates.

School districts will usually report the percentage of graduates planning to attend college. Little mention is made of those planning to enter employment or their success rates. Seldom will districts know how successful their graduates were in completing college, since districts are not required to have such follow-up data for past graduates.

The Cheektowaga Transition Project represents an effort of four school districts in the town of Cheektowaga (NY) to design and implement a follow-up system of former graduates 1, 2, 3 and 4 years after high school graduation. The project also involves an exit survey for all graduates from the four districts.

The idea is to develop a valid data set on high school graduates and their transition experiences to either employment or further education. The data will allow the four districts to make comparisons between and among graduates during a four year period of time.

The data should provide information on needed changes in the curriculum and teaching–learning strategies for the districts involved in the project.

Pautler (1992) in the *Cheektowaga Transition Project* can provide additional information regarding this project. The initial data was collected from 1991 high school graduates in the four districts so this project is at an early stage.

Secretary's Commission on Achieving Necessary Skills (SCANS)

The United States Secretary of Labour appointed the Secretary's Commission on Achieving Necessary Skills (SCANS) and charged the Commission with the following:

To
- define the skills needed for employment;
- propose acceptable levels of proficiency;
- suggest effective ways to assess proficiency; and
- develop a dissemination strategy for the nation's schools, businesses and homes.

During June 1991 the United States Department of Labour published, *What Work Requires of Schools* — A SCANS Report for America 2000. SCANS research verified what was called workplace know-how and defined competencies and foundation.

Five competencies were defined and are as follows:

Resources:	Identifies, organises, plans and allocates resources.
Interpersonal:	Works with others.
Information:	Acquires and uses information.

Systems: Understands complex interrela-
                             tionships.

Technologies: Works with a variety of
                             technologies.

These competencies are more clearly defined and spelled out in
detail in the SCANS report.

A three-part foundation was suggested and is as follows:

Basic skills: Reads, writes, performs arithmetic
                             and mathematical operations, lis-
                             tens and speaks.

Thinking skills: Thinks creatively, makes decisions,
                             solves problems, visualises, knows
                             how to learn, and reasons.

Personal qualifications: Displays responsibility, self-esteem,
                             sociability, self-management, and
                             integrity and honesty.

This three part foundation is spelled out in more details in the
actual report of the SCANS commission.

The final SCANS report *Learning a Living: A Blueprint for High
Performance* (1992) is divided into two parts. The first part
'Learning a Living' is concerned with solving the skills problem
and a high performance future. The second part presents a blueprint
for high performance which presents what SCANS calls 'A
Learning-a-living System' which includes the following:

- reinventing schools;
- fostering work-based learning;
- reorganising the workplace;
- restructuring assessment.

Those interested in more details concerning the SCANS reports
should contact the US Department of Labour in Washington, DC.

National Center for Research in Vocational Education

The National Center for Research in Vocational Education
published a report by McDonnell and Grubb (1991) *Education and
Training for Work: The Policy Instruments and the Institutions* which

details the last thirty years of education and training for work in the United States. The report represents an initial effort to understand the complex education and job training system and the policy instruments that drive it.

The report examines five education and training policy areas in depth. These areas are as follows: secondary vocational education, post-secondary vocational education, Job Training Partnership Act (JTPA) programmes, state-funded training programmes, and welfare-to-work programmes.

Those readers interested in a more in depth analysis of educational and training for employment are encouraged to obtain this report from the National Center for Research in Vocational Education, University of California, Berkeley, CA.

America's choice: high skills or low wages?

The National Center on Education and the Economy is a not-for-profit organisation created to develop proposals for building the world class education and training system that the United States must have if it is to have a world class economy. This Center funded by the Carnegie Corporation of New York, The State of New York as well as other sources, established a Commission on the Skills of the American Workforce in 1989. This Commission sponsored by the National Center on Education and the Economy issued their 1990 report *America's Choice: High Skills or Low Wages* to the public.

In the time since its publication it has become a most quoted document in the press, media, and professional journals. It makes the point that the top 30 per cent of the US population grows wealthier while the rest become poorer.

The section describing how children are prepared for work suggests that too little is invested in education for the front-line workers. The group being discussed is the so-called forgotten half which has been mentioned earlier in this chapter. It makes the point that these young people exit schooling and are left to 'sink or swim' in the workforce of America.

The Commission and the report makes some excellent suggestions regarding changes needed in the educational system including the development of a Certificate of Initial Mastery. Such a certificate would be based upon standards that would mean something to employers.

Many of the concepts and ideas are not new, but, the ideas and design of the model are worth serious consideration. The report is worth serious review, consideration, and discussion by those responsible for the policy decisions dealing with schooling and manpower development for the United States.

America's Choice: High Skills or Low Wages and other reports of the National Center on Education and the Economy are available from their offices in Rochester, NY.

This section has attempted to identify some general trends that are worth noting in dealing with the preparation of those in the 14–19 year age group. Many are concerned about the quality of the future work force in the United States and especially those preparing to enter the work force with only a high school education. We are labelling this group the forgotten half.

Summary and conclusions

In the **American curriculum experience** I have attempted to present an honest and objective view of the curriculum in place in American schools. Of major concern is the curriculum for those in the 14–19 year age group and the level of preparation in place allowing those youngsters to transfer to more education or employment upon high school graduation.

An attempt was made to describe the control of public education as well as the organisational structure of American public schools.

A discussion then followed on high school completion requirements and successes and failures. A good deal of this information was taken from *The Condition of Education* (1991) which is based upon census data from the Federal government.

A brief discussion of High School Transition theory and practices then followed. The last section of the chapter then presented some general trends and major projects underway in the United States dealing with school to employment transition issues.

This writing and research effort has been a real challenge and one of extreme professional interest. I have come to the conclusion that every high school graduate should be handed over to some 'next' agency or employer.

- Those graduates continuing their education are handed over to that school or organisation.

- Those seeking and obtaining full time employment are handed over to the employers.

- Those seeking but not finding employment are handed over to the appropriate state employment agency.

- Those not continuing their formal education or seeking employment or entering the military remain the responsibility of the school for at least the short term.

No graduate is just turned out and left to 'sink or swim' in the world beyond high school.

References

Hull, D. and Parnell, D. (1991) *Tech Prep Associate Degree* Waco, TX: Center for Occupational Research and Development.

Kozol, J. (1991) *Savage Inequalities: Children in America's Schools* New York: Crown.

McDonnell, L. and Grubb, W. (1991) *Education and Training for Work: The Policy Instruments and the Institutions* Berkeley, CA: Rand Corp.

National Center on Education and the Economy (1990) *America's Choice: High Skills or Low Wages* Rochester, NY: National Center.

New York State Education Department (1991) *A New Compact for Learning* Albany, NY: The University of the State of New York, The State Education Department.

Pautler, A. (1992) *Cheektowaga Transition Project* Buffalo, NY: Graduate School of Education, University at Buffalo.

Pautler, A. (1993) *High School to Employment Transition* Ann Arbor, MI: Prakken Publications.

US Department of Education (1991) *The Condition of Education 1991* Washington: National Center for Education Statistics, Office of Educational Research and Improvement (Volume 1, Elementary and Secondary Education).

US Department of Labor (1991) *What Work Requires of Schools: A SCANS Report for America 2000* Washington: The Secretary's Commission on Achieving Necessary Skills.

US Department of Labor (1992) *Learning a Living: A Blueprint for High Performance* Washington: The Secretary's Commission on Achieving Necessary Skills.

William T. Grant Foundation (1988) *The Forgotten Half: Non-college Youth in America* Washington: Commission on Work, Family, and Citizenship, The William T. Grant Foundation.

PART II: THE THEORETICAL CONTEXT

4 Curriculum policy development since the great debate

Denis Lawton

One of the problems in writing about educational or curriculum policy is that the word 'policy' normally has connotations of careful thinking and planning; the additional word 'development' should reinforce that impression. 'Policy development' sounds good as rhetoric, but unfortunately policy in practice tends to be contaminated by ideology, expediency and even by personal ambition. Cynical observers of educational policy since 1976 might suggest that every new education minister 'needs' a bandwaggon of some kind; in the case of curriculum since 1988 'development' of the National Curriculum has been confused both by the politicisation of curriculum and by individual ministers wishing to set their stamp on one aspect of policy or another.

The period 1976–1992 does not, therefore, present a clear narrative of progress towards the goal of a better curriculum 5–16 or 5–19; the development has been distorted by inadequate planning, impulsive changes of direction and the sudden emergence of new goals. But let us start at the beginning — 1976 — even if that was not really the beginning (a number of writers, for example, Chitty 1989 and Knight 1990 have shown that the origins of the right turn in education and curriculum go back to the 1960s). Nevertheless, 1976 was a significant date. The Labour Party Prime Minister, James Callaghan, in his Ruskin speech ventured boldly into the secret garden and publicly raised the question of a core curriculum. His Education Secretary, Shirley Williams, took up the issue in the Green Paper *Education in Schools* (DES 1977a) and in DES Circular 14/77 *LEA Arrangements for the School Curriculum* (DES 1977b).

The National Curriculum

The swing to central control had begun in a mild bureaucratic way. Meanwhile, HMI had for some years been at work on a professional approach to an 'entitlement curriculum' which was in accord with the drift towards comprehensive secondary education. Their document *Curriculum 11–16* also appeared in 1977 (DES 1977c). It is probably safe to assume that the combination of political, bureaucratic and professional pressures from within the DES would have produced some kind of national curriculum had the Labour Party been elected in 1979. But they were not, and we can be equally safe in assuming that the kind of national curriculum that emerged during the Thatcher years was different in some respects from what might have emerged as Labour Party policy.

First of all it is not without significance that during those 13 years of Conservative rule, there have been two Prime Ministers, and more importantly, six Secretaries of State:

1 Mark Carlisle (1979–81) apparently showed little interest in the idea of a National Curriculum, and spent his time struggling to retain a reasonable share of the diminishing Public Expenditure (and carving out enough money for the Assisted Places Scheme).

2 Keith Joseph (1981–86) was ideologically opposed to the idea of a National Curriculum which was, however, raised for discussion in his time (*Better Schools* 1985 explicitly rejected a National Curriculum).

3 Kenneth Baker (1986–89) was the enthusiast for and driving force behind the National Curriculum. He seized upon the idea eagerly and wanted results very quickly — for reasons about which we can only speculate. But the haste was destructive. And, ironically, despite the haste, Baker did not have the chance of putting his plan into operation: he was 'promoted' in 1989 to be Chairman of the Party.

4 John MacGregor (1989–90) was left with the job of implementation. He was beginning to appreciate the difficulties and the complexities involved (some say he listened; others say he 'went native'). He was moved on.

5 Kenneth Clarke (1990–1992) was appointed by Margaret Thatcher to apply the same kind of diplomatic skills to education that he employed in damaging the National Health Service. He wanted common sense simplicity — an end to 'elaborate nonsense'.

6 John Patten (April 1992–?) has made noises about the importance of religious education and moral training in the

curriculum, but his bandwaggon appears to be encouraging all schools to opt out, thus obliterating LEAs from the face of God's earth.

In discussing the National Curriculum, we are really focusing on the brief period from Kenneth Baker's North of England speech at the beginning of 1987 to the second half of 1992. On 9 January 1987 Kenneth Baker, as Secretary of State, made a speech to the North of England Conference in Rotherham (DES 1987). He suggested that the English education system was 'eccentric' — less centralised than that of France or Germany. He complained that standards were not high enough and that there was lack of agreement over a curriculum for the 14–16 age group:

> These weaknesses do not arise in those West European countries where the schools follow more or less standard national syllabuses. In those countries the school system produces results which overall are at least as satisfactory as those produced here; and the teachers are no less professional than ours. Nor do these countries show any sign of wanting to give up the advantages of national syllabuses. . . .

If you ignore the rhetoric, Kenneth Baker was apparently saying that he wanted a school system that was more efficient, with higher standards and with better accountability. This does not seem to be an unreasonable set of desires. What went wrong with his curriculum policies?

There are at least three kinds of explanation for the problems that arose:

1 Ideological contradictions within the Conservative Party.
2 Operational problems about the National Curriculum: it was bureaucratic not professional.
3 Implementation strategies were ignored or not understood.

It may be helpful to look at each of them a little more closely.

Ideological contradictions

Secretaries of State for Education have to gain support from all sides of the Party. I have elsewhere (1989) suggested that there are four (overlapping) ideological positions on education which would have been important for curriculum planning, at least three of which could be found in the Conservative Party in 1987:

1 the privatisers (who would prefer to abolish state schools and let people pay for what they want and can afford);
2 minimalists (who accept the need for state schooling but choose not to use it for their own children, and prefer the state to provide something less expensive — they tend to talk about 'the basics' and see schooling in terms of training for work rather than general education);
3 pluralists (who would like state education to be so good that there would be no motive for having private schools — nevertheless they argue in favour of the continued existence of independent schools on grounds of social diversity, freedom of choice and academic differentiation);
4 comprehensive planners (who would like to plan for a single system catering for all social and intellectual types of children). If there were any 'comprehensive planners' in the Conservative Party in 1987–8, they kept their heads down.

The kind of National Curriculum that Conservative politicians would have supported depended (*inter alia*) on their ideological position. Privatisers preferred no National Curriculum (Sexton 1988); minimalists wanted a concentration on basics (the three core subjects); pluralists would have advocated something like the HMI Entitlement Curriculum for all (if they had known about it). A compromise was needed, but compromises run the risk of incoherence.

The National Curriculum began by resembling an entitlement curriculum 5–16 in some respects; but the unnecessary concept of 'core' was introduced presumably as a sop to the minimalists; and the idea of a National Curriculum was made acceptable to some privatisers because it was an essential framework for the assessment figures which would be published in league table form and used by parents to choose good schools. Bad schools would close; the market would rule. Sadly, policy coherence was sacrificed for the sake of appealing to minorities within the Conservative Party.

Kenneth Baker also had to convince his Cabinet colleagues that he had not been unduly influenced by the 'educational establishment' within his department. Thus the National Curriculum *content* was expressed in a very conventional way — a list of subjects that any MP would immediately recognise and regard as 'sound common sense'. The HMI Entitlement Curriculum Model (based on 'Areas of Experience' rather than subjects) was ignored. It was unfamiliar and looked suspiciously like 'educational theory' — an increasingly taboo concept in right-wing circles.

Unfortunately, the 'list of subjects' approach to curriculum was considered by most curriculum planners to be quite inappropriate as a basis for 'reform' in the 1990s: so many vital issues (for example, health education, political awareness etc.) were not included in the subject structure; hence the repair work which later had to be undertaken by the National Curriculum Council in the form of cross-curricular themes.

Curriculum planners were carefully ignored in 1987; but assessment experts could not be. The different sections of the Tory Party were promised greater national accountability and more market competition. A new assessment system was needed which could deliver data demonstrating the efficiency (or lack of it) in every state school, as well as providing test scores which could be used *competitively* and published in league table form (thus satisfying minimalists as well as privatisers). I will return to this under 'implementation'.

Operational problems

The National Curriculum was bureaucratic rather than professional. There is a good deal of literature available showing that successful curriculum change should start from the professional concerns of teachers, making use of their knowledge and experience, not as a top down plan imposed on teachers by civil servants. Since 1988 teachers have, however, felt deskilled and demoralised as a result of National Curriculum arrangements. No attempt was made to give them 'joint ownership' of the curriculum. Most teachers behaved very professionally and did their best with the unsatisfactory curriculum model, but although the principle of a National Curriculum is now generally accepted, they still regard the 1988 version as something alien which has to be accommodated.

Another policy design error was to move from very general aims to lists of content expressed as objectives (or 'statements of attainment') without any intervening justification or explanation.

Implementation strategies

In many parts of the world (OECD 1988) hard lessons have been learned about the difficulty of putting curriculum policies into practice. The reasons for the difficulties of implementing curriculum change are no longer a mystery: the practical problems are extremely well documented (Fullan 1982), and it would have been possible to overcome them.

The National Curriculum itself, although very traditional, did involve some difficult changes: for example, fitting more subjects into the 14–16 timetable, or making sure that enough teachers would be available for subjects such as technology and modern languages. Such problems were ignored, and only when the results of the technology curriculum began to be particularly disastrous was action taken to rethink the nature of the subject and how it might be taught by existing teachers.

Even more importantly, from an implementation point of view, the excellent assessment scheme devised by the Task Group for Assessment and Testing (TGAT) should have involved adequate time for co-ordination between the Subject Working Groups; time for making teachers familiar with the new ideas and procedures; time and resources for adequate training and moderation exercises. The most common error in the implementation of curriculum change is to underestimate the time and resources needed. The 1988 National Curriculum will now become another example of neglecting the lessons of previous studies.

Since 1988 several changes have been made to the National Curriculum which have watered down the idea of entitlement. Students 14–16 may now choose to drop either history or geography at key stage 4, whilst music and art also become completely optional. A further move in the direction of minimalism.

Moreover, the National Curriculum Subject Working Groups developed quite distinct concepts of 'profile components' and 'attainment targets' (ATs) which resulted in the mathematics and science ATs having to be reconsidered 1991; the number of ATs was reduced from 14 and 17 to 5 and 4 — just when teachers were beginning to get familiar with the mark 1 model.

As for assessment, the TGAT model possessed a number of advantages, even conceptual innovations of considerable power. Central to the assessment process was the Standard Assessment Task (SAT). The SAT was intended to be a form of assessment which would avoid many of the disadvantages of conventional 'paper and pencil' tests (not least for 7 year olds). The idea was that good examples of teaching–learning situations would be used by teachers in a standard way with built-in assessment opportunities for the teachers. Such assessment need not be either disruptive or intrusive. Some politicians were always suspicious about this approach which was eventually dismissed as 'elaborate nonsense' by Kenneth Clarke and replaced by more conventional tests — with all the disadvantages that TGAT had tried to avoid, and with little hope of validity and reliability.

What might have happened with better policy planning? First, it would have been sensible to have encouraged and extended the HMI experiments with LEAs on school-based curriculum development using the 'Entitlement Curriculum' as a set of guidelines for improving practice. Second, the policy should have planned for assessment introduced over a much longer period, allowing for the work of the individual subject groups to be co-ordinated, rather than each going their own way. Third, a sensible policy would have planned for the National Curriculum 5–16 to have been integrated not only with GCSE but also with the developments 16–19. (I will return to this 'missed opportunity' below.) Fourth, good policy planning would have worked with teachers rather than against them, giving them partial ownership of the curriculum and assessment procedures.

It may not yet be too late to change policies and to incorporate some important principles. Teachers now should be given every possible opportunity of making the existing curriculum structure work, even if it is a less than perfect model. Changes should be made only to remove intolerable bureaucratic burdens or to put right innovations which are professionally unacceptable. The major example of that kind is that test results should no longer be used to compare LEAs, schools and teachers themselves. Comparisons based on raw scores, regardless of the standards of the pupils in the first place, are clearly misleading and unfair. In the long run there would be advantages in separating the two functions of assessment by returning to APU testing (on the basis of light sampling *not* every child) to monitor standards, and use National Curriculum Assessment for formative and diagnostic purposes.

Curriculum development 14–19

I have already referred to the missed opportunity of considering the development of policy for the 5–16 National Curriculum in conjunction with much needed and long overdue reforms at 16–19. This was a major error of planning — or lack of planning. It was quite clear by the mid-1980s that the A level route to higher education and employment was obsolete in a number of damaging ways: A levels were part of a 'failure system' rather than a success system; they encourage over-specialised and unbalanced curricula; they segregated academic from vocational and technical courses in a way which was no longer appropriate.

The main story begins earlier than 1976. The General Certificate of Education (GCE) A level examinations, together with O levels came into existence in 1951, following the recommendations of the Norwood Report (1943). But soon it was recognised that the A level examinations were having undesirable effects on the curriculum of the 16–19 age group. In addition, the Early Leaving Report (1954) was concerned about the large number of able young people who left school at 16 or earlier. This was a loss of opportunity for the individuals as well as a national problem of wastage of talent. In 1959 the Crowther Report returned to the theme, indicating that the education of the 15–18 age group was unsatisfactory. The system was failing to attract sufficient school-leavers into further education or higher education.

During the 1960s the problem of over-specialisation and lack of balance were seen as major problems. Schools themselves attempted to solve the problem by a kind of 'self-denying ordinance' in the form of the Agreement to Broaden the Curriculum. This was a well-intentioned attempt to supplement A level courses by general education, but the Agreement faded away after a few years. Faced with ever-increasing demand for places, universities took the easy way out by requiring higher A level grades. The Robbins Report (1963) recommended the expansion of higher education. This eventually mitigated the problem, but the supply of additional places failed to keep pace with the dramatic increase in demand. A level grades in two or three subjects remained the first priority.

In 1964 the Schools Council for Curriculum and Examinations was established. Solving the A level problem was one of its first tasks. In 1966 the Schools Council suggested a broader and more balanced curriculum by replacing the typical three A level diet by a broader pattern of two major subjects, two minor subjects, plus general studies. This prescription for a broader curriculum was generally supported, and in 1968–69 the Council produced a concrete proposal in the form of a two-stage structure: Qualifying and Further Examinations (Q and F). The suggestion was that young people who were destined for university or the professions would take about eight O levels at 16, about five subjects at Q level one year later, and only in their final year (age 17–18) specialise in three subjects at F level.

One objection to this Q and F proposal was that young people would be subjected to major public examinations three years in succession, at age 16, 17 and 18. The Q and F solution was rejected in 1969. An alternative proposal was put forward by the Schools Council in 1973. This was a development of the Q and F idea, but now became N and F. A mixture of normal and further level subjects would be taken at the end of the second year in the sixth form, thus avoiding an examination at age 17. This was considered by some universities to involve a lowering of standards which would only be acceptable if the university first degree course was extended from three years to four. This was clearly unacceptable to government on financial grounds. In 1980 there was an attempt to revive the principle of Q or N in the new form of 'Intermediate' levels which would have preserved the A level standard. The Department of Education and Science was not in favour of this solution.

In 1984 the DES itself made a proposal: A levels would remain at their existing standard, but would be supplemented by courses *at the same* standard, but involving only half the amount of content and study time of the A level. These 'half subjects' were to be known as 'advanced supplementary' (AS). They were intended to be used both to contrast with A levels and to complement A level subjects in a way which would provide a broader curriculum of at least four subjects.

By the early 1980s the A level problem was complicated by another development which had come about particularly since the initiation in 1965 of the Certificate of Secondary Education (CSE) for the 40 per cent of pupils who were below the 20 per cent considered suitable for O levels. The result of this examination, together with a desire for extended education, was what came to be referred to as 'the new sixth form'. Schools were faced with the problem of students who wanted to remain at school (or at colleges of further education), but were regarded as insufficiently academic for A level courses. Some vocational qualifications were available, but many of them were regarded as unsatisfactory. Examination boards were encouraged to devise a Certificate of Extended Education (CEE) which began in 1976. The DES was not completely happy with this development and set up the Keohane Committee. The Keohane Report (1979) suggested a broad-based, common course. This was rejected by the DES which decided to abolish CEE and replace it by the Certificate of Pre-Vocational Education (CPVE) in 1983. This was also a common core examination but more vocationally oriented. There was a further development in 1986 when the National Council for Vocational Qualifications (NCVQ) was established to co-ordinate vocational courses.

By the mid-1980s, there were two separate but related problems: the inadequacy of A levels for 'academic' students; and the increasing demand of other young people to have worthwhile curricula. In addition, further complications were added by the Education Reform Act (1988), particularly the National Curriculum, and the fact that at long last, in 1988, the GCE O level and CSE examinations were replaced by a single examination for the 16+ age group — the GCSE. This new examination was designed to be much more broadly based than O level, involving more practical work, school-based assessment and course work of various kinds, all of which would have a knock-on effect for 16–19 courses, including A level.

The Higginson Report (1988)

The Vice-Chancellor of the University of Southampton, Dr (later Sir) Gordon Higginson was asked to chair a small committee to make recommendations about AS and A levels. The Report recommended a five-subject structure, made up of a mixture of AS and A, but it was also recommended that A levels should be leaner and tougher, that is with less factual content but just as demanding in other respects. The clear intention was to achieve greater breadth without a loss in standards. Such a proposal would not have solved all the problems (it would have achieved breadth but not necessarily balance), but it received a good deal of approval in the educational world. The Secretary of State, Kenneth Baker, had given the Report his informal approval, but he was over-ruled by the Prime Minister, Margaret Thatcher, who reverted to the argument that standards would be threatened and that the 'gold standard' of A levels must be the first priority. The problem was referred back to the DES who handed it over to the School Examinations and Assessment Council (SEAC).

In November 1989 the DES held a conference to establish general policy guidelines. Mrs Angela Rumbold, Minister of State, delivered a speech stressing four points. First, she pointed out that there was already a trend towards more balanced courses: nearly one-third of A level students were choosing a mixture of arts, social sciences and physical sciences. AS courses were intended to accelerate that process. But she thought that a mixture of A and AS would not be enough and floated the possibility of a list of core skills for all 16–19 year olds (which the National Curriculum Council (NCC) were already working on).

Mrs Rumbold's second point was that the A level failure rate was too high (about 25 per cent on average for all subjects; about 10 per cent of candidates failing to pass any A level). She suggested that for bright young people to have nothing to show for two years' work was unacceptable. There was also a high drop-out rate. Her third point was that it was desirable to have more opportunity for transfer between A level and vocational courses, with appropriate arrangements for credit transfer. Finally, she referred to the underlying problem that more young people were needed to continue training or education from 16–19. (The CBI had recently suggested a target of 50 per cent achieving NVQ Level III, the equivalent of A levels.)

Mrs Rumbold's speech was well received. But her four valid points made A level reform even more complex. The problem was now not simply achieving a broad and balanced curriculum, but also increasing the participation rate. How could a target of 50 per cent be achieved, without lowering standards, when A level — the gold standard — was designed for the most academic 20 per cent?

The question since 1988 has essentially been one route or two: whether the A and AS route could be improved and offered as one possible route with improved vocational courses providing a second (but equal) route; or should integration take place to provide a single route with options within that route?

Since the Higginson Report, educational and employer opinion has moved towards something broader and more balanced that the A/AS solution. There has been a preference for some kind of common, broader qualification, at least at 17, before choices are made for the final year. In April 1990, Sir John Cassells wrote a Report for the Policy Studies Institute (PSI) *Britain's Real Skill Shortage*, recommending a new unified set of qualifications covering academic, technical and vocational subjects. In May 1990, Sir Christopher Ball, produced *More Means Different*, stressing the need to widen access to HE, and questioning the continuation of A levels. In July 1990 the Institute for Public Policy Research (IPPR) recommended a more radical reform in *A British 'Baccalaureat': Ending the Division Between Education and Training* (Finegold 1990). It was suggested that tinkering with the present system would be a waste of time; A level and vocational courses should be abolished, with all young people studying in tertiary colleges, covering three areas — social and human sciences, natural sciences and technology, and the arts, language and literature. The proposal was clearly modelled on the courses in European countries such as France and Germany, and is similar to the International Baccalaureat in some respects.

The debate continued throughout 1991 and 1992. In April 1991, the Secondary Heads Association (SHA) published *16–19 The Way Forward* suggesting five foundation subjects in the first year and a choice of three or five A or AS, or advanced vocational courses, all within a modular structure with credit transfer. The Committee of Vice-Chancellors and Principals said that they did not regard 'the existing A level system and the confusing number of other qualifications as providing a suitable base for a wider admission system to higher education'. They preferred a more radical solution. The Association of Principals of Sixth Form colleges

(APVIC) recommended a national post-16 framework with a single award which would include A, AS, BTEC and others. The Royal Society said that A level was irrelevant to industry and HE, and should be replaced by an Advanced Certificate and Diploma (Royal Society 1991).

Those advising the Conservative politicians in power, however, remained committed to two separate routes. Margaret Thatcher, still Prime Minister, in an answer to a Parliamentary question in October 1990, had indicated her support for A level standards in their existing form; in November 1991, Kenneth Clarke, promised the House of Commons that A levels would remain the gold standard; in December 1991 Tim Eggar, who had replaced Angela Rumbold as Minister of State, promised to retain A level standards, whilst admitting that the government wanted a large increase in the numbers staying on for vocational qualifications. Kenneth Clarke, said, 'It is the level of qualifications that matters, not whether it is academic or vocational'. But he wanted far higher numbers reaching NVQ levels II and III, with equal value for the two routes.

These Conservative views were eventually enshrined in the White Paper: *Education and Training for the 21st Century* (DES 1991). But the debate continued. Even the Tory press were critical of the government's timid recommendations. Despite the departure of Mrs. Thatcher, the gold standard view of A levels still prevailed. The White Paper was based on the fallacy that there could be two separate routes with parity of esteem. There was a further compromise in the shape of a common Diploma (provided that certain minimum requirements were met on either of the two routes). The National Council for Vocational Qualifications (NCVQ) was encouraged to develop the second route, and in particular to establish General National Vocational Qualifications (GNVQ). In July 1992 Sir Bryan Nicholson, Chairman of NCVQ, announced that GNVQ syllabuses had been prepared in five subject areas and the courses would be piloted in 100 schools or centres, starting in September 1992. Ministers had been convinced that this vocationally-based alternative to A levels would be sufficiently rigorous. The five GNVQ courses are: leisure and tourism; manufacturing; health care; business and administration; and art and design. GNVQs at level III (to be awarded by BTEC, RSA and City and Guilds) will be regarded as the equivalent of two A level passes. All GNVQ courses include core skills — problem-solving, communication, personal skills, numeracy and information technology. Ministers had, however, insisted that, contrary to previous NVQ practice, all courses would have to have terminal written examinations.

In July 1992 another White Paper, written by the new Secretary of State, John Patten, *Choice and Diversity: A New Framework for Schools* (DES 1991) moved the educational debate away from examinations and qualifications, towards structural questions concerning grant maintained schools and the future of LEAs. No mention was made of 16–19, perhaps on the grounds that the recommendations of the previous White Paper were still being discussed and implemented. This did not stop other bodies making more specific recommendations. In particular, the National Commission on Education (NCE) had produced a number of Briefings from February 1992 onwards. Briefing No.3 *Participation of 16–18 Year Olds in Education and Training* (NCE 1992a) by David Raffe came back to the theme of the low participation rate of 16–18 year olds in the UK as compared with other OECD countries. The UK rate was 33 percent, exactly half the average for the other twelve countries. Raffe suggested that the British 'mixed model' was very inefficient compared with other advanced countries. Briefing No.5 *Breaking Out of the Low-Skill Equilibrium* (NCE 1992b) took the argument several stages further and made some suggestions for reforming the system from the point of view of employment and training.

In October 1992 a Discussion Paper was produced: *Towards a Framework for Learning to Age 18/19 in the 21st Century* (NCE 1992c). We are told of the urgent need for more education and training for this age group, the need to avoid rigid boundaries between academic, vocational and technical routes, as well as the importance of reducing (or even avoiding) failure 16–19. The NCE proposal consisted of extending the National Curriculum upwards to age 18 or 19 for all (full or part-time) with a General Education Diploma replacing existing awards at 16 and 18. The GED would be available for the majority of young people at 18 or 19, but if minimum standards had not been reached, a Record of Achievement would show whatever levels of progress had been reached. Pass/fail would give way to a detailed transcript of achievement. This proposal has the merit of providing a unified system which does not threaten existing standards. Details have yet to be worked out, but it is just possible that the time for real reform has come. If so, better late than never!

In summary, it has to be said that curriculum policy since 1987 has been divided in two (5–16; 16–19) when it should have been unified. The 5–16 curriculum development has been distorted by gross political interference; the 16–19 opportunity has been delayed by the worship of the sacred A level cow.

References

Ball, C. (1990) *More Means Different* RSA.
CACE (1959) *15–18* (The Crowther Report) HMSO.
Cassells, J. (1990) *Britain's Real Skill Shortage* PSI.
Chitty, C. (1989) *Towards a New Education System: The Victory of the New Right?* Falmer.
Department of Education and Science (1977a) *Education in Schools* White Paper HMSO.
Department of Education and Science (1977b) LEA *Arrangements for the School Curriculum* Circular 14/77 HMSO.
Department of Education and Science (1977c) *Curriculum 11–16* HMSO.
Department of Education and Science (1979) *Proposals for a Certificate of Extended Education* (Keohane Report) HMSO.
Department of Education and Science (1985) *Better Schools* HMSO.
Department of Education and Science (1987) Secretary of State's speech to North of England Conference. DES Press Release.
Department of Education and Science (1988a) *National Curriculum Task Group for Assessment and Testing, First Report* DES.
Department of Education and Science (1988b) *Advancing A levels* (Higginson Report) HMSO.
Department of Education and Science (1991) *Education and Training for the 21st Century* White Paper HMSO.
Department for Education (1992) *Choice and Diversity: A New Framework for Schools* White Paper HMSO.
Finegold, D. et al. (1990) *A British Baccalaureat* IPPR.
Fullan, M. (1982) *The Meaning of Educational Change* OIES Press (Ontario).
Knight, C. (1990) *The Making of Tory Education Policy in Post-War Britain 1950–1986* Falmer.
Lawton, D. (1973) *Social Change, Educational Theory and Curriculum Planning* Hodder and Stoughton.
Lawton, D. (1989) *Education, Culture and the National Curriculum* Hodder and Stoughton.
Lawton, D. (1992) *Education and Politics in the 1990s* Falmer.
Ministry of Education (1954) *Early Leaving Report* HMSO.
National Commission on Education (NCE) (1992a) *Participation of 16–18 Year Olds in Education and Training* Briefing No.3 NCE, May.
National Commission on Education (1992b) *Breaking Out of the Low Skill Equilibrium* Briefing No.5 NCE, July.
National Commission on Education (1992c) *Towards a Framework for Learning to Age 18/19 in the 21st Century* Discussion Paper NCE, Mimeo, October.

OECD (1988) *School Development and New Approaches for Learning: Trends and Issues in Curriculum Reform* Paris: OECD.
Royal Society (1991) *Beyond GCSE* Royal Society.
Secondary Heads Association (1991) *16–19 The Way Forward* SHA.
Sexton, S. (1988) 'No nationalised curriculum' *The Times* 9 May 1988.
Williams, R. (1961) *The Long Revolution* Penguin.

5   Public education and local democracy

Stewart Ranson

Introduction

The present phase of the Conservative Government's movement to reform education has taken a decisive turn. Under the mask of continuing the changes begun in 1988 the legislative proposals of 1992 in fact mark a final break with the post-war values of universalism in favour of an earlier tradition, never eliminated, of private and selective education. At the centre of the new programme lies an attack upon the public and democratic foundations of education and upon the equal opportunities they strive to constitute. This chapter seeks to discuss the Government's quiet revolution to undermine public education and to present an alternative agenda for an empowerment curriculum the foundation of which lies in extending rather than eroding the conditions for local democracy.

The 1988 Education Reform Act sought to recast the government of education in the most radical reform of the service since 1944 while, arguably, retaining some of the defining characteristics of the post-war period. The 1988 agenda for reforming the quality of education revolved around a number of key principles. First, establishing *an entitlement curriculum*: the creation of a National Curriculum would provide an entitlement to broad and balanced learning for all five to sixteen year olds and would improve achievement by providing a better definition of what is to be taught and learned. Clearer assessment of what has been achieved would enable planned progression from stage to stage of the learning process. Such close monitoring of progress in learning would enable parents to know more clearly what was being studied, what objectives were being set and what was achieved individually and collectively. Second, *public accountability:* this would substantially increase the amount of public information available to parents about the curriculum, achievement, and the use of resources would enable schools and the service to be more accountable to parents. Third, *public choice:* the availability of such evidence about the performance of institutions would enable parents to make more informed choices. Open enrolment together with 'pupils as vouchers' formula funding of schools (Thomas 1990) would encourage competition between schools and lead to improved standards of education. Fourth, *local management:* better management and a better curriculum go hand in hand, and the 1988 reforms sought to delegate decision-making as close as possible to the point where the decisions bite. Schools and further education colleges would be granted the flexibility to use resources more effectively to respond to their own needs as articulated by the governors and parents as well as the teachers.

Although the ERA redefined responsibilities, both centralising and devolving powers away from the LEA, it nevertheless accorded it, potentially, a leading role in the reform programme. The challenge for the new style LEA was to set aside its traditional commitment to controlling the routine administration of local education and to concentrate instead on clarifying strategy, supporting and assuring quality in schools and colleges. A 'providing' authority was to give way to an 'enabling' authority. The system was maintained but authority redistributed within an integrated but devolved framework of institutional governance for post- as well as pre-sixteen local education.

The juxtaposing of entitlement and public choice within this reformed system suggested an uneasy compromise between the universal values of post-war social democracy and the emergent perspectives of consumer democracy. By 1991 the agenda appeared to be subject to radical revision in a series of legislative proposals and shifting policy priorities that were realised during 1992. In March the Education (Schools) Act 1992 and the Further and Higher Education Act 1992 received the Royal Assent and in July by the White Paper *Choice and Diversity: A New Framework for Schools.* The implications of this legislative programme needs to be explored further.

Education and training for the 21st century (White Paper 1991, FHE Act 1992)

On 21 March 1991, the Government announced its intention that further education colleges would be given independent corporate status and be funded direct by an FE funding council from April

1993. Within a couple of months this idea provided the platform for a much more far reaching and extensive initiative. On 20 May 1991 the Prime Minister launched a major programme of reform of post-compulsory education and training for the 21st century. Its primary objectives are: to ensure that virtually the whole of the 16 to 19 age group are drawn into education and training; to reform post-16 qualifications; to raise the status of vocational studies; and to provide employers with a dominating voice in the new system.

The FE legislation in effect creates a new 16–19 college sector of education. From 1 April 1993, colleges of further education together with tertiary and sixth form colleges have been 'incorporated' and form a new directly funded sector focusing upon the needs of over two million full and part-time students. It is believed that in time most of the current distinctions between different types of colleges will disappear as, for example, sixth form colleges take on vocational courses and part-time students. The colleges will become a legally independent corporate body with powers: 'to provide education for those over 16; to employ their own staff; to enter into contracts on their own behalf; to manage assets and resources, and to act otherwise as a legal body undertaking activities in furtherance of their purposes as providers of education.' With charitable status funded through two Further Education Funding Councils (FEFC), one each for England and Wales and advised, in England, by nine regional advisory committees with offices and staff. These new councils, with strong industrial, commercial and professional representation, have been appointed by the Education Secretary in consultation with the Employment Secretary. They have wide ranging powers and responsibilities for the new sector, including the planning of provision, incorporating the power to determine what kind of courses colleges should offer, controlling the allocation of annual funding as well as capital resources, and monitoring the quality of college performance.

The LEAs will have formally only a tenuous link with the new college sector, being asked merely to *liaise* with the colleges while local councillors will only be able to serve on the governing bodies of the colleges if invited to do so. The Government, some have interpreted, 'is determined to ensure a complete rupture between the colleges and their present masters' (*Times Educational Supplement* 24 May 1991, p.4). The Training and Enterprise Councils (TECS), however, are to be accorded the right to become governors.

> After the reforms instruments of government will no longer provide for formal LEA representation. The legislation will, however, remove the provision in the 1988 Education Reform Act which prevents people who are local authority members or

employees from being co-opted on to governing bodies. Governing bodies will be able to co-opt two additional members. This means that some governors may well combine their public service on the governing body with membership of a local authority. They will be co-opted for their individual qualities, and not as delegates or representatives of the local authority. . .Existing employment interest governors should be supplemented by a representative of a local TEC. This will reflect the TECs' important contribution to training locally and their increasing involvement in vocational education.

The colleges will be funded in part from an education and training council grant. This will comprise two components: a cash limited block grant together with a further amount based upon student admissions. Colleges will continue to derive funds from: TEC grants under the work-related further education programme, grants from polytechnics if they undertake some higher education work; fee income from employers and students; and from consultancy and other services. The colleges will be able to offer training credits, which are vouchers for 16 or 17 year olds to pay for part-time vocational educational and training. The scheme will be managed by the TECs. Now being piloted in eleven areas of the country, the White Paper proposes that by 1996 all 16 or 17 year olds will be offered training credits to pay for vocational education and training.

This wide ranging reconstituting of the governance of post-16 education and training is designed to support reforms which will ostensibly break down the divide between academic and vocational systems of learning and qualification. A vocationally oriented competence based curriculum and assessment is to be given parity of esteem with the academic:

Young people and adults need a clear framework of qualifications to measure their success in education and training. We need to build up a modern system of academic and vocational qualifications which are equally valued. They must both set a high standard and offer ladders of opportunity after sixteen and throughout working life. . .
Vocational qualifications in this country have been undervalued and underused. A major reform is underway to produce clear, nationally recognised qualifications. The reform is led by the National Council for Vocational Qualifications. . .the NCVQ should work with others to develop criteria for accrediting more vocational qualifications.

At the same time, a framework of principles will be designed to ensure the quality of all A level and AS syllabuses. New diplomas will encompass these academic (e.g. A levels) and vocational (NVQ) qualifications. A range of general NVQs will be developed for young people to cover broad occupational areas and enable a variety of career choices. The Government intends that these principles should control the development of syllabuses, limiting assessment by coursework and establishing examinations at the end of courses as the norm. Other changes include:

- school sixth forms to be allowed to admit part-time and adult students, and to accept training credits or to charge fees for them;
- education compacts to be extended nation wide; these are bargains between young people, employers and colleges. Young people work towards personal goals and in return employers provide a job with training for those who achieve their goals;
- vocational adult education to be funded through colleges; leisure/social adult education expected to be funded by fees.

Local authorities and the teacher associations have been critical about the implications of these reforms: firstly, for preventing the development of coherent strategies and plans for the post compulsory education and training which had been at the centre of the 1988 Education Reform Act; secondly, the narrow, utilitarian conception of the purposes of education and training; and thirdly, special educational needs post-16. The influence of the TECs and a tendency to output measurement of performance were already leaving students and trainees with SEN at the margin. The *Times Educational Supplement* concluded that 'even if reducing local taxation is no longer an electoral imperative, the government is going out of its way to strip the local authorities of responsibility or influence in further education and its support services' (24 May 1991, p.4).

Despite the high expectations of the launch of the FE White Paper in 1991 and the urgency of the 'skills revolution' required to support the regeneration of industry, a special report in *The Times* (23 November 1992) reviewed the failures of training policy: 'only 37 per cent of 16 to 18 year olds in full time education and less than 20 per cent of the rest on the Youth Training Scheme'. Moreover, the Minister for Employment acknowledges that school leavers face an 'alphabet soup' in which 4000 qualifications are offered by 300 different bodies. *The Times* concludes that 'the promise of local diversity has often withered into confusion and apathy; worse, the divide between academic and vocational tracks remains all but absolute in spite of new modular courses which should allow interaction between the two;. . .shamelessly. . .training (is thought of) as a way of dealing with the less able, instead of encouraging a broader definition of ability itself; public recognition of vocational qualifications remains low, a problem compounded by their omission from the school league tables launched last week'. Educationalists contributing to *The Times* report were particularly critical of the narrow focus of the existing NVQs: Professor Smithers believes that 'the qualifications have lost touch with reality. They are tailored to specific jobs. Rather than setting a core standard for maths for example, you just have to know the maths related to one job. This may be alright in the short term but what about a job in five years time'. Hilary Steedman, of the National Institute for Economic and Social research argues that: 'NVQs need significant amendment to be suitable for young people because they are too focused on one or two areas and have no perspective of what will be needed in ten years time. They will be alright for adults because they encourage people to get recognition for skills they have already acquired and this can improve morale. But it does not improve skill levels. It simply certifies levels which already exist'. This narrowness raises the significance of the new GNVQ which intend to emphasise cross-curricular themes and core skills. Yet, the new scheme, is being piloted this year as a vocationally programme complement to the 'gold standard' of A and AS levels.

The agenda of the FHE legislation seems clear: the nationalising and regionalising of further education, the stratifying of education and training rather than their integration, institutional differentiation subject to market forces, and the de-democratising of local education. Green (1991) concludes: The creation of a more integrated national system of post-16 institutions 'is clearly not this Government's intention. . .(preferring) to let free-for-all competition between institutions prevail. . .In any case the bifurcation of control between LEAs (for sixth forms) and the councils (for colleges) will rule out any further comprehensive reorganisation and put an end to further tertiary college development. Even the nascent "tertiary systems" will be jeopardised, since these carefully nurtured cross-institutional networks have relied on the good offices of the LEAs and an ethic of cooperation which is unlikely to survive in an atmosphere of open competition. Our inefficient and confusing "mixed institutional system" seems here to stay. . .In this Government's hands we seem to be progressing fast back to the old tripartite division of academic (A level), technical (now GNVQ) and vocational (now NVQ) tracks, delivered through the same multiply-fragmented institutional system'. These trends towards regulation, differentiation and de-democratising of local education are at the centre of and reinforced by the White Paper and Bill on *Choice and Diversity*.

Choice and Diversity (White Paper and Bill 1992)

The White Paper was published with a fanfare by the Secretary of State as the most important reform since 1944, 'a landmark document. . .setting out an evolutionary framework for the organisation and funding of schools into the next century' (DES 1992a). Yet the 1988 Education Reform Act had purported to provide the same radical change to the government and management of education. The question must be raised whether the proposals for change which have emerged since 1991 are indeed an evolution of the 1988 reforms or amount to a fundamental recasting of the agenda and the return to pre-war educational policies.

Although there is the semblance of continuity between 1988 and 1992 there is actually a fundamental shift of policy. In place of 'progression', 'entitlement' and 'local management' is substituted a new emphasis upon 'standards', 'specialisation', 'selection' and 'autonomy'. The elements of the new paradigm will be discussed in turn.

Table 5.1: From 1988 to 1992

	1988	1992
Mission	Public choice and accountability (entitlement)	Choice and diversity (differentiation)
Learning process	An entitlement curriculum progression assessment	Specialisation Standards Testing
Institutional system	Local delegation (LM)	School autonomy (GM) College incorporation
Government	National education, locally administered The enabling LEA	Nationalisation of education Demise of the LEA, especially, the role of local democracy
	Governing body	Regional funding agencies Foundation governors
	Parental choice	Parental power
	Quality assurance/ development	Quality control/ inspections
Context	Economic crisis	Economic and social crises

Standards

The Prime Minister in the forward to the White Paper says that 'the drive for higher standards in schools has been the hallmark of the Government over the last decade' and is now to be carried forward. The White Paper emphasises that the Government is:

> absolutely committed to testing. . .as the key to monitoring and raising standards in our schools. (p. 9)
> Tests are. . .critical in spotting under-achievement and in pinpointing the need for 'remedial' work.

The White Paper reinforces other Government announcements about standards. The proportion of course work in GCSE has been reduced while that of exams has been increased. The concern about standards in GCSE was reiterated following the publication of the exam results in August when the Secretary of State announced a review of marking following a confidential report from inspectors which claimed a decline in standards. In earlier years simpler tests are being introduced to assess a more basic curriculum. Standard attainment targets (SATs) have been simplified with an increase in pencil and paper tests and some of the key curriculum orders are being reviewed. Only three years after publishing its Orders on the teaching of English, the Government has now announced a review of the subject. The traditional 'basics' are to be reinforced with greater emphasis given to spelling, grammar and to the speaking of standard English. In October the Prime Minister, on the radio, emphasised the importance of teaching facts in history.

What is emerging fitfully but surely is a different conception of learning within the National Curriculum: a move away from an emphasis upon progression in understanding, skills and capacity taking into account the needs of the child as a whole person as well as the requirements of learning through the National Curriculum. The move towards a basic standards model of the curriculum entrenches even more securely than the subject based National Curriculum a conception of learning as the inculcation of disaggregated bodies of knowledge, a 'collection code' curriculum, and of assessment as the sorting and differentiating of young people. It reinforces a notion of fixed levels of ability, the 'normal curve' of achievement, and of different 'types' of aptitude and ability.

Specialisation

The White Paper celebrates 'choice and diversity': 'diversity and parental choice allow schools to develop in different ways. In particular they encourage schools to play to their strengths. Some schools stress an all ability curriculum; others, in addition to the National Curriculum specialise in one or a small number of subjects' (p.9). Diversity offers parents and children greater choice: private and state schools, county and voluntary; comprehensive schools of variety, grammar and bilateral; CTCs and grant maintained schools. Some schools will choose to specialise in music or technology or in languages. Diversity, it is proposed, extinguishes the anathema of uniformity which 'in educational provision presupposes that all children have basically the same educational needs. The reality is that children have different needs. The provision of education should be geared more to local circumstances and individual needs: hence our commitment to diversity in education' (pp.3–4).

This discussion implies, however, that specialisation might proceed beyond different emphases of subject into different types of learning and school — academic, technological and creative. These distinctions recall the terms of tripartite education — grammar, technical and modern — outlined in the 1938 Spens Report and the 1943 Norwood Report and introduced into the secondary system after the Second War. Indeed, the 1992 White Paper refers affectionately to this tripartite system of secondary school which, it implies, would have proved an ideal education system if it had only been supported by a National Curriculum to provide equality of opportunity! Like the 1940s Reports, the 1992 White Paper expresses its commitment to 'parity of esteem' between different types of school. It is argued that schools can develop such specialisation 'within existing powers': 'it generally does not constitute a significant change of character requiring the approval of the Secretary of State. If schools wish to develop in this way responding to the aspirations of parents and local economic needs, then it is entirely appropriate that they should use the discretion vested in them to do so'.

Selection

While the White Paper celebrates diversity and alludes to the virtues of a tripartite education system it denies that any such specialisation or differentiation of institutions entails selection. 'Specialisation is often confused with selection. . .a school that specialises is not necessarily one that applies rigid academic criteria for entries to a non-selective school can also choose to specialise'. Yet the word 'selection' appears in a title of prescribed values together with 'specialisation' and 'standards' and, moreover, the White Paper acknowledges that selection *could* take place through parental choice:

> as schools develop their strengths, they may become more attractive to parents and pupils. The greater demand to attend the school the greater the resources that will flow to the school. . . the selection that takes place is parent driven.

Notwithstanding the implication that choice itself can lead to selection and social differentiation of schools, it is clear from emerging evidence (Echols *et al.* 1990, Bowe *et al.* 1992; Walford 1992, Ranson 1993) that a market place of schools leads increasingly to schools selecting parents while getting rid (excluding) pupils who are believed not to be consistent with their chosen image and profile.

Institutional autonomy

While the 1988 Education Reform Act introduced the possibility of schools 'opting out' into grant maintained status it is a contested issue whether the originating conception for GM schools was as the future of all schools, or as a privileged sector like the old 'direct grant' schools, or as an exception (for schools seeking to escape purported 'undesirable LEAs'!). The norm was, arguably, intended to be 'locally managed schools' within an LEA but accorded considerable discretion over the use of resources within local strategic policy planning. Yet since 1991 Ministers have been promoting a very different policy that 'GM status should become a norm not an exception'. Institutional autonomy rather than discretion has now become the key value of Government.

> More diversity allows schools to respond more effectively to the needs of the local and national community. The greater their autonomy, the greater the responsiveness of schools (p.2) . . .

especially to parents who 'know best the needs of their children' certainly better than the professionals. Now, the autonomy provided by GM status supposedly becomes the key to future quality of schools.

The demise (final curtain) of the LEA

By 1991 the LEA was once more in the eye of the storm as the purported cause of the service's problems and the very conception of education government embodied in the ERA — of a strategic LEA leading an integrated, albeit devolved, system of institutional governance giving way to a very different vision of autonomous institutions with the local administration retained to provide for 'residual' services and special needs. The Prime Minister in May 1991, spoke of the need to break up the monolith of the local education *system* while a senior civil servant spoke of the need to 'plough the ground' a metaphor for dismantling the local system of education. The introduction of a new Funding Agency (FAS), controlled from Whitehall, is to be introduced to control finance but also the rationalisation of institutions. As opting out accelerates, the FAS is conceived as replacing the role of the LEA in relation to primary and secondary schools. Any obstacles which may resist increasing the 'organisational flexibility' of the LEA in the evolution of its residual functions will be removed, 'in particular the requirement to establish an Education Committee. Some local authorities may soon be in sight of no longer needing them'.

Thus the emphases of the 1992 legislative changes and proposals of 1992 mark a significant change for the government of education. They establish a new consistency of governance to replace the contradictions of entitlement and choice. Now the principles of student differentiation and selection sit harmoniously with the established policy of institutional differentiation. The changes, by reinforcing market forces, will entrench the reintroduction of tripartite education. The Conservative Party's agenda represents a Platonic vision of education to secure social selection and social control during a period of social and economic crisis.

Perhaps the defining characteristic of the present restructuring of the government of pre- and post-16 education is the attack upon the democratic foundation of local education. Its attempt to remove education (schools and colleges) from local politics presents the most significant indication of the termination of the post-war social democratic era in which local government played the pivotal role in the development of public services for all. The de-democratising of local education is not a peripheral element: it is, arguably, its central purpose. At this stage, the analysis of an American study which has been influential with the Government (a civil servant indicated that ministers had made it prescribed reading) needs to be critically examined.

The attack on local democracy

Chubb and Moe in their, *Politics and Markets in America's Schools* (1990) (popularised in the glossy *Sunday Times* magazine in

February 1992) seeks to argue that local democracy is the source of the problem of failing schools. This argument proceeds through a number of stages. The presenting problem is that schools are failing in their core academic mission — maths, science, foreign languages etc. Children are not learning enough, nor the right things, nor learning how to learn.

Two waves of reforms, designed to remedy this situation, have helped only marginally. The first wave of reforms introduced: tighter standards for teacher certification, higher teacher salaries, career ladders, merit pay, stricter disciplinary policy, more homework, and standardised tests. The second wave of reform, looking remarkably like our own 1988 reforms, encouraged: school based management, teacher professionalism, and controlled choice for parents and pupils. These reforms, though contributing a little, were deemed to be failing because they were not identifying and addressing the underlying cause. The reforms therefore were destined to fail. The task was to develop a theory which explained failure. Such a theory was to be found in institutional analysis. Because schools are shaped by their institutional settings, the kinds of organisation they become are largely a reflection of the institutional contexts in which they operate.

While the reformers believed that the source of the problems lay in and around schools, that schools could be made better within existing contexts, Chubb and Moe argue that existing institutions cannot solve the problem because they are the problem. The very institutions which are supposed to solve the problem are the source of the problem — that is, institutions of direct democratic control. This institution, Chubb and Moe believe, is incompatible with effective schooling: direct democratic control undermines academic performance.

The institutional characteristics of the public sector, it is argued, create problems for schools. The game of local democracy constitutes a perpetual struggle for power that creates winners and losers. This makes democracy an essentially coercive institution: the winners impose their policies at the expense of the others. The *raison d'être* of democracy is for the winners to impose their higher order values which they realise through rules and procedures. Bureaucratic and hierarchical control, therefore, arises naturally and inevitably out of this process of democracy because of the need to ensure compliance.

Schools are trapped within these institutional arrangements. They can't set their own agendas because these are determined by politicians and administrators who impose their values upon schools: for example, 'sex education', 'socialisation of immigrants', 'the mainstreaming of the handicapped', 'bilingual education', 'what history to teach'. The ensuing paraphernalia of rules stifles the autonomy of schools and demotivates the teachers. Institutions work when people choose them. The key to better schools lies, thus, in institutional reform which reinforces choice and therefore commitment. The appropriate institutional setting for education lies in (or in some semblance of) the private sector in which society controls schools through the market rather than democratic politics.

- Authority is radically decentralised, enabling discretion, promoting autonomy.
- No one makes decisions for society.
- All participants make decisions for themselves.
- Markets are myopic, they offer what people want, through selection and sorting, organisations and consumers are matched.
- To be successful schools need to find a niche — a specialised segment of the market to which they can appeal and attract support; the obvious way to do this is through the strategic design of their curriculum, targeting particular values — discipline, religion, socio-economic and ethnic make-up of students.
- The market allows and encourages its schools to have distinctive, well-defined 'mission'.

Although markets have imperfections these are preferable to those of public authority: democratic control tends to promote bureaucracy, while markets tend to promote autonomy. Thus according to Chubb and Moe the institutional conditions for effective schools are to de-democratise institutional setting and to create market setting which constitutes: decentralisation, competition, choice, autonomy, clarity of mission, strong leadership, teacher professionalism and team co-operation.

Critique of Chubb and Moe

While Chubb and Moe correctly identify the focus upon the key issue of the institutional structure of democracy, or the structure of the polity, their analysis is mistaken. Markets cannot provide what is needed for education or society. The unintended consequences which follow from individuals acting in isolation ensure that self-interest is often self-defeating. More importantly markets are formally neutral but substantively irrational or biased. Under the guise of neutrality the market actively confirms and reinforces the pre-existing social order of wealth and privilege. The market is a crude mechanism of social selection. Markets are, therefore, the supreme institution of winners and losers, with the winners imposing their power on the losers without redress because of the structure of social selection: markets produce survivals and extinctions in a Darwinian zero sum game. Markets are politics: that is, a way of making decisions about power in society and they ensure that the already powerful win decisively.

Markets cannot reduce the problems we face: indeed they ensure that we stand no chance of solving them. The problems we face derived from the transformations of the time: the restructuring of work; environmental erosion; the fragmentation of society. These transformations raise questions about what it is to be a person, what is the nature of the community, what kind of polity we need to secure the future well being of all. These present issues of identity, well-being, rights, liberty, opportunity, and justice. These predicaments that confront us cannot be resolved by individuals acting in isolation, nor by 'exit' because we cannot stand outside them. Markets can only exacerbate these problems: they ensure that we stand no chance of solving them and are unlikely to be legitimated by the majority of people who will be defeated and excluded by markets.

The predicaments of the time are collective or public in nature and require public action to resolve them. The only solution to these problems lies in the public domain. Only the public domain can solve the physical problems of the environment the conditions for which lie in collective action and only the public domain can solve the moral and social problems facing our society: issues of membership, recognition, value, space, opportunity, having a purpose for living a life. What are the qualities of the public domain which provide the conditions for resolving these issues?

- A process which enables individuals and groups to articulate and reconcile the values and needs that are believed to be central to their own development as well as that of the communities in which they live. This is inescapably a political process. It requires:
- a commitment to learning, listening, reasoning, and judging the public as well as private good;
- institutions which support and sustain discourse, learning, public choice.

These institutional conditions are those of democracy and government. The structure of the public domain which best provides the conditions for motivating people to engage in individual and collective development lie in *democracy*, because democracy enables the (political) process of articulating and reconciling differences and thus establishing the conditions (individual and collective) for living a life in which all citizens can flourish, which acknowledges their values, accords them identity and sustains them materially.

Developments which became preconditions for the educational development of many young people — bilingual teaching, a multicultural curriculum, equal opportunities for a gender neutral learning, comprehensive schools — did not emerge from Whitehall nor from isolated individual assertion but bottom up through local discourse and public action in response to the articulated demands about the need to learn and an understanding of the conditions for learning. The challenge for our time is to reconstitute the conditions for a learning society (Ranson 1992a) in which all are empowered to develop and contribute their capacities.

Towards learning for empowerment

A number of local authorities facing the issues of disadvantage and hopelessness in 'the inner city' have recognised the need for a more fundamental review of the purposes and conditions of learning which can provide an alternative agenda for educational reform. They have defined the problem as an intrenched loss of self-esteem, dignity and confidence. In the context, the task has been to understand 'the long term process of transforming the way people think about themselves and what they are capable of and of shaping our methods of implementation accordingly'. Initially, the LEAs perceived the management challenge as one of clarifying their vision of education, in the direction of enabling local people to develop the confidence and capacity to handle their own futures. Subsequently, they attempted to articulate this vision in development plans that could both manage change and help to regenerate education. Such plans often began by expressing the new values and principles which would shape the reform of provision, teaching and learning, the curriculum and relations with parents and the community. These will be summarised in turn.

Valuing capacity

Values were carefully chosen to celebrate a distinctive vision about the reservoirs of capacity in individuals: the purpose of education being to create active rather than passive learners, empowered with the skills to make responsible choices about the direction of their own lives as well as to co-operate with others to improve the quality of life for all in the community. The LEAs believed in (i) valuing the identity and dignity of each, to develop the self-esteem which is a precondition for learning. Education helps young people to form positive attitudes to themselves as well as others and thus to dissolve prejudice. (ii) Belief in individual capacity and achievement: 'that no limit should be assumed to the individual's capacity for achievement: this must be the basis of expectations of young people from all backgrounds'. (iii) Valuing assertiveness, self-confidence: to learn is to reach out, to examine something beyond the self; to encounter a different environment and the strangers within it: The value of self-confidence is especially important for those groups — girls, the black and ethnic minorities — which have, traditionally, been disadvantaged by education. (iv) Agency: empowerment for autonomy and responsibility: enables students to become independent learners: they manage what they are doing, make decisions about the best way of doing it and have access to resources. (v) Responsibility for others and the wider community: the LEAs wished to encourage an outward looking education: 'schools and colleges should help young people to form constructive and co-operative attitudes to each other, to their work and to the community so that they can play an active and responsible role in society'. There was also some movement towards active citizenship and an understanding of the importance of taking decisions.

Provision for entitlement

A number of values established objectives for schools and colleges: what is offered in terms of opportunities, resources and facilities. Thus it was argued that provision should enable the principles of: entitlement to a comprehensive and continuing education for all to achieve personal growth throughout their lives; responsiveness to the expressed educational needs of all in the community; accessibility to enable members of the community to take up learning opportunities, which require flexibility of provision in schools and especially in further and higher education to enable students to transfer courses and maintain progression in learning. Resources remain a vital condition for educational quality and these LEAs invested considerably in staff development; indeed they strove to protect expenditure in the face of pressure to contract it.

A belief in quality development was expressed in the growing commitment to the monitoring and evaluation of provision.

These characteristics are best provided in a tertiary system of schools and colleges for 14 to 19 year olds as Chitty *et al.* argue (1991): 'there is an urgent need for the widening of access to higher education; that this can be achieved only by moves towards a more coherent, unitary and integrated public system of 16–19 education and training; and that the tertiary college provides the institutional structure most ideally suited to a comprehensive system of post-compulsory provision' because of its commitment to equal opportunities for all young people.

Comprehensive curriculum

Teachers, lecturers and advisers sought to develop principles which would encourage a comprehensive curriculum that would be relevant to learners, enabling them to draw upon their experience of living within the community. This proposed curriculum should be broad and balanced in the learning offered, modular in its form, though ensuring coherence and integration across the experience of learning, enabling continuity and progression, and supporting young people with formative and positive assessment to help them understand their achievements and progress. The most persuasive recent account of a comprehensive curriculum for the 'transition age group' has been produced by the Institute for Public Policy Research (1990) whose proposals strive to integrate the academic and vocational divide within a unitary post-16 system which gives education the initiative:

> A unified system would require the abolition of both A levels and the various vocational awards, and their replacement with a single qualification, though not a single exam, at 18 plus. A modular curriculum would allow students to pursue different levels of intellectual and practical study according to their aptitudes and interests. With the curriculum consisting of three areas of study – – natural sciences and technology, social and human sciences, and arts, languages and literature –– a common core could be established to build coherence as well as choice into the system. (Miliband 1990)

The qualities required of students at advanced level, industrial workers and citizens in a developing democracy are increasingly the same: the ability to question conventional wisdom and practice, analyse, form judgements in debate and carry them into practice. A reformed comprehensive curriculum for 14–19 year olds should strive to explore the interdependence of theory and practice, placing knowledge at the service of society and the environment upon which it depends. The IPPR model provides the prospect of developing young citizens with understanding, skills and social confidence that would be welcomed by employers as well as university admission tutors.

Active learning

If learning is to be effective it should motivate young people by engaging their interests and by being related to their experience. The process of teaching, moreover, should seek to involve students in, and negotiate with them, a process of active and collaborative learning: 'We must shift from a teaching approach to a learning approach'. The values emphasised: (i) Student centred learning: education should begin from the needs and strengths of the individual and not merely the benchmarks of preconceived standards; 'Learning should be appropriate to the needs of individual students and provide a challenge to each one . . . We must take time and involve students, to share the ownership of learning. It is no good if the "problem" is ours and we tell the answers. It is only when the young person owns a problem in learning that they will really want to learn "to write" or "to read". We need to listen to young people'. (ii) Participation and dialogue: motivation is more likely if learning grows out of a process of agreeing with pupils and students the tasks to be undertaken. (iii) Active learning: there is a strong belief amongst educators in disadvantaged LEAs that if the learning process is to be involving it needs to be a more active experience than it has proved traditionally in most schools. Active learning can encourage students to take responsibility for their own learning experience and that of others. (iv) Learning can serve others: learning, even within the traditional subject curriculum, can be given purpose by serving the needs of others in the community. (v) Collaborative learning: if students are to achieve the educational value of respecting other persons and cultures, then the very process of learning must encourage collaborative as well as individual activity. Students need to be given the responsibility of developing projects together so that they decide the ends and plan the means: 'Learning is most fulfilling as a co-operative activity rather than a solitary or competitive enterprise'. Your ideas and knowledge provide the spark to my discovery, your progress is necessary to mine. (vii) Learning as enjoyment: 'Learning should be interesting and challenging, it should be an exciting experience: it should be fun: too many schools are still boring environments'.

Partnership with parents and the community

Partnership with parents is regarded as the key to improving student motivation and achievement, while service to and involvement of the public reflects the broader responsibility of school and college to promote education within the community. Characteristics of partnership for improving learning quality include: (i) Welcoming parents into the life of the school as partners: establishing a new style in which schools will listen to and respond to parents: 'As teachers we need to listen, learn and respect: the great mystique about teacher autonomy needs to be unmasked'. (ii) Parents as complementary educators — in the home: parental contribution to schemes of reading is encouraged because of its acknowledged influence upon motivation, confidence and attainment scores; and — in school: the wide range of skills and experience amongst parents which can support the learning process is increasingly recognised. (iii) Developing shared understanding of the curriculum: establishing a closer match of understanding within the partnership takes time, given the differences of perception, but 'teachers, pupils and parents as well as others need to know what is intended, how it is to be pursued and achieved'. (iv) Dialogue in curriculum design: listening to parents and members of the community about how the curriculum, enriched by local knowledge and experience can enhance a school's multi-cultural and anti-racist understanding. (v) Partners in assessment of learning progress: establishing regular communication with parents about the progress their child is making; involving the parent in assessment and in agreeing a strategy about future development. (vi) Partners in evaluation and accountability: schools having the confidence to report to parents about performance, to listen to the 'accounts' of parents and to involve them in evaluating achievement.

Democratic governance of local education

What we learn from the strategies pursued by disadvantaged authorities is the significance of developing a new conception of the purposes and conditions of learning. That we cannot learn without being active and motivated, without others (i.e. the support of society) and without shared understanding about justice and rights to equal dignity. This suggests that if we are to establish the conditions for all to flourish, to be motivated and to take their learning and lives seriously, then reform needs to address the wider public purposes and conditions of public education:

- Learning is inescapably a *system*. Learning is a process which cannot be contained within the boundaries of any one institution. Discovery and understanding occur at home, in the community, on a scheme of work experience as well as in college or school. Progress, furthermore, will unfold more securely between stages of learning when they are mutually comprehending and supporting. Improving achievement, it is proposed, depends for its realisation upon enabling a wider system of learning: one element cannot be treated in isolation from another if each is to contribute to the effective working of the whole. Ensuring, for every school, the appropriate numbers of pupils, the provision of resources and teachers to support a balanced and comprehensive curriculum with choices at key stages to enable progression in response to diversity of need are characteristics which have to be managed at the level of the system as a whole, as well as the school, if all young people are to provided with opportunities to realise their powers and capacities.
- Education needs to be a *local* system. The system of learning is more effective if managed locally, as well as nationally and at the level of the institution. The different tasks need their appropriate tier of management and by creating a local system which delegated *and* enabled strategic leadership, the 1988 reforms enacted the conditions for excellence in the local management of education within a national framework. A local system of management is needed to ensure understanding of local needs, responsiveness to changing circumstances, and efficiency in the management of resources within geographic boundaries consistent with identifiable historical traditions. Such local systems need to be properly accountable and this requires location within a local democratic system.
- Education needs to be a local *democratic* system. If education is, as it should be, a public service of and for the whole community rather than merely the particular parents, young people and employers who have an immediate and proper interest in the quality of the education provided, then education must be responsive and accountable to the

community as a whole. The significance of learning for the public as a whole suggests the indispensable location of the service within a framework of democratic local government which enables all local people to express their views and to participate actively in developing the purposes and processes of their education service. A learning society — enabling all to contribute to and respond to the significant changes of the period — will depend for its vitality upon the support of local democratic institutions which articulate and take responsibility for developing all members of the community.

A flourishing public domain requires the vitality which local democratic governance brings to education. Upon local authorities lies the inescapable task of both re-interpreting national purpose to local need and generating the shared sense of purpose that is the precondition for public confidence and commitment. Only a very sophisticated social institution could bring off this demanding task. The challenge for the future is to extend rather than extinguish, the qualities of equality and justice which local democracy bring to the educational opportunities of local communities.

This paper builds upon earlier writings, Ranson 1992a and 1992b (see references).

References

Bowe, R., Ball, S. and Gold, A. (1992) *Reforming Education and Changing Schools* Routledge.

Chitty, C. (Ed.) (1991) *Post-16 Education: Studies in Access and Achievement* Kogan Page.

Chubb, J. and Moe, T. (1990) *Politics, Markets and America's Schools* DES Brookings.

DE/DES (1991) *Education and Training for the 21st Century* DES.

DES (1988) *The Education Reform Act 1988* DES.

DES (1992a) *The Education (Schools) Act 1992* DES.

DES (1992b) *The Further and Higher Education Act 1992* DES.

Echols, F., McPherson, A. and Willms, D. (1990) 'Parental choice in Scotland' *Journal of Education Policy*, 5, No.3.

Green, A. (1991) 'The White Paper on Education and Training: the rhetoric and the reality' *Forum* 34, No.1.

Institute for Public Policy Research (1990) *A British Baccalaureat: Ending the Division Between Education and Training* London: IPPR.

Miliband, D. (1990) 'Time to ditch the system' *Guardian* 2 October 1990.

Ranson, S. (1992a) 'Towards the learning society' *Educational Management and Administration* 20, No.2.

Ranson, S. (1992b) *The Role of Local Government in Education: Assuring Quality and Accountability* Longman.

Ranson, S. (1993) *The Changing Governance of Education* (forthcoming).

Thomas, H. (1988) 'Pupils as vouchers' *Times Educational Supplement* 2 November 1988.

Walford, G. (1992) *Selection for Secondary Schooling* London: National Commission on Education.

6 A philosophical perspective on 14–19 curriculum change

Richard Pring

Introduction

The system and the content of education are in a state of change to an extent that has rarely been equalled in previous times. And there seems to be no sign of it diminishing. But the more changes there are, the more confusion there seems to be concerning the purposes and the control of education.

This is particularly true of changes taking place at the latter end of secondary schooling. Such are the confused messages that it is important to look beneath the plethora of qualifications, behind the political manoeuvrings of many different pressure groups, beyond the disjointed ad hoc reforms and innovations, to the deeper educational traditions which these changes either embody or contradict.

This chapter aims to be philosophical, not in any profound sense of that word, but in the sense of pointing to the nature of these deeper traditions which are rarely acknowledged in the current debates.

To understand these traditions we must necessarily enter into essentially philosophical territory concerning what values are worth pursuing (answering the perennial educational question raised by Herbert Spencer in his essay 'What knowledge is of most worth?'), concerning the nature and organisation of that knowledge, and concerning the relationship of the state to educational activities. Ethics, epistemology and social philosophy are at the heart of this book's concerns, and, indeed, failure to see this is the cause of so much superficiality and incoherence in current attempts to address the problems of the 14 to 19 curriculum.

I shall therefore in this chapter do the following things. First, I shall briefly point to the array of changes which require some attempt to look for more stable principles to guide the choices to be made. Second, I shall put these changes within a wider political and social context — in particular, the criticisms in response to which the changes are being made. Third, I shall make explicit the underlying philosophical issues. Fourth, I shall by way of conclusion outline three distinct educational traditions which vie for allegiance amongst these many changes.

Changes

The changes affecting the 14–19 curriculum are of three kinds.

Qualifications

First, there is the fairly massive reshaping of qualifications. Until fairly recently, there were, on the one hand, relatively simple and well understood academic qualifications, but, on the other, quite disconnected and very complex vocational ones. The more able students would take GCE O level at 16 and some of those who were successful would proceed to take A levels as the matriculation requirements for university. The less able would, at 14, opt for the Certificate of Secondary Education (CSE), a form of examination designed in the 1960s to reflect the more practical and school initiated curriculum for those without academic aspirations. After the age of 16, those who wanted to acquire additional qualifications, but for whom the academic route of A level was deemed inappropriate, could, either full-time or part-time, pursue vocational qualifications at colleges of further education. The vocational route, however, was a veritable jungle of disjointed qualifications, obscure to potential trainees as well as to the public at large, organised by a range of examining bodies such as the City and Guilds of London Institute (CGLI), the Business Education Council, the Technical Education Council (now joined together as BTEC), the Royal Society of Arts (RSA) and many others.

In the last few years, there have been various attempts to change these qualifications – to build bridges between the academic and the vocational and to bring some order into the mess. First, the GCE O level and CSE have given way to a unified form of examination at 16 which, nonetheless, through an emphasis on course work and practical projects, has endeavoured to incorporate the educational principles underlying much of the CSE work. But the GCSE was also an attempt to emphasise criterion referenced rather than norm referenced assessment, which increasingly characterises the 14–19 qualifications. Concern for standards, which to many people were preserved through the O level rather than GCSE system, has led to the development of national assessment in National Curriculum subjects at 14 and 16, and no doubt GCSE will change again as it becomes the vehicle for delivering national assessment at 16.

After compulsory schooling, A levels (and more recently AS levels) remain roughly untouched as they are perceived as the 'gold standard', 'the flagship', 'the jewel in the crown' of the educational system. But the vocational area is changing radically and is doing so in such a manner that A levels, and the idea of academic studies, cannot remain unaffected. First, there has been the growth of the pre-vocational courses and qualifications, geared to those who want a course with a practical and vocational orientation but who are not ready for specific vocational training. There have been in the space of the last few years, following the Further Education Unit's *A Basis for Choice*, very popular CGLI 365 courses adopted by schools pre-16 and by schools and colleges post-16. These eventually gave way to the Certificate of Pre-Vocational Education (CPVE), to the BTEC First Certificate Courses, and to the CGLI Diploma in Vocational Education. But these in turn either have been abandoned or are being reshaped by GNVQ (the General National Vocational Qualification). Meanwhile, the very many vocational qualifications are being made to fit in with the framework set by the National Council for Vocational Qualifications (NCVQ) which is establishing criteria for five different levels of qualification across the vocational field.

The details of these changes are too great to be spelt out here, but for my purposes certain features need to be remembered. First, there is both a reassertion and a questioning of the academic and vocational distinction. Is it adequate for describing the complex range of educational purposes and modes of learning which constitute our system of education and training from 14 to 19? Second, the process of tidying up the qualifications and of 'building bridges' affects the transaction which takes place between teacher and student. Can the 'conversation between the generations of mankind', as Oakeshott describes the educational transaction, be put into an administratively convenient straight jacket? Third, the messy world of education, which may infuriate the bureaucratically minded, may indeed be a more appropriate reflection of the complex purposes which education serves and of the autonomy of educational traditions. What relationship is defensible between central government (or central qualification bodies), who increasingly control both the curriculum and how it should be taught, and the teachers, who structure the learning which takes place on the basis of their authority within an educational tradition and on the basis of their knowledge of the needs of the learner?

Institutions

The second kind of change affecting the 14 to 19 curriculum is institutional. Not long ago, arrangements seemed, in their general shape, to be relatively simple. Secondary schools took students through to 18 — if they wished to remain in the academic mainstream. Colleges of FE catered for full-time and part-time vocational students. There were slight variations on this, and some 'mission drift'. For example, a few schools had no post-16 studies, and students would go to a sixth form college for A levels, or to colleges of FE which increasingly provided A level courses. Nonetheless, schools themselves were for academic rather than vocational learning. And since all institutions came within the LEA, it was possible to ensure a comprehensive system of academic and vocational courses for all young people.

That now is changing as the innovations introduced by the 1988 Education Act and the 1992 Further and Higher Education Act have their effect. Schools and colleges are seen to be autonomous units competing for 'business' in an educational market. Many of the restrictions defining who does what have gone with the demise of LEAs' financial and administrative controls. Schools are now able to offer vocational awards, adult education, part-time courses. Over one-third of the colleges have franchising arrangements with universities for teaching their degree courses. Schools apply for 'technological status' as they conform to the present Government emphasis upon 'choice' and 'diversity' and 'specialisation'. There are city technology colleges and technology schools, differently funded and of different legal status.

Certain aspects of this need to be picked out for the purposes of this chapter. First, the changed institutional provision for the 14 to 19 group reflects a blurring of boundaries between education and training which makes distinctions between the academic and the vocational less easy to sustain. Second, judgements about what is educationally valuable, and the ethos and mission of the institution, are inextricably mixed up with what is marketable in a competitive system of financially autonomous 'businesses'. Thirdly, collaborative relationships have, with the demise of LEA control,

given way to competitive ones which are proclaimed as a vehicle
for raising standards.

Curriculum

It is impossible to give a brief summary of curriculum changes over
such a wide range of academic, pre-vocational and vocational
courses, but two important changes are worthy of note.

First, it is seen to be important to incorporate a greater degree
of vocational relevance even in the academic curriculum. Thus, the
Technical and Vocational Education Initiative (TVEI) launched in
1982 aimed to make the curriculum for all more relevant to the
economic needs of society and of the individual concerns. This did
not entail much encroachment upon the professional authority of
the teachers, since the money made available to TVEI depended
upon the curriculum meeting only broad criteria established by the
Department of Employment, not upon detailed prescriptions.
Nonetheless, the curriculum would be seen to be vocationally
relevant –– fostering those general skills, knowledge and
understandings which prepared students more effectively for the
world of work. It would ensure continuity from school to further
education and training. It would provide the habits and techniques
which would support continuing learning after school. It would
provide the guidance and counselling that enabled the student to
make wise choice of career, training or further education. Partly
arising from TVEI has been the development of core skills which
transcend particular subjects and their content — the personal
qualities needed to be effective within the adult world,
communication skills, numeracy, problem solving skills, and
economic awareness. Such 'core skills', it is argued, will be
incorporated in A-level syllabuses as well as in their assessment.

Second, there has been a shift, under the influence of certain
models of vocational training, towards a much greater precision in
curriculum planning and assessment – with clear statements of
attainments and precise quantification of performance measured
against those statements. This is often seen as a more rational
approach to teaching in contrast with more sloppy, ill thought out
ways.

For my purposes, the main questions concern, first, the extent to
which the integrity of subjects can be preserved once such
deliberate efforts are made to embody a vocational aspect; and,
second, the extent to which rational curriculum planning is the sole
mode of rationality as we describe the transaction which takes place
between teacher and learner.

Context

These changes, which upset a relatively stable world of education and training, must be understood against a background of mounting criticism of schools and colleges — or at least against a much deeper critique of the value that society at large places upon education — schools and colleges being but the victims of a much deeper malaise. These criticisms are summed up in Sir Claus Moser's presidential address to the British Association (1992). There he says that:

> this country is now in danger of becoming one of the least adequately educated of all the advanced nations — with serious consequences for the future socially, economically, technologically and culturally.

There are four sorts of interconnected criticisms.

Economic

First, it is argued that the system of education and training has not provided the future workers with the skills, attitudes, knowledge and personal qualities that a sophisticated economy needs. This criticism is pitched at various levels. Thus, many young people start work without even basic standards of literacy or numeracy, in a society which is ever more dependent on such basic skills. But even those who are literate and numerate lack other skills which the modern economy should be able to take for granted — skills in communication, in thinking or problem solving, in information technology. They lack those qualities of enterprise and entrepreneurship which a modern competitive economy requires. Though knowledgeable about the Reformation or about the achievements of the Romans, they remain ignorant of the world of business and commerce. Moreover, the most able, encouraged by liberal educational values, treat with disdain the practical and industrial world which sustains them. In brief, the world of education is disconnected, both in content and in values, from the world of work.

This criticism is one which needs to be taken seriously, though not as self evident. It is well argued by Finegold (1988) that Britain seems satisfied with a low-skill equilibrium — with an educational and training service which produces relatively low skilled workers because industry itself seeks little more. From the teenager's point of view, it is quite rational to opt for work without further training if the financial returns on being trained are very small. At times of prosperity, employers entice young people from further education and training rather than encourage long-term investment in higher qualifications. In other words, the connection between education and vocational preparation is a disputed one — both the nature of that connection in terms of skills, attitudes, qualities and understandings that need to be fostered, and the attribution of responsibility for whatever defects there are in the connection. For my purposes, however, the key question concerns the aims of education — the extent to which it can serve liberal ideals whilst being determined by economic needs.

Standards

A second major criticism has been that standards of both education and training have been lower than they should have been. This is partly borne out by cross-national studies in mathematics and science in which British students at 14 and 16 do not on average achieve as well as their German, French or Japanese counterparts. But also there is much anecdotal evidence produced in newspapers. And there are various studies which proclaim to show low standards in literacy and numeracy. Furthermore, the training system (so it is argued) does not produce the craftsmen and technicians to the same level of competence as that required by our major economic competitors.

By no means are these allegations proven, and indeed it is difficult to unravel the political content from the educational in the often acerbic debates. Objectivity is not helped by press commentary or by the superficial league tables now produced based on a few performance indicators. But for my purposes, we need to pick out such concepts as 'standards' and 'performance indicators' and to see how they relate to a wider set of concepts which require further clarification. 'Standards' presuppose particular values and purposes. They do not stare one in the face. Different judgements will be made depending on what one sees to be the aims of education — and on whom one believes to be the arbiters of those standards.

Social relevance

Society is more than a network of economic units for which the next generation has to be prepared. It is a mix of individuals, groups of individuals, and institutions, held together by a set of values which reflect personal and social norms. These norms determine the relationship between people and groups; they are internalised and shape how we behave — what we acknowledge to be right and wrong and what we expect as appropriate behaviour from others. Thus, an education service is expected to develop the virtues of honesty, of perseverance, of respect for persons (whatever their class, ethnicity or gender), of respect for the truth. It is expected, too, to develop the responsibilities and qualities of citizenship — the consciousness of civic obligations including political participation.

Where there seems to be a deterioration in such virtues and civic values, blame is often attributed to schools for lack of firm discipline and authority. But, again, there are limits to how far schools can, or should, fight against social attitudes which more often than not are linked to the wider social context of which school is but a part. 'Citizenship' contains within it some element of political participation and is a contestable concept within our own society. There are, therefore, deeper, more philosophical problems concerning the teaching of such contested concepts and concerning the authority of the teacher to decide what sort of society should be promoted through the curriculum. One consequence of the government becoming final arbiter in matters of curriculum and assessment is that it, the government, has wrested that authority from the teacher. It is as though what counts as citizenship is a political, not an educational, decision.

Personal relevance

The poor participation rate after the date of compulsory schooling has been blamed on several factors, not least that of a curriculum which is not seen to be relevant to so many young people. Others, however, would blame not the curriculum but the quality of teaching. Yet others would blame the perceived disconnection between further study and financial gain.

One of the most significant features of 14 to 19 changes has been the attempt to provide a vocationally relevant curriculum which calls upon more active learning approaches. Around TVEI and CPVE was a wide spectrum of innovations using information technology and flexible applications of teaching facilities to transform motivation in learning. These changes were in most cases far from cosmetic. They depended on a deeper, often unarticulated relationship between theory and practice, between knowing and doing, and between understanding and purposeful activity, which too often had been ignored in more traditional and didactic modes of teaching.

There has, however, been some confusion here which needs to be addressed. Interestingly, the more student centred approaches to learning, which found circulation through the publication of the Plowden Report 25 years ago, thrive mostly in the vocational context of further education. CPVE, the Diploma in Vocational Education, BTEC National and Higher National, all emphasise the importance of learning through structured activities and projects, through which practical competence and problem solving are inextricably linked to theoretical understanding. This is certainly a matter to be taken up when we seek a more philosophical understanding of events and as we establish a more philosophical critique.

To conclude this section, therefore, we have seen how the changes outlined in the first section are to be understood against a background of mounting criticism of the system of education and training. This criticism is fourfold — economic, standards, social relevance and personal relevance. Each criticism could with profit be expanded, for the sake both of seeing how valid each is and of understanding the underlying rationale of the changes. But for my purposes, it is more important to understand the ideas which are implicit in such criticisms. For there are inconsistencies which need to be examined in the light of more philosophical considerations. There is, in consequence, the need to think anew the aims of education which will accommodate the vocational purposes, which will have a defensible notion of standards and which will be seen to be both socially and personally relevant.

Philosophical issues

Educational values

Aims

Education is centrally concerned with the process of learning. But not any learning is accepted as educational. Learning which is narrowly conceived or which is indoctrinated or which is confined to trivial matters would not be so evaluated, for education is an evaluative term as much as a descriptive one. To call someone educated is to say more than that they have learnt something. It is to say that they have acquired 'worthwhile learning' — and that they have internalised it in a significant way. The educated person is someone more than the merely well trained one, although it necessarily involves training in a wide range of skills.

The significance of these conceptual points is that education (and thus the schools and the teachers which are there to promote it) is committed to certain sorts of learning rather than others; only certain sorts of learning are thought to be valuable and have an approved effect upon the learner. Such a learner, if successful, becomes an educated person. But what sorts of learning are valuable, and what counts as success in such learning? Are there certain books, and not others, which should be read and understood? Are there certain skills, but not others, which the educated person might expect to possess? And are such personal qualities as enterprise and entrepreneurship the ones to be expected of an educated person?

To sort out what sort of learning is valuable or what sort of person should be deemed educated is one aspect of ethics. It is a central element in our conception of 'the good life'. But there are confused voices here, never more so than in the present debate on the curriculum. On the one hand, there is a tradition — a dominant one from the 19th century — that the values to be pursued concern the 'perfection of the intellect', those studies that develop the power of reasoning and of imagining. In defending what would now appear to be a narrow curriculum of classics, mathematics and divinity, Copleston of Oriel College argued in 1810 (according to Slee's account of liberal learning at Oxford University) that through the teaching of classics, and the same argument was used later for mathematics, the university was aiming not to train its alumni directly for any specific profession but rather to develop an elevated tone and flexible habit of mind. The mental discipline of the classics and of mathematics plus the exposure to a particular literature and culture provided the mental training which 'liberated' the young person from the fashions and utilitarian influences of the day.

This conception of a liberal education has had a pervasive influence in the curriculum of 'public' schools, then the grammar schools, and subsequently the comprehensives. It has created a contrast between liberal and vocational learning which has entered into our institutional arrangements as well as the curriculum.

There are, however, contrasting ethical arguments which underpin the current debate. The first concerns the connection between education and development as a person, where 'person' requires more than 'the perfection of the intellect'. The second concerns the connection between education and the social, including economic, context in which education is provided.

Thus, to be a person, and to develop as a person, requires more than intellectual prowess. It requires more than the refinement of the imagination. It requires, too, the acquisition of those dispositions or virtues which are associated in society with being 'a good person'. It requires the acquisition of physical and social skills which will enable both survival and fruitful relationships. It requires the strength of character to provide self confidence in approaching difficulties. And, in so far as these qualities, dispositions and skills can be learnt, so too might they be seen as part of an educational programme. Therefore, learning to be more fully a person, as an aim of education, shifts the focus from mere intellectual development to wider personal qualities and dispositions, to emotions and values, to skills and habits, which either as individuals or as members of society we cherish. Much that has happened in the curriculum reflects this wider educational perspective — the recording of achievement which goes beyond academic success, the building of self confidence and self esteem through a range of achievements not always academic, the promotion of habits of co-operation, the development of empathy and tolerance.

Furthermore, there is implicit within these developments a questioning of the 'perfection of the intellect' — the academic achievement — as the main or sole purpose of education, where that treats the person as an individual disconnected from wider social and economic relationships. Thus, education, as a system of learning, might be seen as the acquisition of whatever values, knowledge, understanding or skills prepare young people for the adult world. Of course, that adult world could be conceived widely enough to embrace dissidents as well as conformists, critics as well as supporters. But it would include relevant economic awareness, skills relevant to earning one's living, the capacity to participate in political life, the readiness to adapt to changing social conditions. In other words, education would include a set of qualities, knowledge and skills which derived from a consideration not simply of individual perfection but also of living within a particular social and economic world. To understand the changes currently taking place — the assertion of the virtues of enterprise, the emphasis upon economic awareness, the promotion of 'core skills' — is to grasp this shifting concept of education, and the values which it embodies.

Academic and vocational purposes

Connected with this conceptual, and moral, shift is a questioning of the erstwhile clear distinction between the academic and the vocational. This distinction is often made as though it is self evident, and yet, upon examination, it clearly is not. Thus, A levels are seen to be academic; BTEC courses are vocational. Physics is an academic subject; crafts, design and technology is a vocational one. There is indeed a confused area in the middle. Medicine is obviously vocational but it demands academic qualities; engineering is academic, but its subject equivalents lower down the educational ladder are vocational.

This distinction, which is related to differences of status and value with which different studies are perceived, is related to a particular concept of 'the educated person' — one whose intellect has been perfected or at least refined by particular disciplines. Such disciplines have no obvious utility. They train the mind; they put the learner in touch with the best that has been thought and said; they arise from disinterested enquiry.

However, with a wider, more generous concept of 'the educated person', the distinction becomes much more blurred. Where the educated person is one who has an economic and social value, or where such a person is defined equally in terms of personal qualities and dispositions and skills acquired through systematic learning, then those studies are also of *educational* value which promote such awareness and virtues. Significant distinction lies, not in 'academic' and vocational', but between studies or disciplines which either do or do not promote these personal qualities, wider social and economic perspectives, valued dispositions, and mental qualities. Mathematics may or may not be educational depending on how it affects the mode of thinking and feeling as measured against these broader educational aims. So too training to be a carpenter or a car mechanic is educational or not, depending on the qualities of mind, personal dispositions or mental skills which it promotes. Vocational studies can be as much the vehicle of education as what traditionally have been called academic studies. The disconnection of utility from specifically educational aims has been a damaging myth.

Standards

'Standards' is a key concept in current educational changes. Standards are said to be too low or to be falling; standards in British schools compare badly with those in competitor countries; standards need to be improved and, to ensure that, performances will be measured against defined standards and thus comparisons made between child and child, between school and school, and over a period of time. It is assumed that what counts as standards are obvious, self evident, in no need of argument.

However, standards are incomprehensible outside a context of values — and in so far as people embrace different values, so they will refer to different standards. What exactly is valued in the teaching of English? Is it the appreciation of poetry? If so, then standards will be related to what counts as appreciation and to the kind of poetry deemed worthy of appreciation. Is it the clear communication of needs or wants or ideas? If so, then standards relate to such clarity in relation to whatever audiences are seen to be significant. It is often regarded as self evident that 'academic' students conversing intelligibly with their tutors on medieval poetry are demonstrating high standards. But the criticism, emerging from those who feel less convinced by the values of our education system, is that such students, though succeeding in this mode of conversation within universities (and appointed to academic posts to ensure its continuation) may at the same time demonstrably fail to converse with those outside that community. Happy in the Bodleian, they are at sea in the world of industry or of commerce. 'Standard' relates to the purpose of the activity. Should one change one's conception of 'the educated person', and should one thereby change the nature of the studies which are to count as educational, then one changes the standards whereby performance is to be judged.

Possibly the most significant challenge to traditional standards has been the TVEI innovations already referred to, and this was reflected in the battles fought within the examination boards. TVEI represented a different set of values — the value of practical skills and learning, personal and social qualities relevant to the world of work, communication skills, economic awareness. These values presupposed a different set of standards whereby success was to be judged and performance evaluated. Once one recognised the value of more practical modes of learning then performances previously rejected become recognised in the standards set. And this had profound consequences for the examinations and for the grading of work. TVEI set different standards because it challenged prevailing views concerning educational success.

Educational knowledge

Learning

Of the interconnected concepts through which we describe education — the values to be pursued, the academic and vocational studies through which they are pursued, the theoretical and the practical knowledge to be acquired, the standards by which success is measured — 'learning' is the most central one.

Current changes have been characterised by an insistence upon the importance of 'the process of learning' or of 'learning how to learn' or of 'learning skills'. But there is something very odd and misleading about such phrases because one does not learn in a vacuum. *Something* has to be learnt. And for learning to take place there must be the acquisition of new knowledge or skills or habits. Moreover, for that learning to be a success, then such acquisition has to 'come up to standard'. Hence, the spelling out of educational aims in detail requires the detailing of the subject matter to be learnt — and also the standards or the benchmarks according to which one might judge that learning to have taken place. Such detailing cannot avoid questions about the organisation and content of different forms of knowledge.

The traditional, academic curriculum has provided a particular, and some would say limited, map of knowledge characterising what is to be learnt and the criteria of successful learning. Therefore, the broader concept of 'the educated person' has required a different mapping of knowledge and new 'subjects' — technology, design, business studies and economic awareness, social studies and personal understanding. Moreover, the nature of the subject matter has, more often than not, required different learning strategies and different modes of assessing that learning has been successful. Success might lie in the intelligent performance rather than in the intelligent writing about performance. Different voices are being heard in the 'conversation of mankind'.

Oakeshott's metaphor of the conversation, however, in which students are introduced to the voices of poetry, of history, of science, of politics, is increasingly threatened by those who conceive learning much more behaviourally and narrowly. One characteristic of a good conversation is that, although there are clear standards implicit within it (attending to the point, taking seriously the evidence, following the logic of the argument), no one can prescribe or foretell exactly where it is going to end. An educational encounter is essentially open ended. Students try to make sense of their lives, and that sense might not be exactly as teachers or parents would have liked. The most one should hope for is that the conclusion is justified in the light of evidence and remains open to further development in the light of criticism. However, from a narrowly vocational model, one can see how such a notion of learning (and thus of the educated person) is being jeopardised by those who seek to prescribe in precise terms the end of the conversation — or, at least, deny that there should be such a process.

Explicit bits of knowledge or skills or behaviours are prescribed by vocational examination bodies or by government, and learning becomes not the internalisation of the standards of a conversation as expressed by various voices within an educational tradition but the repetition of knowledge or of behaviours as prescribed by those external to the educational transaction. This threat to educational values (in the extension of education from a privileged minority to the majority), which are tied to a particular concept of learning, is most obvious in the increasing stranglehold which NCVQ has over vocational qualifications such as BTEC. National Vocational Qualifications, including GNVQ, describe at different levels the exact tasks one should perform and the finite list of successful behaviours which count as having learnt to perform those tasks correctly.

Theory and practice

Under the influence of a particular understanding of 'academic', itself logically connected with specific (and impoverished) views of an 'educated person', educational has been linked to theoretical knowledge, to propositional knowledge, to 'knowing that', to what can be written down and read — and even dictated, as many A level students know. Practical knowledge, or knowing how, or being able to 'do' intelligently, wisely, intuitively, skilfully, is regarded as atheoretical and not part of a distinctively educational programme. Perfection of the intellect, not professional preparation, is the role of universities as John Stuart Mill reminded his audience in his inaugural lecture at the University of Aberdeen over 100 years ago.

Once again, however, this is a false dualism which needs to be (and is being) challenged by present curriculum developments. The defence of A levels as the 'gold standard', the attack upon course work in GCSE and A level, the low status attributed to 'vocational' awards such as BTEC depends upon, first, the distinction between the theoretical and the practical, and, second, the superiority of the former. 'Rigour' is associated with the theoretical, which in turn is linked to propositional knowledge.

However, fundamental to our understanding of what currently is happening is an appreciation of the fact that the practical can be more or less intelligently engaged in, that 'doing' can be informed by reflection, imagination, intelligence, and that theory itself is so often the reflection upon intelligent action. Theology depends on religious practice. Ethics depends on moral strivings. Mathematics depends on everyday calculations. Literary criticism depends on people writing novels and poetry. The educated person should be seen as *capable*, not just knowledgeable, *practically intelligent* in many spheres, not just theoretically astute.

Educational control

To be educated is to have acquired valuable forms of knowledge, valued skills and habits, moral virtues and dispositions which are judged to be worthwhile. As I have indicated, there is no ready consensus on what in detailed substance is to count as educated because there are disagreements about these values. And, indeed, the current changes in education, especially from 14 to 19, must be understood precisely in these terms. Those from the vocational areas question a concept of education which ignores the useful and the practical. Those from the academic camp treat with disdain the attempt to mix education with vocational preparation.

Nonetheless, the debate is essentially an educational one which does itself belong to a tradition of argument about 'the good life' and about what is worthwhile. The different voices in the argument are themselves speaking from within traditions of literary criticism, scientific argument, theological dispute, vocational preparation, and moral debate. What is wrong is for such a conversation to be hijacked by any one body, especially by government, and to be coerced through various forms of control (financial or legislative). The wrong lies not simply in such bodies, especially government, going beyond their legitimate role, but in a deep misunderstanding of what constitutes an educational process and an educational tradition. Education is tied to the values which are held within society and therefore must be argued about and defended in moral terms. The 'educated person' cannot be defined by government but only within a tradition of argument to which many, including government, make a contribution. There are distinctive educational traditions, ever open to development through criticism, which define the educated person.

There is always a danger that, through the control of knowledge and of institutions, this tradition can be distorted. There is a danger, too, that different metaphors might be promoted that distort our conception of 'educated persons' and of the educational processes which produce them. Thus, metaphors produced from business, in which 'education' is a commodity to be bought and sold in a market, the curriculum is something created by government and 'delivered' by teachers, standards are defined by clients' wants, learning is measured by a few performance indicators, quality is assured by quickly trained lay inspectors, facilities are audited by accountants — such metaphors begin to transform our conception of education and of the role that the state might legitimately play in defining the 'educated person'.

Conclusion: competing educational traditions

To understand the changes in the 14–19 curriculum, it is necessary to see the different educational traditions, defined in terms of the philosophical disagreements outlined above, which compete to dominate the changes occurring in the curriculum and institutional arrangements for 14–19.

Academic tradition

This tradition sees the purposes of education to be essentially concerned with 'the perfection of the intellect', and thus with initiation into those subjects or disciplines deemed to be central to intellectual development. It gives low status to the practical and the vocational and, generally speaking, would distinguish clearly between intellectual formation and personal development. It is reflected in traditional O level and A level courses, and its standards are intrinsic to the nature of reasoning and thinking which characterise those subjects. Within such a tradition, questions of utility or relevance hardly arise. Knowledge is pursued for its own sake and, in so far as the majority is not hooked on such motivation, then the academic tradition is embraced only by the minority. Educational objectives or attainment targets, in so far as they have to be declared, arise from within the nature of the subject.

Vocational tradition

This tradition derives much more from an examination of utility, of the competences necessary to do a job effectively, of economic and social needs. Education does not point to intrinsic goods but to means for achieving extrinsic ends. It elevates the practical and the useful, and it looks to those outside education (the 'industry led bodies', for example) to define what the ends of education should be. Teachers, far from being the voices in a developing academic tradition, are the technicians making things happen. Standards are derived from one's estimate of a job successfully completed. Knowledge is a means to an end, and is broken down into bits and pieces which are more easily digestible. Schools become workplaces. Part-time studies were welcomed as a way of integrating theory and practice rather than of keeping them apart. In breaking knowledge down into its bits and pieces, so external bodies (such as NCVQ) specify exactly what facts, principles, skills and habits should be learnt and what performance indicators show that they have been learnt successfully.

Pre-vocational tradition

The academic and the vocational traditions seem worlds apart in terms of ends to be pursued, values to be treasured, modes of learning to be fostered, authorities to be respected, and standards to be measured by. But it is the purpose of my analysis to show that reconciliation is possible, and this is implicit in developments that to the discerning eye have been occurring within the 14–19 curriculum. The pre-vocational tradition of TVEI, of CPVE, of BTEC has sought to get rid of the false dualism between academic and vocational, between theory and practice, or between liberal and useful, and has demonstrated how the practical project can demand intellectual rigour, or how the useful can be a vehicle for the aesthetic and the academic, or how vocational learning can be geared to general rather than to specific ends. Indeed, reflection upon these developments indicates a reformulation of liberal learning which, based on a broader vision of the educated person, incorporates the preparation, in an understanding and imaginative way, for participation in the political and economic world of adults.

Possibly the most critical aspect of current curriculum policy and institutional changes is the failure of policy makers to grasp this point although it is implicit in so much good practice.

References

Finegold, D. and Soskice, D. (1988) 'The Failure of Training in Britain: Analysis and Prescription' *Oxford Review of Economic Policy* 4, No.3.

Moser, C (1992) *Our Need for an Informed Society*, London, British Association.

Slee, P.R.H. (1986) *Learning and a Liberal Education: The Study of Modern History in the Universities of Oxford, Cambridge and Manchester 1800–1914*, University of Manchester.

PART III: THE PRACTICAL CONTEXT

7 The organising, co-ordinating and stimulating contribution of the local education authority

John Braithwaite

Once upon a time, and certainly throughout most of the 1980s, education ministers adopted a friendly attitude towards local education authorities, seeing them as the natural and equal partners in the organisation and delivery of education in their own areas. When for example the TVEI programme came on stream in the early 1980s it was axiomatic that the planning and execution would be in the hands of local education authorities, and this illustration is but one of many where there was no question that local education authorities had a major role and that it was taken for granted by central government.

Indeed this continued to be the viewpoint as the decade progressed. When the White Paper *Better Schools* (1985) was published it stated:

> the needs of sixth formers can usually be adequately met with a reasonable use of resources *only if the LEA succeeds in securing effective arrangements for co-ordinating the programmes of individual pupils between the school and one or more other institutions.*

This recognition of the local education authority's role (highlighted by my italics) was reiterated in 1988 when Kenneth Baker addressed the CLEA Conference, emphasising the 'strategic role' of local education authorities, and he urged them 'to avoid gaps and wasteful duplication' in the FE sector, and stressed that the introduction of schemes of local management would 'reinforce and strengthen the planning role'.

How encouraging it was to know that central and local government were at one on this issue, but as we reflect in 1992 we must wonder whether what had seemed so bright a concept of partnership in the 1980s was merely a mirage rather than reality. After all, the 1992 White Paper, talking about local authorities having an education committee, says 'Some may soon be in sight of no longer needing them'. Speaking of the 1992 meeting of CLEA the former senior chief HMI Eric Bolton said, 'The Government is calling the tune in ways that make it clear that it no longer regards education authorities as its major partner in a national system of education that is locally administered'. What the CLEA audience heard in 1992 differed dramatically from what their counterparts heard only four years previously!

What follows is in a sense a case study, being an account of one local education authority's approach to the reorganisation of 11–18 education which spread across this fascinating period of the 1980s into the early 1990s, in other words from the halcyon days when the local education authorities were courted by governments to the present when they feel like betrayed suitors.

The context is a medium-sized town with sixteen secondary schools (two of them single sex) all serving the 11–18 age range, one large college of further education, and Roman Catholic provision consisting of one sixth form college and three 11–16 schools. The brief was not just to produce the best blueprint for post-16 students, but also to ensure that the students in the 11–16 age range should receive the best education possible. There was a precedent to consider in the Roman Catholic field for reorganisation had taken place there only a relatively short time before. One lesson which arose from that reorganisation was the importance of choosing the right site for the new sixth form college, for if the school previously on the site had not enjoyed a good reputation the new college would have to work extra hard to shake off the historical reputation. A second lesson concerned the way in which staffing should be handled.

Within the local authority schools, as in those of many towns and cities elsewhere, there was massively uneven provision for the students in terms of curriculum, pastoral care, buildings, and especially in what was happening post-16. There was one school with literally no sixth form students whereas only six miles away there were nearly 400 students in one school's sixth form; the other schools provided figures across the range between these two extremes. Geographically, there was a mismatch between the viable sixth forms in schools in the east and west of the town and the inadequately sized sixth forms in the north. Inevitably this led to a much richer curricular diet for the former than for the latter, a situation which could not be allowed to continue — *clearly a role the local education authority had to take on.*

The socio-economic nature of the areas was to a large degree reflected in the staying-on rates in the schools, and this meant that some students in the east and west remained in school to take post-16 courses which were not geared to their needs. On the other hand, in the north many academically able students left school at 16 because there was little encouragement at home for them to continue their education; also, some left because their school was unable to offer a wide range of courses or subjects, even some 'core' A level subjects not being available. An element of joint provision occurred, but it was minimal and often unsatisfactory. Timetabling in the two establishments was often difficult to organise in order to accommodate the joint provision, and more pertinently students were resistant to travelling between schools, feeling they belonged to neither place.

There was an inevitable, but very unfair, perception that those schools with large sixth forms were 'better' than the others, this viewpoint totally disregarding the excellent work being done with the younger students in all the schools and being a most unfair slur on those teachers in the schools with the small sixth forms.

In the midst of all this, apart but yet involved because of the implications which would arise from any reorganisation, stood the large further education college situated in the centre of town. As well as catering for post-19 students it offered a full academic and vocational curriculum for students at 16+, and it was a particular attraction to students in the north of the town as well as to many others who preferred the FE culture.

Such was the background to the work which the local education authority set in motion in the early 1980s. It was by no means unique, countless authorities having wrestled with similar problems both from pragmatic and from philosophical standpoints, *but it was one which seemed to fall naturally into the lap of a local education authority.* A working party was set up to audit the status quo and to investigate possible ways forward. The group consisted of representatives of the various teachers associations and of the Education Division. At the time when it met there was a long-standing tradition of institutional autonomy, the schools and the college having been free to create their own pattern of courses for the post-16 age group, to recruit students, and to allocate staff and resources within the boundaries determined by the Education Committee. The further education college, unlike the schools, had for a long time been accustomed to negotiating with the Education Division before it set up a course. Minimal co-operation had taken place between schools and the college, though the advent of the

Technical and Vocational Education Initiative in 1984 had assisted in breaking down boundaries. It seemed certain that when the working party was created some surrender of this cherished autonomy would have to occur.

The working party met regularly for many months, consulted its constituents, and eventually following the working party's deliberations the Director of Education was able to present a review of educational provision for 16–19 year olds in the town to the Education Committee at its meeting in June 1985. It reviewed in principle all the possible ways forward for the future pattern of 16–19 education in the town, bearing in mind the background of falling numbers of students and the changing needs of students. The review also kept firmly in the foreground the needs of children in the 11–16 age range. The Education Committee resolved that the Director of Education should bring forward a further report to a future meeting of the Committee in which various options for action should be considered. The Committee had recognised the need to make structural changes which would permanently achieve equality of educational opportunity for young people in the town, and it also recognised the need to consult widely with all those affected before it took final and irrevocable decisions.

In August 1985 a report was published which was basically the work of the Director of Education but which relied heavily on the teacher/officer/adviser working party and on the representatives of the party groups on a finely-balanced council. The report presented three principal options, these being:

1 a significant reduction in the number of 11–18 schools;
2 separate provision for 16+ education;
3 different forms of organisation across the town.

The report stressed that whichever system was eventually chosen there would be a need for co-operation at all levels whether the 16+ system covered the whole town or only part of it, *and this co-operation would clearly be facilitated if the local education authority were to play a leading role — that was still taken for granted in 1985!*

The report underlined the need for full and extensive consultation, a modus operandi which had been used with a variety of previous major issues. At the outset of the consultative process the Director's reports had already been circulated to headteachers and principals, the staff of establishments, the teacher associations, the four MPs whose constituencies embraced the town, and the press. The actual consultation process had seven main features, these being:

1 The Director of Education and his officers met with the staffs of all the institutions concerned.
2 There were discussions with the teacher associations involved, initially with the officers but also through the normal consultative machinery.
3 The relevant governing bodies considered the issue.
4 Reference was made to the area committees.
5 Consultation was held with the Roman Catholic diocesan authorities.
6 Open meetings were held at secondary schools where parents, students and the wider public would have the opportunity to make their views known.
7 Informal consultations were held with the DES and the Inspectorate.

What is abundantly clear is that such an extensive consultation programme could not have been conceived or carried out without the oversight of the local education authority.

The public meetings were very well attended, numbers ranging from 1,050 at one school to around 80 in the smallest audiences. In the northern area there were eight meetings, attended by a total of just over 3,000 people; the four schools in the east had total attendances of just under 700 people, and the west's four schools held public meetings which brought in about 1,100 people. Although the meetings were held in secondary schools a letter had been distributed to parents of all 8–14 year old pupils, and the governors of all primary schools were notified about the programme so that they could attend one of the public meetings. In all cases those present were able to listen to, and to question, the Director of Education or his representative and the Chair or Vice Chairperson of the Education Committee. People were also invited to write in with their comments, an opportunity seized by many.

There was no doubt that if the future of a specific school was thought to be in jeopardy the mood of the audience was more militant, and in these cases passion often outweighed reason in the discussions. There was also a feeling in some places that the decision had really been taken in advance by committee, the 'different forms of organisation across the town' being the presumed choice. This presumed outcome was particularly resented in the north where there was a feeling that the more favoured areas in the east and west would be allowed to keep their sixth forms. It was interesting to note that the differences between sixth form colleges and tertiary colleges were not uppermost in most people's minds, the status quo — the known 'animal' — being what most people were happy with, especially in the east and west.

There was considerable concern over pastoral matters, over maintaining the liaison between primary and secondary schools (which were a striking feature in many places), and a wish that if a split were to occur at 16 the transitional process should be as carefully handled as it is at 11+. Whilst it would not be fair to say that the academic issues were ignored, they often fell below the time spent on pastoral matters.

In November 1985 Committee received the Director's report in which the outcome of the consultations was set out. Committee was invited to focus its attention on certain issues in reaching a decision. The Director advised Committee to view option 1 with a degree of scepticism, to see option 3 as preferable, but to consider option 2 most seriously. Whilst mixed provision in a town is not unusual the report expressed unease about the boundary between one system and another in this particular town. The report went on to draw attention to the growing realisation nationwide that bringing together post-16 students into larger establishments is the most effective way of meeting their needs, a fact illustrated by the numerous precedents all over the country. It was stressed that a far wider range of courses would be possible, participation rates would be likely to rise, the pastoral systems would be better than many people had believed in their comments during the consultations, and teaching methods could be more easily changed to reflect the older age group.

The Director in the report finally recommended a carefully phased approach with reorganisation in the north, followed possibly one year afterwards in the east, then a further year or two afterwards in the west. The Committee was also invited to consider the related issues of adult education, special education, and the joint use of buildings.

Having read the report and listened to the arguments the Committee at its meeting that November made certain resolutions:

(a) that the authority should move in planned stages to a system of school organisation that is consistent across the whole of the metropolitan borough; and

(b) that the most appropriate system, ultimately, for the whole of the borough would be the one where pupils aged between 11 and 16 were educated in schools providing only for that age range, and at 16 they had access to three colleges, one in each area, which would approximate to the sixth form college model.

The implication of (b) was that the authority would need to commit considerable capital expenditure at the earliest stages and regard had to be taken of the ability of the authority to fund the projects within the allocations made by the government and council. In addition, staffing redeployments would have to be achieved in good order. Therefore a phased programme was put forward, phase 1 in the northern area to start as soon as possible with phase 2 following within two years, but the precise timing would depend on capital programmes, and, even more importantly, be calculated to cause the least possible disruption to pupils and staff. Phase 3 would probably begin four years or so after phase 1.

The working party continued to meet and to consider such issues as staffing, accommodation and curriculum, and one of the most significant points to emerge and to be agreed was that the staffing issues should be resolved within the boundaries of the area being reorganised, only the post of the college principal being opened up for national advertisement. The group met through 1985, 1986 and early into 1987, and it was late in 1986 that ministerial approval was received for the scheme. It was then all hands to the pump as steps were taken to put everything into place in time for the first college to open in September 1987, along with the schools which were to be 11–16 in scope. One interesting aspect was that the incipient 11–16 schools would be able to admit sixth formers for a further two years, whilst the proposed college would, on a year-by-year basis, phase out its younger pupils. The point to bear in mind, however, is that the package agreed by government in 1986, owing to the phased nature of the scheme, was one which would still be in process of implementation in the 1990s; LMS, grant maintained status etc. were not in the frame at that time!

Though reached after negotiation with all interested parties, there were certain features which provoked very mixed reactions amongst professionals and lay people alike. The principal ones related to the phased approach, the giving to teachers the opportunity for selecting where they wished to teach, and allowing schools to take in sixth formers at the same time as the college in the area was trying to get off the ground.

The phased approach was seen by cynics as being a way to safeguard the sixth forms in the west particularly, but also in the east; however, there was sense in making a start where the needs were the most pressing, namely the north, but with all parties on the council and all the local MPs committed to the other areas coming in at the appropriate time — a strategy endorsed by ministers. Surely, therefore, the process must be sacrosanct — mustn't it? What could not have been foreseen at the time was the change in attitude to local education authorities by central government so that when the west began its reorganisation the climate had shifted.

Giving teachers the opportunity to select the school/college in which they wished to teach was much appreciated by the associations, and the outcome in the scheme has been about 95 per cent success in teacher placements across the borough. Headteachers and principals were not able to pick and choose who they wanted, and provided that curriculum gaps were not left in the school from which a teacher wished to move nothing could prevent that move occurring. Opportunities for professional development and for new starts by teachers who may have felt they were in an inescapable rut were obvious benefits, but it may also have been felt that some teachers, especially in the college in the north, were not in the environment best suited to their teaching abilities. To ensure as little discontinuity as possible in the 11–16 schools some teachers deferred their move for a year or two, and others were leased back to their original schools. *All this required massive co-ordination, a job undertaken by members of the education division with sensitivity and understanding.*

The opportunity given to the 11–16 schools to admit sixth form students for two years after reorganisation did arouse some hostile reaction, especially from those committed to getting the colleges off to a flying start. In the north there was quick, though not unanimous, agreement by the headteachers that they would not take up this option to have incoming sixth formers, for they preferred to devote all their resources to the 11–16 pupils. However, two schools did admit sixth formers in the first year though inevitably the numbers were small and arguably they were less well served from a curriculum and a social point of view than if they had gone to the college. However, it has to be stressed that this choice made by students and their parents was legitimised by the agreement. In the east two of the designated three 11–16 schools elected to carry on running sixth forms, and in the west all of the schools did, but by this time the DES was giving positive encouragement to schools to pursue their own individual wishes.

Another significant decision had been taken by the Committee and that concerned the further education college which was told it would not be able to run advanced level courses for full-time students in the 16–18 group, a decision clearly taken in an attempt to assist the new sixth form colleges to make a successful start. However, as the latter began to respond positively to the Government's encouragement to them to mount vocational courses there was a growing and understandable feeling of resentment amongst all connected with the further education college. Their feeling that this was one-way discrimination is hard to refute, but the local politicians were adamant that the embryonic colleges must be protected.

The whole issue of what courses should be on offer at the various colleges was the principal agenda item for the strategy group which met for the first time in 1988. This group consisted of the college principals, a representative secondary headteacher, the TVEI co-ordinator, the principal careers officer, and various officers and advisers. The meetings were chaired by an assistant director. As part of its curriculum remit this group agreed a curriculum entitlement. The idea of entitlement was of course also on the national agenda, and Kenneth Baker's core skills were very similar to what the strategy group had recommended and what the town's Education Committee adopted as its statement on curriculum planning. The main problem with which the group wrestled was the conflict, if such existed, between imposing an overall entitlement whilst acknowledging that each institution would wish to have its own individual characteristic; and, of course, there was the fact to be acknowledged that the further education and schools sector colleges were different in culture.

The history of the strategy group reflects the ways in which the colleges have developed for each has assumed a unique identity, and as this has happened the group's aim of consensus has been harder to achieve. One college has very much stressed the importance of advanced and GCSE courses, another has introduced vocational courses and encouraged a wider age participation, a third has introduced the International Baccalaureate, and the fourth has opened up negotiations with the further education college to create joint courses and to facilitate progression; this college has also developed a very strong community dimension. After strenuous discussions within this group and elsewhere the sixth form colleges were enabled to introduce mature students on an infill basis by enrolling through the adult education centres. This is but one of several initiatives which local education authority development funding has facilitated through the further education budget.

As the colleges have developed unique features there has been an increasing tension regarding the advertising of courses. Initially there was a 'gentleman's agreement' that colleges would advertise only in their own area of the town, but then feelings arose within the group that what each college was offering should be made more widely known. The issue was how this should be done, and a central approach seemed to be the obvious answer, and this was eventually agreed, albeit lukewarmly in certain quarters. The growing entrepreneurial attitude being encouraged nationally made it all the more difficult to maintain the aforementioned 'gentleman's agreement', a fact welcomed by some principals more than others. Students and parents, not to mention governors, began to demand full knowledge of what was available in the town, they sought the right to visit all institutions, and efforts were made to encourage all colleges to participate in affairs such as careers conventions being held in schools. The original *raison d'être* of the strategy group to ensure co-operation and consensus was being severely buffeted. This was a great pity for the original aim of greater participation had been handsomely achieved, 52 per cent at the outset having risen to 75 per cent in four years, to a great extent, though not exclusively, owing to the spreading of a college culture.

Working alongside the strategy group but meeting separately was the group of principals alone, under the chairmanship of the senior tertiary adviser. This provided a forum in which the principals could rather more informally discuss problems, air differences, and generally be more frank than they might be in the larger strategy group. Even in this more intimate gathering, however, the rift amongst the principals began to grow wider, and one could imagine government ministers rubbing their hands in glee if they had seen what effect their policies were having on people who had on the whole set out to work in harmony.

One of the products of the strategy group was the post-16 strategic plan. On its very first page underlines the fact that co-operation was central to its conception.

> The first strategic plan is the work of. . .Education Authority in partnership with. . .College and other post-16 providers.

The plan submitted seven strategic aims, these being:

1   student entitlement;
2   partnership;
3   progression;
4   equality of opportunity and access;
5   responsiveness to the economy, employment and the environment of change;
6   efficient use of resources;
7   high quality: the value of people in the service.

Whilst no one of these is more important than the others, there are some which are more germane to the purposes of this chapter. For instance, under the heading 'partnership' everyone agreed the wording should be:

> In the interests of the range and coherence of the offer to students, the LEA will promote co-operative partnerships between providers, encouraging responsiveness to change without dissipation of energies.

Then in the section on 'progression' it states that:

> The LEA will seek to ensure continuity of provision to allow individuals to experience success, develop higher level skills in a context of academic rigour, progress to higher education and enter and re-enter education and training at whatever stage of their lives. Within this continuum particular providers will have distinctive major roles and minor roles.

However, there is no doubt that the respective roles of the local education authority and the individual establishments is best set out in a further paragraph on the topic of 'partnership', and it articulates clearly the whole spirit of the reorganisation as initially envisaged and as carried out until central government began to create a different climate.

> Decisions on the majority of provision will lie with establishments without reference anywhere else, but where there is potential overlap, in the area of minor roles, providers have acknowledged the need to collaborate in the interests of students, through the forum of the post-16 strategy group, TVE and the action groups formed under them. The LEA's role is to plan provision in the interests of clients, to set the budget and avoid wasteful duplication in its use.

Then the context changed, the local education authority's significance began to weaken and strategic planning became more difficult. What must now be the hope is for the regional committees of the new funding council to sustain the coherent approach which an earlier minister had sought. The era of market forces may or may not encourage students to remain in education in the same way as has been so eminently successful in recent years. For example, it is questionable whether the Act's requirement that those with learning difficulties should be regarded will actually ensure the continuation of the situation there is now with a special unit at one of the colleges. It is equally doubtful whether the present development of joint courses will be pursued as keenly as heretofore. The principals will be even more hard pressed to maintain their erstwhile partnership approach. It seems unlikely that the co-ordinating role of the local education authority will be maintained in the future when such an organisation is challenged.

However, in spite of the original reorganisation scheme having been endorsed by the Government, the funding council has not recognised the west area college on the grounds that younger pupils are still present. As an assistant director wrote in *Education*, 'It is left stranded in some strange limbo untouched by current preparatory work. The local coherence is threatened'.

The story of this particular reorganisation has been one in which a great variety of people, many with vested interests, have worked together to ensure a smooth but radical restructuring of twenty institutions. *Without the organising, co-ordinating and stimulating contribution of the local education authority it is unlikely that the current healthy situation would have been reached.*

The following story may well be a parable which relates to the present position where the value and constructive role of the local education authority is dismissed as summarily as the essential features of the symphony. If the consultant's views had been acted upon the world would have been the poorer; will the world of education be the worse if local education authorities are treated in a similar cavalier fashion?

Art of the efficient

A company chairman had been given tickets for the performance of Schubert's *Unfinished Symphony*. He couldn't go, and passed them on to his work study consultant. The next morning, the chairman asked him how he had enjoyed the performance, and was handed a memorandum which read:

'For considerable periods, the four oboe players had nothing to do. The number should be reduced, and their work spread over the whole orchestra, thus eliminating peaks of inactivity.

All of the twelve violins were playing identical notes. This seemed unnecessary duplication, and the staff of this section should be drastically cut.

Much effort was absorbed in the playing of demi semi-quavers. Now this seems an excessive refinement, and it is recommended that all notes should be rounded up to the nearest semi-quaver.

No useful purpose is served by repeating with horns the passage that had already been played by the strings. If all such redundant passages were eliminated, the concert could be reduced from two hours to twenty minutes.

If Schubert had attended to these matters, he would probably have been able to finish the symphony after all'.

(*Church News Service*: as printed in an edition of the Church Magazine of St. Chad's Church, Far Headingly, Leeds).

8 The National Curriculum and the 14–19 curriculum

Duncan Graham

The debate about the 14–16 curriculum has, since the Education Reform Act of 1988, been conducted within a defined framework, largely statutory in nature. Whatever the problems created by the great Key Stage 4 nightmare, there are solid gains which should not be overlooked. One of these is that most youngsters now have a more balanced subject diet than they had before. As recently as 1989 DES statistics revealed that a sizeable proportion of youngsters tackled neither mathematics nor English, one science at best, and no language. Gender bias was rampant in the area of crafts and home economics, and lip service was paid to the arts. While many schools did ensure balance, some did not: even one defaulter was one too many. The National Curriculum core has surely put paid to that. The regret is that opportunities have been lost to be definitive about the whole curriculum, what is compulsory and what is optional.

The Key Stage 4 problem stemmed from an absence of clarity about the aim and purpose of the last two years of compulsory education; as regards post-16 education there is still none laid down. If a National Curriculum is essential pre-16, why should the state be happy with no more than an aggregate of syllabuses after that age? The wholeness where it exists, depends upon the good offices of schools, further education colleges, and the idealism of BTEC, City and Guilds and RSA. It has become embarrassingly clear that while 120 years of state education have given rise to many academic theses on the whole curriculum, it had not brought a working definition, still less a statutory one. Equally clearly while the government felt comfortable with 'subjects', it saw the 'add-ons' as distractions at best, the liberal backlash at worst. Values were OK as long as they were Tory ones.

The potential for disaster was identified by Peter Watkins, NCC's Deputy Chief Executive, long before the 1988 Act was enshrined in statute: I suspect that many other headteachers and ex-headteachers also had serious reservations. In essence his argument was that it would not be possible to teach all ten subjects in their entirety unless everything else was excluded, whether additional subject — such as a science, language, the classics or economics — or social and personal education. The logistical problems presented by GCSE as it was then defined were insuperable. It is a matter of record that ministers, civil servants, and HMI ignored the pleas of NCC officers for early consideration of the options. The delays and obfuscations made a mockery of the forward planning schools were being encouraged to undertake, and made the position of music, art and PE increasingly parlous.

The National Curriculum Council added to the size of the problem, justifiably in my view, by its working definition of the whole curriculum as the ten subjects, RE and in addition dimensions, skills and themes. These were defined in Circular Number 6 (October 1989) and were well received by schools, and significantly and encouragingly by industry and business. They were founded on the preamble to the 1988 Act where a statutory responsibility was placed upon schools to provide a broad and balanced curriculum which:

> promotes the spiritual, moral, cultural, mental and physical development of pupils at the school and of society; and
> prepares such pupils for the opportunities, responsibilities and experiences of adult life.

Dimensions were defined as those essentials which should **permeate** the whole curriculum, and be ever present, e.g. a commitment to equal opportunities, preparation for adult life in a multi-cultural, and pluralist society, and equality of access to the curriculum irrespective of ethnic, cultural, and social background. These compel a set of values as a curriculum component, and eradication of gender bias.

Skills were defined as, at minimum, communication, numeracy, study skills, problem-solving, personal and social skills, and information technology skills. These could of course arguably be fostered entirely within the statutory curriculum, in which case an audit of attainment targets and programmes of study would be necessary to identify where. I can vouch for the fact that no subject working party was asked to identify and incorporate skills in its report. NCC was commissioned by John MacGregor when he was Secretary of State to do a retrospective identification exercise: this

has not yet materialised: it had sadly been as stillborn as the
NCC's essay on core skills post-16, which though well received
by so many bodies, fell foul of the gold standard obstacle. It was
concluded by ministers that all A level syllabuses already subsumed
all the skills! That was presumably safer than having a really close
look. The time will surely come. . .

The themes, although by no means an exclusive list seemed to
most people to contain a minimum five to be covered either within
the ten subjects, in addition to them, or by a bit of each. They are
economic and industrial understanding, careers education and
guidance, health education, education for citizenship, and
environmental education. Most schools accept these and have
incorporated them in their curriculum planning; the series of
curriculum documents produced by NCC has been well received
as helpful and supportive. Taken together with personal and social
education and values education they provide a minimum basis for
the non-statutory elements of the curriculum. They add to the
pressures on time and resource. The years since 1989 have seen
tension between government attempts to keep the curriculum
narrow and statutory, and the endeavours of schools and
businessmen to broaden it out. More recently the Government, no
longer able to say that we must concentrate solely on the
introductory phase, has taken to fairly overt attempts to define the
values. This raises, as do other developments, fundamental
questions about political interference in content. It conflicts with the
NCC's advice that the purpose of values education is to foster the
ability in each youngster to develop his or her own set of values
and principles.

There were and are differences in the attitudes of schools and
government. Teachers have traditionally sought to put subject
teaching into a wider context. One way or another there was going
to be a whole curriculum. This intensified the pressure on the ten-
subject curriculum and brought up starkly the question of what
should be compulsory and what optional. Was the great principle
of the Act sustainable? Did it matter? Were there ways of squaring
the circle? One serious question underlying it all was what degree
of choice is necessary up to the age of 16. The greater the choice,
the more doors may be closed prematurely.

In essence three fundamentally different views emerged from the
consultations which NCC conducted extensively during 1990. They
were those of the government, and of the independent sector, and
of the vast majority.

Once Baker and idealism were gone and out of fashion ministers
began to turn to narrowing, to resurrecting the academic pecking-
order. They were tempted to revert to a core of three (not least the

then Prime Minister, Margaret Thatcher) and certainly to downgrade art, music and PE. At one point PE seemed likely to become an extra-curricular activity (as in a time sense it is in the independent sector) and art, music, drama and dance to become non-statutory. This would get ministers off a lot of GCSE examination hooks; in effect they were no longer interested in solutions which delivered what they claimed to want — breadth and space for other things.

The independent schools' lobby wanted space for three separate sciences, and for extra subjects. They could have ignored the National Curriculum. Instead, possibly fearing its success, they chose to put pressure on ministers to reduce the requirements, and were supported by those HMI who, for quite different reasons, wanted a return to the *laissé-faire* of the eighties. Perhaps the latter thought they could get back to areas of experience. In that sense and in others the National Curriculum represented a defeat for HMI which foreshadowed worse to come.

The majority, and it was considerable, based on the objective evidence of a national survey and consultation by NCC, took the view that a homogenous curriculum of ten subjects to 16 was broad enough. If forced to choose they would plump for that. If they could have the best of both worlds, these and space for extras, their cup would be full. There was talk of half courses in GCSE and of combination GCSEs embracing two National Curriculum subjects, or one plus an additional subject, e.g. geography and economics. SEAC advised that this was feasible. Some few, including myself, began to mention the unmentionable — need we have both GCSEs and National Curriculum assessment?

My own belief was that it would be folly to surrender the gains already made in creating a curriculum embracing a range of academic and aesthetic subjects. A country whose state education service had been bedevilled by patchiness and a complete absence of entitlement had at last acquired a truly National Curriculum which it should hang onto at all costs, while finding a *modus operandi* within it.

The first piece of my thinking was that five subjects formed an irreducible extended core — English, mathematics, science, a modern language and technology. Angela Rumbold was the first to see the force of the arguments. She had the ear of Margaret Thatcher. And so, it came to pass.

With that agreed, NCC set about the task of looking for workable solutions. After considering many options, it finally recommended that the extended core be contained within 60 per cent of the timetable, with 10 per cent divided between history or geography, either as combined subjects, or as single subjects, 10 per cent to art, music and PE, to be allocated at the discretion of schools, 5 per cent to RE and personal education, leaving no less than 15 per cent for other subjects.

All that was wrong with the solution was that the political agenda had changed, and Clarke had succeeded MacGregor as Secretary of State. Publicly only the independent schools objected to the 70/30 solution (extended core plus history/geography) as it became known. The decision would have little to do with logic. The Secretary of State (Kenneth Clarke) with magnificent disregard for what had gone before, announced that 'the curriculum must not become prescriptive and exclude the whole variety of options that people want to exercise'. We were on the way back to square one. He later said that we should 'not impose a rigid curriculum'. Well, yes, but!

What has happened since has been predictable. While the extended core has prevented reversion to the worst practices of the eighties, it is once more at the discretion of schools as to how they tackle, or avoid the cultural and the aesthetic. Good schools have preserved the balance, less good have not — the 'patchiness', so much abhorred before the Act in 1988, has recurred in a new guise. Sadly, too, the pressure on able pupils to acquire excessive numbers of passes at the expense of a broad liberal education has reappeared. It is ironic that good independent schools, having had their way with ministers, use the extra time at their disposal to cover all the ground which is now restricted in state-schools.

Whatever one's views about the events and the outcome, one thing is clear. There has been and still is a complete absence of thought about what should in subject terms constitute a 14–16 curriculum, as a vital part of a 14–19 curriculum. It is assumed that choice at 14 is desirable, but the costs are not calculated either for the pupil or the school. A study needs to be undertaken about the nature and range of choice which is desirable at the various stages of the age range 12–19. This needs to take account of the choice available within subjects, as well as between them. Exercising choice is a part of the growing-up process which needs to be set against the opening and shutting of doors to career opportunities. There is a consensus that work experience is a key component of the 14–16 curriculum. Until that is undertaken, in conjunction with careers education, choice can be a mixed blessing, made without the relevant experience.

In an ideal world, educational considerations would not be affected by those of resource. In the nineties this cannot be so. The costs of choice at key stage 4 are substantial in terms of accommodation, equipment and teaching staff. The place of art, music and PE, now leaves them vulnerable as staffing formulae bite:

to accommodate wide options at key stage 4 schools have to increase class size at Key Stage 3. None of this has been taken into account in legislation about Key Stage 4, any more than the fundamentals of what education is about in a 14–19 context.

Confusion about choice reflects more than a lack of definition of aims and objectives, and conflicts about resources. It is part of the politics of education — the battle between the modernists and the traditionalists — or between the forces of 'evil' (the former) and the 'good guys' (the latter). The outcome will have an immense bearing not just on the curriculum but on assessment, teaching methods, and the extension of the curriculum through its links with the workplace. The modernists are perceived to have tried to restrict choice ('over-prescribed') in order to impose a dull conformity; the traditionalists are portrayed as trying to open it up ('sturdy independence, freedom for the individual, what we always had').

Who lurks behind the epithets? The traditionalists (most evident in the right wing think tanks, and increasingly in the membership of NCC and SEAC) saw the National Curriculum as a salvation — back to well defined, statutory enforceable basics. They met two set-backs: one has been discussed and their reaction noted — it was too big, too all-embracing. The other was the personnel chosen to oversee its introduction. These people were perceived to have come from those who had 'gotten us into this fine mess' — universities, local government, the civil service. They were (perhaps awkwardly!) reinforced by the support of leaders in industry and commerce as we have seen. The 'Tory modernists', epitomised by Lord Young, had through MSC and TVEI pushed breadth, experience and context which required a different approach from 'chalk and talk' and fitted well with group methods, modular approaches, and course-work assessment. It has to be said that the success of the National Curriculum at Key Stage 4 has had much to do with these influences, but they have not been popular with the Right.

It was not long before battle was joined with implications which are and will be profound. The scope of the National Curriculum (Kenneth Baker had moved it from the Thatcherite three-subject core) was attacked for its complexity and over-prescription. Willing allies (unwitting) were found in independent headteachers and some overworked teachers. 'Complex' things are always bad — 'soft' deliberately unclear 'liberal'. 'Simple' things are much better — hard, clear, resistant to professional manipulation. While the National Curriculum, as with all innovations rushed through, could do with measured trimming based on research and experience, that is not really the purpose of the game. It is to get it back to basics. These turn out to be 'knowledge-based' — hence the relentless thrust as subject orders appeared towards knowing rather than doing, which reached its climax in music where knowing Mozart's date of birth became more important than making music, and in art and RE. Each ministerial push in this direction, does most harm at Key Stage 4, increasing as it does the gap between education to 16 and what is required beyond.

The next thrust was directed at assessment. This is not the place to rehearse the saga of the descent of National Curriculum testing from an elaborate and well intentioned attempt to test positively and diagnostically to penal simplistic paper tests. It has been the complex/simple process rerun. It panders to the gut reaction that formal testing is good and what 'we all had in our day'. As so often, in education in England, the debate has been conducted more with heat than light, with polarised caricaturing and little attempt to compromise. The decision to go back on course-work in the GCSE exams can only be seen as a victory for prejudice and traditionalism. Course-work is harder, its results more reliable, it allows a wider range of students to succeed, it accords with common practice post-16, in the services and industry, and in the private sector in general. Recent GCSE results testify to its success, but not to its desirability in the eyes of right-wing ideologues. What do they want of education? Why do they fear success? Education at key stage 4 will be severely set back. If the target really is the best trained workforce we can get, we are going an odd way about it.

The pressures on assessment are measured by those on teaching methods. It is one of the great strengths of ERA that it did not give control of these to ministers. They remained in law at least the birthright of the teaching profession. It would be naive to see that as an exclusive right of course. There must be legitimate debate. When this is balanced and informed it invariably results in two conclusions — there is no holy grail: a mix of methods is best. In recent years though 'child-centred, learning by doing' has been seen as 'complex' and 'chalk and talk' as 'simple' (as well as cheap!) Hence attempts by ministers to lean on first primary teachers and later more widely. In the 14–16 range this places at risk all the gains of TVEI and the rich fabric of work experience, group methods, problem solving and so on. There is evidence in many schools of a stout disregard for right-wing pressures; in others 'market forces' are pushing in the other direction.

The curriculum at key stage 4 is particularly vulnerable in the political-educational battle. It is in a positive sense vitally transitional, it is critical to a 14–19 continuum in which, post-16, leaving aside the eccentricities of A level provision, there is a coherent progression towards a skill-based system, modular delivery, and assessment by credits and course work.

There is every reason to encourage the same process at key stage 4 (and earlier: it is a 5–19 continuum we need). The National Curriculum is well placed to underpin this, not least if the tangled web of relationships with GCSE is unravelled. Neither youngsters nor employers need a terminal examination nor do our competitor nations. What we do need is clear information for employers, positive incentives to 16 year olds, and cashable credits for trading post-16.

A number of things seem to be preventing the wide debate that is surely called for. One is the strangle-hold which a relatively small right-wing group seems to have on national policy. Its arguments should be the subject of much greater scrutiny than at present they are. The group's success has been to give the campaign the feel of a moral crusade, good against evil. This effectively discourages scrutiny of the arguments, throwing everyone else on the defensive. Professional advice is at a premium in Government circles and is in any case suspect and unwelcome (the White Paper *Choice and Diversity* of 1992 makes this abundantly clear). Even a qualifying word or a reservation voiced is sufficient to relegate the perpetrator to that vast group of 'left-wing trendies' which is now a very catholic church indeed. A critical comment recently led to the *Financial Times* being described as 'crypto-socialist'! With the decline in influence of LEAs and their advisers, the discrediting of academics, and the emasculation of HMI there are precious few voices left to put the centrist case. At a time when governors and parents are finding greatness thrust upon them, it is unfortunate that they are so bereft of balanced advice.

Another obstacle to debate lies in the examination system. At GCSE the problems are those already rehearsed — vested interests, the immense effort put in to setting it up, and whether it is an anachronism. This has recently become inextricably confused with the quality debate more closely associated with A levels and the gold standard. As long as Government stands implacably and inflexibly behind two dubious theses debate is sterile. The first is that if a system is perceived by ministers to be superb, then any change or modification will inexorably lead to a fall in standards. The progress of civilisation would not have got far on that basis. The A level problem casts its distorting shadow not just over the 16–19 academic/vocational debate, but directly over key stage 4 as well. Continuity with A levels requires pandering to its constraints. The implication at every turn is that nothing must jeopardise the smooth transition for a minority to A level. Little has changed in 50 years.

The other thesis is that GCSEs must be judged by GCE standards. The knee-jerk reaction to the good results of 1992 illustrates the point clearly. If grades fall, the system/teachers have failed. If they rise, things are not what they were. Apples and pears can be compared, it seems. Apart from the psychological and moral damage, the effect is to engender despair about the prospects of rational discussion, dispassionate research leading to positive action. There seems little prospect of rational debate about key stage 4 at the present time. It is tempting to shrug the shoulder and point out that it has been that way since Forster's Act in the 1870s; so why bother now? But two things are different. One is the magnitude of the importance of getting it right. A large part of the country's future lies in positive change, and quickly, in 14–19 education. It sounds pretentious but how else are we going to avert the peasant economy which beckons beyond if not before the millennium? We need a thorough revision of our national institutions, starting with the political: we need to resume making and selling things.

The other new factor is that we have to hand for the first time the components which could take us forward quickly. The years since 1988 have been full of confusions, contradictions, retreats, policy on the hoof: in spite of that real progress has been made.

The National Curriculum provides a framework, more clearly delineated than ever before, of what the subject content of the curriculum should be. There is little disquiet among teachers, parents and pupils. The changes which seem to cascade to schools on the backs of envelopes seem based more on prejudice than on research. How can we, for example, 'restore' Shakespeare to a curriculum which already contains him? If we can put aside the trendy/traditional distractions, we have the stuff of progress.

In the field of assessment and provided that testing at 14 is not regressive, GCSEs are markedly successful at encouraging positive achievement by a wider range of youngsters, together with a system of attainment targets which can provide the information needed for a modular, credit approach. Both require a range of teaching methods which are appropriate to post-16 education. There is enough positive merit here for a way forward to be found, without perpetuating terminal exams at 16, or misplaced claims about standards. There was no suggestion when the National Curriculum was framed that it needed to be artificially sub-divided into academic and vocational components and courses. Such paths should be eschewed. The dividing lines delineating compulsory, 'optional but compulsory', and choice within and without the National Curriculum have been established. The NCC documents which recorded the discussion and consultation provide a rich resource for informed debate within individual schools. The evidence is that for the most part they are for now preserving balance and an aesthetic content. Predictably the less adventurous schools and the weakly led schools are reverting to the narrower. Was this not what a National Curriculum was set up to eliminate?

There is now, in however rudimentary a form, a whole curriculum framework which commands a wide measure of agreement outside the pressure groups. The dimensions, skills and themes have preserved and strengthened breadth and balance and kept the question of values alive. The attempts to infiltrate or colonise them are a measure of their success! The broad liberal thrust of education has in my judgement survived and prospered since 1988. For that reason it will need to be defended vigorously from the insidious insertion of biased values, from attempts to impose values rather than encourage their formulation through each young person's self-development, and from attempts to downgrade them by thrusting them down the priority list. This may well be done by emphasising the basics, as if the choice is 'either/or' rather than 'both/and'. The whole curriculum illustrates where we stand in microcosm — better informed opportunities, greater risks of regression.

Another area awaiting positive development is that of skills and their correlation with what is happening post-16. The skills listed in *Curriculum Guidance 3 The Whole Curriculum* (NCC 1990) and those recommended by NCC in *Core Skills 16–19: A response to the Secretary of State* (1990) have much in common. While Secretaries of State have pointedly ignored the latter, presumably because they suggest areas of weakness in A level provision, John MacGregor did invite NCC to investigate how skills implicit within the National Curriculum could be made overt, and, presumably, reconciled with those emerging *de facto* post-16 through the efforts of NCVQ, BTEC, City and Guilds *et al.* The opportunity to build on consensus in 1990 was lost. There is common ground and good will to be exploited. There are strong arguments for a coherent, well-planned curriculum continuum from 14–19 (and with a broader 5–19 framework). The strengths of the National Curriculum must be extended beyond the compulsory phase, and in turn the best assessment practice post-16 be infused into key stage 4, with greater emphasis on school-based, externally moderated, testing.

Post-16 education has the advantage of some semblance of quality control and assurance. There may be differences about the philosophy and purpose between NCVQ and others: they appear to be at one in terms of monitoring and accreditation of courses and institutions. Pre-16 there is no credible machinery. With the demise of LEA advisory services and the emasculating transition of HMI into Ofsted, there is little in the way of quality assurance other than market forces. If industry needs BS5750, schools need a more participative role than that provided by four-yearly external inspections. There is a real risk that a government which introduced a National Curriculum to raise standards will be unable to tell whether or not standards are rising. If it discredits GCSE and the rest of us rightly refuse to take crude league tables seriously, how will we tell? Other policies relating to the administration and financing of schools (LMS, opting out etc.) will increase the differentials in provision, privilege and deprivation. How will allowances be made, the 'value-added' calculated?

The advances in subjects, whole curriculum and skills have had a beneficial effect on the provision for less able pupils, taken in conjunction with the gains from GCSE and TVEI. The clarity of the curriculum, the adaptability of and flexibility of attainment targets and programmes of study have assisted the extension of the curriculum to pupils of all abilities.

Expectations that the levels would simply reinforce failure appear to have been largely unrealised, although there are dangers. More dangerous will be attempts to carve out a 'vocational' (i.e. for 'thickies') version 14–16: it is an historic fact that all such attempts, however well-meaning, mean watered-down, less rigorous, courses. These pupils stand to gain enormously from the replacement in time of GCSE with credits based on modular courses. They bring things of value in the jobs market place and equally importantly motivation.

The balance sheet to date is of progress set against retreats and lost opportunities. Nonetheless we are farther forward than perhaps we deserve. Wide ranging debate based on informed evidence and rational examination of the facts could propel us where we need to go. That will require a universal self-denying ordinance. No more polarising, no more caricaturing, no more moral right claims substituted for argument — is that too much to ask for with the tools for change in hand, and the only economy in the Western World where manufacturing production is in such decline?

9   Bridge or blockage? The need for a coherent 16–19 system

John Dunford

A level has been described as 'the gold standard' of the education system of England and Wales. This analogy, which has been used by government education ministers to defend an important part of their education policy, has produced a halo effect around A level. Many people, however, see this halo as heavily tarnished and Christopher Ball has commented that the only value of gold is its scarcity (Royal Society of Arts, 1991, p. 1). This could serve to strengthen the analogy, for only a small percentage of the 16–19 age group successfully completes A level courses.

The strengths of A level

The supporters of A level can point to a number of advantages for the examination. The most obvious of these is its public acceptability as a qualification both for 18 year olds and for mature students. A level is well known, widely recognised and acknowledged to be thoroughly validated. It provides a known benchmark at the end of secondary schooling. Its tough grading structure — around 20 per cent of subject entries culminate in one of its two failure grades — sets a high standard of performance which is reasonably consistent from year to year. A level is academically challenging and provides a good test of certain skills. In some A level syllabuses this range of skills is rather narrow, although other syllabuses could justifiably claim to test a broad range of skills within the subject area.

Those who succeed at A level have reached a high level of attainment, which provides a good platform for degree courses at university. This enables the British higher education system to produce graduates in three years in most disciplines and the drop-out rate is small. The level of achievement of these graduates compares favourably with those in other countries which have a broader system of secondary education.

The large number of A level subjects and syllabuses ties in well with provision for adult education in further education colleges. Evening classes in leisure interests can open a gateway to A level study in the same subject area which, in turn, provides a passport to higher education for many who missed this opportunity at the age of 18.

Up to 1992 the variety of methods of assessment at A level was growing; some English A level syllabuses were assessed through coursework for up to 50 per cent of the available marks; a variety of practical assessments was available in science and technology courses; the number of modular courses was growing. Many of these modular courses, such as the Oxford and Cambridge Board's Mathematics for Education and Industry (MEI) course, had proved their success over many years. No-one could describe MEI as an easy way of obtaining mathematics A level.

All these reasons militated against change to the system of A level examinations and, in the period since the mid-1980s, there have been two other important factors operating in favour of the retention of A level. First, Conservative Government ministers have spoken so strongly in favour of A levels as a lynchpin of standards in the education system that it has become impossible for ministers even to hint at changing A level without appearing to be undermining the whole system. Secondly, teachers have been suffering so badly from innovation fatigue as a result of the hail of changes which the Government has rained down upon them that they have not actively sought radical reform of A levels. This has reflected the view among many teachers that the introduction of the General Certificate of Secondary Education (GCSE) and the National Curriculum has been more than enough for one decade.

The weaknesses of A level

The arguments against A level are strong. Fewer than 20 per cent of 18 year olds gain two or more passes and around 20 per cent of subject entries result in failure. Because A level is a two-year commitment, and because it is known to be difficult for all but the most academically able part of the population, most 16 year olds do not even consider starting an A level course. This encourages the view that education 'ends' at 16, an attitude which has dogged the system of education and training in England and Wales. However, because A level is such a prestigious qualification, there is often parental pressure on young people to take this course, even though it may be unsuitable for the individual student.

The obverse side of this prestige is that other qualifications for the 16–19 age group appear to have lower status. This particularly affects vocational qualifications, which are rarely considered by the most academically able students. The 1991 Government White Paper, *Education and Training for the 21st Century*, created an Advanced Diploma which could be earned through either the A level route or through vocational qualifications. The Advanced Diploma was intended to bring parity of esteem to the existing academic and vocational qualifications, but A level and its equivalent vocational courses will never be considered comparable as long as A level retains its 'gold standard' tag. If the opportunity existed to mix A level and vocational studies, then the Advanced Diploma would have some purpose, but it is hard to see how, under the Government's proposals, the Diploma adds any value to the existing academic or vocational qualification. The lack of a bridge between A level and other 16–19 courses is a major disadvantage and creates an inflexibility which hinders curriculum development.

Since 1988 GCSE has dominated the 14–16 curriculum, bringing a change of approach from GCE O level, with greater emphasis being placed on the development of a wider range of skills. The system of assessment at GCSE reflected this breadth; teaching and learning styles were adapted to suit the new courses. A sensibly co-ordinated educational programme would have produced change at A level two years after the GCSE was introduced. Apart from some new syllabuses, which caused some A level teachers to change examination boards, there were no major alterations to the traditional A level pattern. This caused a predictable gulf to appear between GCSE and A level, especially in the sciences, where the reduced content of the GCSE courses meant that schools and colleges were forced to allocate more time to A level teaching.

A level has become out of step with GCSE and, as universities have moved increasingly towards a unit-based curriculum, with credit accumulation and transfer both within and between institutions, the higher education curriculum has also left A level behind.

The lack of links between A level, on the one hand, and vocational qualifications, the world of work, GCSE and higher education, on the other hand, creates a degree of discontinuity which seriously hinders the development of a coherent system of lifelong learning.

The typical A level student studies three subjects, which used to be exclusively in the arts or the sciences. Although an increasing proportion of A level students does not follow such a one-sided combination of subjects, there are no guarantees that 16–19 courses contain breadth, balance or the core skills which employers deem to be essential. Not only does this system produce scientists who cannot write fluently and historians with poor numeracy skills, it also produces too few scientists and technologists for the needs of the country. The proportion of A level candidates who study exclusively the sciences and mathematics has halved between 1963 and 1990 (Smithers and Robinson 1991, p. 30) and the number of entries in these subjects is falling. If this trend continues, a smaller number of quality science graduates will be available to teach these subjects and young people will be less likely to be attracted by the work of inferior science teachers. Technology has never emerged as a strong A level subject; in an education system which rewards theoretical work more highly than practical, technology suffers from an early stage. Perhaps the place of technology in the National Curriculum will begin to redress this imbalance.

A level is a sieve system through which too small a proportion of students pass. Its certification gives only a single grade to reflect the results of two years' work. If that grade is N or U — the two grades of failure — then a student has nothing to show for the positive achievements which have been made during the course.

Advanced Supplementary (AS) examinations

AS examinations were conceived by Sir Keith Joseph in the mid-1980s as a means of creating breadth in the sixth form curriculum (Department of Education and Science 1985). As such, they have failed.

AS courses are half the size of A level courses, but they are pitched at the same degree of difficulty as A level. It is therefore incorrect to use the term AS level, since this would imply a standard of work which is different from A level. In schools and colleges, AS courses are commonly taught within half the weekly time allocation of A levels. In this time students cover half the content of the A level syllabus, but have to work particularly hard in order to acquire more than half the skills of the A level student. There is therefore some substance in the commonly held perception that studying two AS courses is harder than doing one A level.

According to a survey carried out by the Secondary Heads Association in 1990, there are many problems for schools and colleges in delivering AS courses. First, no extra resources have been provided to finance this government initiative. Hence, many institutions have tended not to create separate AS groups, but have taught AS courses within A level groups. Differences between A level and AS syllabuses have sometimes made this difficult. Secondly, institutions have offered more AS courses than have been taken up by their students. Other AS groups are uneconomically small. Thirdly, the headteachers and deputies who responded to the questionnaire reported a low level of credibility for AS among higher education admissions tutors. This inevitably affects student choices at 16.

Fourthly and, in view of the Government's stated intention in establishing AS, most seriously, the survey indicated that the new examination did not appear to have created an acceptable way of providing breadth in the post-16 curriculum. Subsequently it became apparent that some schools were entering lower sixth students for AS examinations in subjects which they would be taking a year later at A level. Where broadening does take place, this is usually for highly intelligent sixth formers who add an AS course to their three A levels, rather than the 2+2 or 1+4 pattern which would have given breadth to the courses of a larger number of A level students. Such combinations are seen as too demanding by the majority of A level students.

For the AS experiment to achieve its objectives, the syllabuses must be tied more closely to the core of A level syllabuses of the same title and higher education admissions tutors must exercise positive discrimination in favour of candidates who have used AS to give breadth to their sixth form studies. In this way, more 16 year olds will consider it worthwhile to embark on AS courses. Until then, however, AS will not provide the answer to the problems of 16–19 education.

Vocational courses

The traditional strength of further education colleges has been in vocational courses and the strength of school sixth forms and of sixth form colleges has been in A level. Tertiary colleges have shown that it is possible to be strong in both and this lesson has not been lost on schools and further education colleges, which have broadened their curricula in order to attract a wider clientele. The colleges, partly because of the way in which they are financed and partly because of their strength in adult education, have offered a much wider range of A level subjects than schools can provide. Schools and sixth form colleges, on the other hand, have moved into the vocational field and have thus begun to offer an attractive and worthwhile sixth form education to those who formerly could be offered little more than O level resits. The pattern of vocational qualifications, however, is far from satisfactory.

Occupationally-specific vocational qualifications are designed by a plethora of over one hundred industry lead bodies. There has formerly been no connection between these separate qualifications, so that a diploma in one occupational area has borne no relation to a diploma in another. This confusion is slowly being rationalised by the National Council for Vocational Qualifications (NCVQ), which has devised a five-level structure in which each vocational qualification is assigned to its appropriate level. Level 2 is equivalent to four or five higher grade GCSE passes. Level 3 is equivalent to two A level passes.

BTEC National courses, two years in length and of A level standard, provide a sensible alternative route into higher education or employment for students who do not want to take A levels. Sixth form colleges and schools with larger sixth forms increasingly offer one or two BTEC National courses. The entry qualification for these is usually four higher grade GCSE passes or a relevant BTEC First course. Since 1991 schools have been permitted to offer BTEC First diplomas. They also offer RSA courses, usually in secretarial subjects.

General National Vocational Qualifications (GNVQs) were originally proposed in the 1991 Government White Paper. They are intended to provide a third alternative route into higher education, placed between A levels and the narrower vocational qualifications. GNVQs will be awarded by BTEC, RSA and City and Guilds at Levels 2 and 3. They are being piloted in a hundred schools and colleges from 1992 and the take-up has been encouraging.

Other vocational qualifications are being adapted to the NCVQ structure. City and Guilds, for example, has revamped its Certificate of Pre-Vocational Education (CPVE), which was itself the successor to the Certificate of Extended Education (CEE), a one-year sixth form qualification which never achieved public recognition. To a lesser extent, the same fate befell the CPVE, which provided a vocational-style course without the clear progression routes which are the hallmark of most vocational qualifications. It remains to be seen whether the GNVQ can establish itself firmly both as the alternative to A level and as a pathway to more specific vocational qualifications.

A feature of the system of vocational qualifications in England and Wales is that the awarding bodies are in direct competition. Although BTEC, RSA and City and Guilds have their own niches in the vocational marketplace, they are commercial bodies which seek to maximise their market share. Furthermore, there are tensions between these bodies and the NCVQ which is charged with the task of bringing coherence into the field. This competitive situation is replicated in the academic examination boards, which offer a bewildering choice of syllabuses. Even where progression should be clearest — from A level to first degree courses — the proliferation of A level syllabuses means that higher education lecturers can assume only a small core of prior knowledge among the students in first year degree cohorts. No such problem exists in Scotland where SCOTVEC is the sole body for vocational awards and where there is also only one examination board. This has the added advantage that the vocational awards body and the academic awards body have much closer co-operation than exists between the equivalent bodies in England and Wales.

Separate systems

The consequences in England and Wales of having separate academic and vocational systems are severe and a high price has had to be paid for this policy.

At the age of 16, a young person has to make a decision which has enormous effect on his or her future and which can be reversed at a later stage only with difficulty. The British tradition and the nature of the academic and vocational curricula mean that 16 year olds have to choose between routes which are seen to be taken by academic sheep, vocational goats and wage-earning others. The division between the first and second is disastrous, but the very existence of the third is itself a scandalous waste of potential for those who take paid employment with no guarantee of further education or training.

The separateness of the two systems inevitably leads to a separate view of those holding the different qualifications. In Britain the academic has always been placed above the vocational in the public mind. This has caused vocational qualifications to have an undeserved low status, a situation which can only be changed by radical surgery to the whole system of 16–19 education; parity of esteem will certainly not be achieved by means of anything so tame as the proposed Advanced Diploma. If the country is to have a properly trained workforce, vocational qualifications need to have a high status, so that people are better motivated to take them and do not see them as second-best.

The lack of bridges between academic and vocational courses is an important part of the twin problems of separateness and low status. Experiments have been tried in which 16 year olds have taken a course in science, for which the first year is common to both A level and BTEC National. After this first year, students decide which route to take. If there were fewer examining bodies, there would be greater hope that such experiments could be replicated across a wider range of subjects. It has been very difficult to take a combination of the academic and the vocational, for example by taking a vocational course with one A level. However, the structure of the GNVQ, which will take up the time of two A levels, will enable it to be taken alongside one A level.

The need for coherence

Such links between academic and vocational courses do not represent even the beginning of a coherent system of 16–19 education. What is required is a system in which students of 16 do not have to commit themselves to one route or the other for the whole of two years, with little opportunity to move between routes unless they put themselves at a severe disadvantage. This requires a system which not only has bridges and ladders within it, but which is closely linked to both secondary and higher education.

Early in 1992 a group of headteachers and principals produced a joint statement with the Standing Conference on University Entrance (SCUE), which outlined the principles on which such a coherent system should be based (SHA *et al.* 1992). The central paragraph of the document stated:

The essential principles of such a unified system are that it should:

(i)   achieve a coherent system which converges and articulates separate pathways, with genuine parity between qualifications in respect of value and utility;

(ii)   promote a high participation rate;

(iii) emphasise success with accreditation of positive achievement at each stage of the course — within the framework of a National Record of Achievement and using processes of credit accumulation;

(iv)   encourage a variety of assessment methods that are appropriate to the context and objectives of the course;

(v)   provide flexibility of provision and participation without endangering coherence — by recognising prior learning and by using credit accumulation and credit transfer;

(vi)   recognise that students learn and develop intellectually at different rates and that too rigid a relationship between age and the conferring of a particular award can impair participation and success;

(vii) secure the appropriate balance in programmes of study, to encourage both breadth and depth of learning;

(viii) incorporate core skills into individual students' programmes of study.

In elaborating on the concept of flexibility, the statement emphasises the different contributions of credit accumulation and credit transfer, which are often mentioned together as CATS:

> Horizontal flexibility relates to the features of credit transfer, articulation between pathways, and the identification of modes of learning that are common within different qualifications.
> Vertical flexibility relates to credit accumulation and to disengaging further the giving of awards from student ages. It encourages participation and learning that is challenging, by allowing the most able to move towards higher education at a faster rate, yet it also permits success through a slower rate of progress.

A growing consensus

Apart from SCUE, the group which produced this statement included representatives of the Secondary Heads Association (SHA), the Head Masters' Conference (HMC), the Girls' School Association (GSA) and the Association of Principals of Sixth Form Colleges (APVIC). This represents a formidably broad consensus among the heads of most of the country's schools and colleges with post-16 provision. In fact, the consensus is much wider than this. Other bodies which are in broad agreement concerning the nature of the changes required in post-16 education include the Royal Society of Arts (RSA). Its report *Learning Pays* provides an analysis of the problems and a range of targets which are in accord with the prevailing consensus. The Royal Society's *Beyond GCSE* has many points of similarity and argues for a radical programme in place of A levels. A British Institute of Management (BIM) survey of its members revealed widespread dissatisfaction with A levels. The BIM paper which followed this survey concluded:

> A broad knowledge and the capacity to learn are essential to prepare individuals for both work and higher education.

Currently, A levels act as a barrier in both these areas. They provide overly specialised knowledge to a narrow elite and reinforce a divide between academic and vocational subjects. This is no longer relevant to a workforce where the distinction between academic and vocational skills is increasingly blurred. Government proposals to enhance vocational qualifications and initiatives that make education and training more relevant to young people are to be welcomed. BIM believes that the Government should now extend this imaginative approach to general education post-16 and grasp the nettle of A level reform. (British Institute of Management 1992, p. 4)

The Labour and Liberal Democrat Parties entered the 1992 General Election campaign with policies for post-16 education which reflected the prevailing consensus. None of these organisations and political parties would claim to have conceived their proposals in a 'Road to Damascus' conversion from traditional A levels. Rather, there has been a gradual development of ideas and a careful formation of policies since the Higginson Report (DES 1988) laid out a five-subject A level programme to which Margaret Thatcher gave such a thunderously negative response.
The main points of the broad consensus are:

- a high participation rate among 16–19 year olds;
- a single system of academic and vocational qualifications, with a choice of pathways to suit individual needs;
- parity of esteem for academic and vocational qualifications;
- breadth and balance in the curriculum;
- core skills within individual programmes of study;
- a modular framework of courses;
- the opportunity for credit accumulation and transfer;
- accreditation for positive achievement during the course;
- a variety of assessment methods;
- the use of a record of achievement.

A coherent system

What is required, therefore, is a system of post-16 education which is built largely, but not exclusively, on modules, with the real possibility of transfer from one part of the system to another. It should be possible for students to gain accreditation for each module and, with some modules which are common to both academic and vocational pathways, students should be able to acquire credits and then move to a related course in a different strand. Such a system of credit accumulation and transfer (CATS) is beginning to work well in higher education and would have many benefits for the 16–19 age group. CATS could also be the building blocks for a system of lifelong learning in Britain, enabling us at last to escape from the disastrous connotation that education 'ends' at 16 or 18. Such a system would have wide support.

A modular system would enable students to build study programmes which are relevant to their individual needs and aspirations. The overall structure would ensure that adequate breadth and balance are incorporated into each programme of study. This structure would also have to ensure that study programmes do not consist of an incoherent jumble of modules which lead nowhere. With suitable guidance from tutors in schools and colleges, proper progression can be guaranteed and all individual programmes of study can be arranged to include the core skills which young people will require for their future and which employers rightly demand in all their employees.

A 16–19 education system which encourages a high rate of participation will not serve the country's needs unless it also creates a high rate of success. A major philosophical problem of the existing education system is that it is based on the need for a high failure rate in each examination, as each stage of the education process carelessly discards a high proportion of young people in order to fulfil its objective of selection for the next stage. O level and A level were designed with this need uppermost. Examinations of this type — especially when they are terminal tests at the end of a long two-year course — are seen as hurdles in the educational sprint race from 14–18.

Education should be a marathon, not a sprint, and the 16–19 education programme should be planned, not in isolation, but in close harmony with the remaining parts of the system. A modular system would not only be more closely attuned to the evolving pattern of the curriculum in higher education, but could be planned as a logical continuation of the 14–16 programme. This would enable us to escape from the millstone of age-relatedness, which tends to produce failure at 16 and 18 because students cannot pass particular examinations at those ages. Grade examinations in music are not age-related, but motivate musicians of all ages to move towards the next highest level of achievement. A modular-based 16–19 system, which fitted into a consistent pattern from 14 to 21, would enable students to study, and succeed in, work which was suited to their ability and aspirations. The system would have the flexibility to meet the needs of all young people. Thus, a 17 year old could study a unit of work which he or she would have found too difficult at 15 or 16; an 18 year old, for whom even the present A level course does not provide sufficient stimulation, could study a module which would count towards a future degree; an adult could study a work-related unit, which would also count towards an academic qualification which contributes to eligibility for a place in higher education. Such a system would render meaningless the terms academic and vocational.

A modular-based 16–19 education programme could become the catalyst for a system of lifelong learning in which credit accumulation would not cease when full-time education ends. AS courses, the Advanced Diploma and the GNVQ represent little more than tinkering with the present system when more radical measures are clearly needed. The Howie Committee in Scotland, in addressing the problems of the Scottish system which is widely acknowledged to be superior to the English, courageously looked beyond its terms of reference to the pre-16 curriculum. Fortunately for the Scots, they have no political sacred cows, such as A level, which inhibit reform in England. Only when this sacred cow is slaughtered will England and Wales develop a 16–19 system which serves the needs of the majority of the population. A modular system, based on the principles which have been widely accepted, would not only solve many of the problems inherent in the present arrangement of separate academic and vocational courses, but would be capable of extension into a more logical, continuous system from the age of 14 onwards.

References

Association of Principals of Sixth Form Colleges (1991) *A Framework for Growth: Improving the Post-16 Curriculum.*
Ball, Sir Christopher (1991) *Learning Pays* Royal Society For Arts.
British Institute of Management (1992) *A-Level Reform — A Wider Choice.*
Channel 4 Commission on Education (1991) *Every Child in Britain.*
Committee to Review Curriculum and Examinations in the fifth and sixth years of Secondary Education in Scotland (Howie Committee) (1992) *Upper Secondary Education in Scotland* Scottish Office Education Department.
Confederation of British Industry (1989) *Towards a Skills Revolution* Task Force Report.
Department of Education and Science (1985) *Better Schools* HMSO.
Department of Education and Science (1988) *Advancing A-levels* HMSO.
Department of Education and Science (1991) *Education and Training for the 21st Century* HMSO.

Halsey, A.H. (1992) *Opening Wide the Doors of Higher Education*, National Commission on Education.

Institute for Public Policy Research (1990) *A British 'Baccalaureat': Ending the Division between Education and Training*.

Institute of Directors (1992) *Performance and Potential: Education and Training for a Market Economy*.

Labour Party (1991) *Investing in Britain's Future*.

Liberal Democrat Party (1992) *Time to Learn*.

Royal Society (1991) *Beyond GCSE*.

Secondary Heads Association (1989) *Planning 16–19 Education*.

Secondary Heads Association (1990) *AS Examinations*.

Secondary Heads Association (1991) *16–19 The Way Forward*.

Secondary Heads Association (1992) *Towards a Coherent System*.

Secondary Heads Association *et al.* (1992) *16–19 Education: A Joint Statement of Principles*.

Smithers, A. and Robinson, P. (1991) *Beyond Compulsory Schooling: A Numerical Picture* Council for Industry and Higher Education.

10   The 14–19 curriculum — a further education perspective

Dick Evans and Jenny Cronin

Setting the scene

The post-16 education training scene, particularly in England and Wales, is one of great complexity and variety. It possesses a greater heterogeneity than other educational sectors. Further education colleges, like many other institutions in other sectors, have been subjected to major reforms over the past decade. Innumerable initiatives have been introduced, many of them motivated by political dogma and/or short-term expediencies and these have done little to establish coherence within the system. A number of important initiatives were introduced after relatively short-term piloting without any evaluation. As a result this has added to the state of confusion that already existed.

The post-16 scene, its qualifications, the variety and nature of the institutions, and institutions' organisation and management, is often referred to as a jungle. One of great complexity and full of contradictions and paradoxes. As a result of this, a great degree of misunderstanding and ignorance exists about the further education sector, and this fragmented and confused picture creates barriers for progression, both within the sector and between other sectors for its students. A bewildering array of qualifications exist which are awarded by a wide variety of agencies. Many, in spite of the work of the National Council for Vocational Qualifications (NCVQ) continue to be autonomous. Many of the examining and validating bodies still exercise a disproportionate degree of power over the institutions. Constraints that they impose must be reduced and a much greater commitment made to allow greater freedom to institutions to recognise non-standard entry qualifications and prior learning. Also greater encouragement and recognition should be given to credit accumulation and credit transfer by examining/validating bodies and by institutions in different sectors.

Colleges, schools and sixth form centres operate under different regulations and have different abilities to offer the various examining and validating awards. Sadly, schools and colleges are often seen as competitors when, with diminishing resources and the final phase of the Technical Vocational Educational Initiative (TVEI), the time is right to enter into partnerships and become collaborators to provide a quality service which possesses continuity for all its students. Post-16 programmes of study should build on pre-16 provision in content, range of experience and assessment methods. This approach would surely increase participation rates and reduce wastage and failure rates. Unfortunately the 1988 Education Act in many ways reinforced the institutional autonomy and historical rivalry and weakened the laudable aims of the TVEI pilots. The opportunity for schools to opt out and the creation of city technology colleges added to the fragmentation and confusion in the jungle. This complexity, coupled with a lack of real sympathy and understanding of the sector by politicians has seriously disadvantaged the sector. After all, everyone understands the school system, as everyone has experienced it! The higher education sector is more understood as the majority of the decision takers have been through that system. FE is different; its greatest allies are employers, but it still lacks a significant lobby in Parliament and the Department for Education. However in spite of these difficulties, the achievements of the FE system are immense.

The current picture is further complicated by the fact that FE colleges and sixth form centres have now to prepare for incorporation following the 1992 Education Act. As from the 1 April 1993, 480 colleges will become independent from their local education authorities (LEAs). The present Government argues that, as independent institutions, they will be able to respond more quickly and flexibly to local/regional demands for their customers — principally students and employers. Although independence will produce a number of distinct advantages, the loss of the LEA's influence causes a number of concerns. Many LEAs have been very supportive of their colleges, and the reputation and achievements of the institutions, and indeed the FE sector, is testimony to that support over many years. In order to establish coherence and pathways of progression, there must be a focus for local strategic planning for all pre- and post-16 provision, and many in the world of education see the LEAs as being the only organisation that can provide it. Their place cannot be taken over by the Training

Enterprise Councils (TECs), or the regional groupings that have been recently proposed.

One of the most important and influential initiatives over the past ten years has been the Technical Vocational Educational Initiative in that it attempted and partly succeeded in embracing the '14 to 18/19 curriculum' across the traditional break at 16. TVEI addressed key management and organisational issues in such areas as curriculum co-ordination, resource planning, and performance evaluation. The Initiative can be seen as both a change facilitator and a change agent, and hopefully the lessons learnt and the examples of good practice that were developed can be carried forward into the future. TVEI encouraged institutions to develop consortia and partnership arrangements spanning the schools and FE sector. The Initiative must not be forgotten. Its achievements must influence and inform the future shape for the 14–19 scene.

The colleges within the new FE sector must plan across all aspects of the curriculum and produce more coherent and relevant curriculum frameworks, allowing greater opportunities to bridge the pre-vocational and vocational and academic programmes of study. The curriculum of the future must be guided by the following principles:

- Breadth
- Balance
- Differentiation
- Entitlement
- Progression.

These five principles should help address the issues of curriculum narrowness and the too early specialisation into which students are currently forced. This has produced low participation, wastage, and low levels of qualification in the population. Any curriculum framework in the future must strike that difficult balance in the equation which comprises: breadth, balance and differentiation. Differentiation can be equated with depth and the curriculum experience must be able to match the expectations of the ablest student but equally important provide achievement opportunities for all the other students. Whatever provision is offered must be of high quality. This country seems to equate quality with rarity, the qualifications system seems geared to produce wastage and has been called a catalogue of accumulative failure. Quality should be equated to fitness for purposes for *all*.

Equally important as these principles is the need for effective and appropriate organisational and management structures, which are able to respond to the current climate, even though it is full of uncertainties, and as recent evidence shows, overt political interference. Members of the senior management team must take a lead on these initiatives and support staff directly in bringing about these changes. Leadership qualities are essential in the future, after all leadership is good management in disguise.

Finally, in this scene setting section, and coupled with the above five principles, is that the curriculum must be driven by the learners, irrespective of source/context of learning. The principle of learner centredness is essential and must be the starting point in any major curriculum development.

The current scene

Having set the scene, we now look at the current curriculum and its developments within the post-16 scene, especially in the Further Education sector. As mentioned above, the 1980s witnessed the introduction of a series of initiatives. Many were piecemeal and were structurally unrelated to each other and most certainly not linked to existing provision. Examples of these initiatives included the Youth Training Scheme (YTS), the Technical Vocational Education Initiative (TVEI), the Certificate of Pre-vocational Education (CPVE) and the new Business Technology Education Council Awards (BTEC First Awards). These developments, amongst other things, tried to make education more practical and vocational and/or to produce new qualifications to attract those who did not participate in post-16 provision. However, the Government's obsession with the maintainance of the so-called 'A level gold standard' and no real significant modification to higher education entry policies accentuated the difficulties associated with the relatively low post-16 participation rate.

A typical further education college offers a wide range and variety of curriculum frameworks, spanning pre-vocational, vocational, academic and professional awards delivered by many modes of attendance. A number of institutions within the sector are also involved with higher education (HE), e.g. higher national diplomas, degrees and professional awards. The sector, being 'sandwiched' between the schools and HE sectors, must continue to be aware of developments in these areas. Curricular provision post-16 must articulate with what young people experience pre-16, so that there is as smooth a transition at 16 as is possible from the National Curriculum. Colleagues in the schools are still battling with the contradictions and paradoxes that have been precipitated by the National Curriculum, especially with the so-called new methods of testing and assessment! In spite of all the added pressure and difficulties that teachers are experiencing, GCSE is having some positive outcomes. For example, the requirements to study science for all pupils, more enlightened teaching and learning styles and greater learner autonomy. Students already show greater confidence and competence in assignment and investigative work, although problems still exist in a number of important areas, e.g. mathematics. This, we would argue, is not the fault of the GCSE system, but is more associated with some of the post-16 curricula, especially the existing A/AS levels and some of the vocational awards, for example BTECs. These programmes of study still use knowledge and understanding in mathematics and science which do not make the bridges to the learning outcomes of the National Curriculum. GCSE is process led and increasingly the assessment regimes are becoming criterion referenced, whilst A levels are still product-led and in the majority of cases are still unduly narrowly subject focused, with an over emphasis on traditional end examination/assessments, and finally are still norm referenced. The mis-match in process/product and the assessment regimes causes real difficulties to students, especially in a number of programmes of study, i.e. mathematics and science. A/AS levels must be significantly reformed otherwise these difficulties will continue and possibly impede other curricular reforms which will be mentioned later in this chapter.

Equally important is that the post-16 institutions work closely with higher education institutions (HEIs). Even though the tight hold that HEIs, especially the universities, have on the qualifications scene has been eroded over the past few years, it still sets the agenda and the traditional methods we operate still resonate around the system. Admissions tutors still exercise a degree of control with scant regard for the changing scene in the post-16 institutions. Many still worship at the altar of the A levels. The polytechnics (now the new universities) have led the way on modularity, credit accumulation and credit transfer and more enlightened methods to non-standard entrance to HE. Universities are now showing real evidence of changing their ways of operating but there is still much to do.

The future scene: GNVQ, NVQ and staff development

GNVQ, NVQ

This chapter, as the initial scene setting conveys, takes a position which is underpinned by the centrality in the 16–19 curriculum of the five principles of breadth, balance, differentiation, entitlement and progression and the prime reference point in enacting these principles of the life-time learner as an individual: hence the expression learner-centredness.

The National Vocational Qualifications (NVQ) framework and the emerging General National Vocational Qualifications (GNVQ) framework are, to labour the point, national frameworks. They also contain a set of principles in common. These are: specification in terms of outcomes; their unit base; facility for credit accumulation; design for accessibility to assessment by individuals; and that they assert the irrelevance of time serving and prescribed modes of learning so long as the evidence presented meets the required standards.

Whichever jargon is adopted — client, customer, candidate — both frameworks are learner-centred, which must be recognised by post-16 education/training providers. They are not awarding body-centred or institution-centred but intended to be tuned to the individual's needs.

We believe that the national policy aim of these frameworks should be the maximum, appropriate participation of 16–19 year olds and adults in post-16 education training. Likewise, the outcomes aspired to in national policy terms should be the maximum number and range of competent and qualified young people and adults contributing to and benefiting from the country's economy. This must be coupled with nation-wide availability of opportunities to move in and out of education-training throughout life in order to continue to contribute to and benefit from the country's economy.

At the level of the local post-16 centre, the institutions which perceive, understand and espouse this view of the future are the ones which will attract, progress and attract again the young people and adults in their local and regional areas. This is not a view bound by the urge to outlive and overwhelm the competition from other providers but is essential to enable maximum opportunities for participation and achievement by learners.

Regardless of whether providers are sixth forms in schools, sixth form centres, further education colleges or further and higher education colleges, they must design, manage and deliver the curriculum for vocational qualifications in ways which enable the movement of individual learners and achievers between and amongst such centres — locally, regionally and nationally, not trap and limit them. This means that the individual's prior achievements and competences in GNVQ and NVQ units must receive recognition regardless of the centre at which they were assessed and verified or the awarding body to which they are accredited as GNVQs or NVQs by NCVQ. Smooth transition from this stage must be agreed and progression enabled by the institutions whether laterally or hierarchically in the GNVQ and NVQ frameworks.

The introduction of GNVQs provides the opportunity for the full range of post-16 centres to offer broad-based vocational education leading to national qualifications. GNVQs have the potential to extricate both learners and providers from the tendency towards segregation of learning routes and the vocational qualifications to which they lead which has characterised the conventional vocational curriculum portfolio to date. The GNVQ framework explodes the relatively independent and idiosyncratic cultures and regimes of the vocational awarding and validating bodies and asserts a national language for vocational qualifications over the traditional range of idioms in ascendancy until now.

From the curriculum development and curriculum design point of view there is now an open invitation to pursue long held aspirations towards flexibility and responsiveness which earlier constrictions and dysfunctions in the vocational qualifications system have inhibited. Alongside the established NVQ framework, flexible, coherent curriculum design and delivery of GNVQs and NVQs becomes both an affordable and necessary reality.

College policies, strategies and management, however, have to be clear about the principles to be enacted and the extent to which learning programmes and qualifications will be networked within curriculum frameworks.

On the basis of the principles asserted in this chapter policies and strategies must emphasise the interconnectedness of learning routes and vocational qualifications. This would make opportunities for individual choice, availability of choices, coherence for the individual in the chosen programme, opportunities to change or extend the route and outcomes for the learner which are recognised by gatekeepers of progression routes beyond.

With this vision fleshed out, curriculum design can deploy in earnest the teaching and learning strategies which separate previous initiatives, mentioned in the scene setting for this chapter, have put forward for attention and implementation.

With unit based, credit accumulation and credit transfer qualifications the notions of guidance and initial assessment, individual action planning and recording and reviewing of learning referenced to a core skills framework come into their own.

Similarly coherent planning and delivery of modular programmes matched to GNVQ and NVQ unit specifications delivered through a variety of teaching and learning strategies including resource based approaches now have the context of an economy of scale which can be developed and managed. The facility to open up multiple start and finish dates and times comprehensively across programmes also emerges.

There are however still major areas of national policy and strategy on which the implementation of potentially wide reaching curriculum frameworks are at least partly dependent and over which thinking at national level is unsettled.

Guidance given by NCVQ in July 1992 states that 'GNVQ at Level 3 has been designed to be of comparable standard to that of A-Levels' (NCVQ 1992). This echoes, with some distortion, a similar reference in the White Paper of May 1991, where 'General NVQs should also. . .be of equal standard with academic qualifications at the same level' (DES 1991). This change of emphasis from 'equal' to 'comparable' is symptomatic of the impossibility of equating criterion referencing with norm referencing, process based with product based qualifications as rehearsed earlier in this chapter.

GNVQs are to be threaded through with core skills units: communication, application of number, and information technology. No such thread runs through A/AS levels in any formally recognised way. Where equality does not exist comparability, unfortunately, has to be earned. Credit transfer between vocational and academic qualifications is still therefore to hove over the horizon.

Core skills, and emphasis on process, we believe, are key concerns to be attended to in all post-16 qualifications, as recognised in GNVQs. Perspectives on assessment are much more closely aligned in GNVQs and NVQs. GNVQs are about ensuring a 'foundation of skills, knowledge and understanding which underpin a range of qualifications'. Their outcomes are to be expressed in a 'statement of achievement'. Assessment for GNVQs is characterised as 'comprehensive, covering all the elements in each unit' (NCVQ 1992).

The relationship between GNVQs and NVQs in outcomes and assessment terms is relatively transparent. Performance evidence must feature in all elements of an NVQ and all elements and performance criteria have to be covered. The underpinning nature of GNVQs for occupational competence is pointed out by these features although the assumption has to be trusted that in NVQs core skills are integrated into the demonstrable performance of job activities.

It is the finer detail of the assessment regime for GNVQs which is troubling. NVQ assessment gives credence to local assessment and internal verification with external verification by the awarding body. In GNVQs these practices are to be augmented by nationally set written tests linked to each unit. A pass is essential in each of these to obtain unit credits. It is as if in the absence of real currency to recognise equality between GNVQs and A/AS levels the nationally set terminal examination is to be the chosen common feature.

Guidance

Colleges are moving increasingly towards learner-centredness. This means that guidance processes must be enhanced and extended. The introduction of GNVQs makes it an imperative. Colleges must move away from the more traditional methods of *admissions* to the recognition of *transition* for the learners, and from the formal processes associated with *selection* to the need for *matching* the appropriate provision to the learner. The eventual universal introduction of training credits by 1996 will empower the learner to seek a quality individual programmes of study. This last initiative will require institutions to establish good and effective working relationships with their local Training and Enterprise Councils (TECs). The importance of records of achievement, accreditation of prior learning (APL) and the changes in the curriculum frameworks, i.e. NVQs and GNVQs, again will put the emphasis on the learner. Also the likelihood of output funding will require greater emphasis on continuous assessment and guidance and a focus on the individual learner.

As more students participate in post-16 education training (many with non-traditional qualifications and backgrounds) initial guidance and assessment becomes even more important. Colleges must develop guidance services which embrace all the following elements:

Pre-entry ➡ enrolment ➡ through learning ➡ exit

A recent policy statement (jointly produced by the Institute of Careers Guidance (ICG) and the Association of Colleges and Principals (APC) states very forcefully the key role of guidance in the post-16 scene. Guidance is a complex and multi-dimensional process with eleven associated and inter-related activities, including informing, counselling, assessing, teaching and managing. The service as mentioned above must attend to the initial stages of guidance as well as the 'through-learning' stages, including careers and occupationally specific guidance. Colleges will need to establish a network of services throughout the institution to deal with the various stages/phases of guidance. A possible model is a central focus for initial guidance and assessment including the processes involved with the assessment of prior learning/ achievement (APLA). This central focus is then complemented by a series of other units which deal with the more specialised aspects including occupationally specific elements associated with the 'through-programme of study' stages of guidance/assessment in the NVQ and GNVQ curricula frameworks. It is important that this approach is managed and co-ordinated in an effective and efficient manner.

Implications for staff development

Staff, particularly in further education colleges have some years experience now of deploying flexible strategies in their delivery of education training for NVQs. Their experience and established expertise in these curriculum developments are a key resource in building the vision to provide learner-centred approaches which emphasise guidance and assessment processes across NVQs and GNVQs.

The most successful and productive methods of staff development in this context have been programme team based. The starting points have been the range of needs of the individual learners/candidates referenced to the requirements of the qualification. It has been these foci which have stimulated the appreciation of the need to provide and meet a range of learning and assessment contexts and media and re-examine the relationship between 'staff' and 'students'. The process through which the learner/candidate needs to be drawn and supported has been recognised as the essential framework from which innovative practice in the relationship between tutor and learner/candidate has been introduced.

All stages including marketing, provision of information, initial advice, guidance and assessment, individual action planning, negotiation of learning and assessment activities, review and agreement of readiness for assessment have found their place. The settings within which learning and assessment take place have been seen afresh and alternative more flexible and learner centred environments created. Within these settings the widest range of learning media and materials are selected, sequenced and inter-related for use by learners. The aim here is to match preferred learning styles, provide variety for the reinforcement of learning and ensure appropriateness for the knowledge, skills and application required by the individual learner/candidate for the competences concerned. The key note in such environments is accessibility of learning media and materials to the individual learner. These are the product of collaborative team work of programme tutors not the guarded preserve of individual lecturers. Modularisation becomes an essential curriculum design framework for these kinds of approaches. The renewed recognition of the significance of the learning process and the opportunities which modularisation offers, also means that programme teams in a variety of vocational areas can help and influence each other as these have transferable application regardless of the specialism.

It is however particularly important that at a strategic management level the decisions are taken to endorse, lead and support such innovative practices and that senior managers communicate that these are the kinds of programmes to which the college is committed and on which its future must be planned.

To summarise, in order to establish coherence in curriculum frameworks and the associated assessment regimes and to create continuous and smooth models of progression, post-16 institutions must work closely with all partners, i.e. school, HEIs, employers, the TECs and the local authorities etc. The institutions must move to create unity in terms of the curriculum framework and institutional management in place of fragmentation, and adopt flexibility in place of rigidity. Finally, it is essential that all college staff are supported by effective and efficient programmes of staff development.

This short chapter only provides a rather crude snapshot of the post-16 scene and is somewhat speculative about the future. Much depends on the environment, especially the political view, of this very important sector of education and training.

References

Department of Education and Science and Employment Department Group (1991) *Education and Training for the 21st Century* vol 1, section 3.8.

NCVQ (1992) Information Note to Specification of GNVQ Mandatory Units.

11 Training credits

Lindsay Martin

Introduction

The development of the idea of a market in training, and of credits as a means of providing access to training in that market, can be traced back to the Confederation of British Industry (CBI) conference in 1989. The CBI had established a task force in 1988, chaired by Sir Brian Nicholson, as a result of concern then being expressed about the skills gap in British industry. It produced a document entitled *Towards a Skills Revolution* which was well received at the 1989 conference and which asserted that it was only possible to meet the identified skill needs by creating an effective training market and that there was no place for employment for 16 and 17 year olds which did not include training.

The document also recognised, as part of its concept of 'careerships' for all 14 to 18 year olds, that it was necessary to rate the needs for individuals more highly than that of training providers. By so doing, it was argued, people would be more motivated to train. They would have individual profiles and the buying power to purchase training leading to transferable skills and qualifications. The CBI called on the Government to fund a credit for all 16 year olds to meet the cost of training leading to a National Vocational Qualification (NVQ) at level III or equivalent.

The Government responded on 27 March 1990 by announcing the training credits initiative for young people on a pilot basis and issued a prospectus inviting Training and Enterprise Councils (TECs) in England and Wales and local enterprise companies (lecs) in Scotland to bid for development funding. The initiative was launched by the Secretary of State for Employment (at the time Michael Howard) following consultation with the Secretary of State for Education and Science (as it then was) and other colleagues.

Outline bids were received on 4 May 1990, thirty-three TECs and lecs having applied with seventeen selected by the Secretary of State to develop with the aid of more detailed guidance. On 27 July 1990 the detailed bids were received and eleven were chosen, nine in England and one each in Wales and Scotland with a balance between urban and rurally-based TECs. Those that were chosen then had until April 1991 to become operational; an incredibly tight timescale if the introduction of training credits was to be anything more than cosmetic.

On 20 May 1991, the Department of Education and Science issued the White Paper *Education and Training for the 21st Century* in which, inter alia, the Government announced its commitment to the extension of training credits to all 16 and 17 year olds by 1996. This is to be done in annual tranches building on the experience of existing pilots. In June the prospectus for the second round of applications to pilot credits was issued with a closing date in October. In November the successful bids were announced, six in England, one in Wales and two in Scotland. These second-round pilots are to be operational from April 1993 and have, therefore, a considerably longer development period.

Criticisms of youth training

It is not suggested that criticisms of youth training (YT) led directly to the decision to introduce training credits as a replacement because the direct evidence for that assertion is not there. There is no doubt, however, that a number of TECs have taken note of those criticisms in order to incorporate improvements to YT in their schemes for training credits. It is worth examining two contrasting pieces of work which provide a critique of YT and exploring the extent to which the design of training credits can overcome that critique.

The first is by David Raffe (1990) in the form of a powerful analysis of the way in which YT works in the context of the provision of skills and employment opportunities. His overall thesis is that YT will not be able to break out of its perceived low status and achieve its employment objectives simply by improving the quality of training. His argument is that to succeed, there must be a demand for the skills produced by the training and Raffe cites evidence that employers are sceptical of the sort of training produced by YT which he describes as 'foundation'. He asserts that the occupational-specific skills produced by YT are not in short supply in the labour market and that YT graduates are, therefore, in competition with more experienced adults. He further criticises training under YT for 'not enhancing the potential job performance of individual trainees' and that it does not lead to credible certification. His final point is that YT has to provide evidence about the abilities and capacities of young people which outweighs the perception (and the reality?) that they are drawn from the bottom of the educational hierarchy.

Raffe proposed two ways in which YT could attempt to overcome the above critique. It needs to:

provide occupationally specific skills in demand in the local labour market and to certify these in a way that retains the confidence of potential employers

and

enhance the context of YT by giving its trainees favoured access to the information networks through which employers recruit. (Raffe 1990)

Does the introduction of training credits do either of these things? As training credits are required to lead to National Vocational Qualifications, or an alternative suitable to the needs of the individual, which are themselves based on specific job competencies identified by lead bodies drawn from representatives of the industry concerned, it can be argued that the first of Raffe's points is met. As far as access to information networks is concerned it is not at all clear exactly what this means. If it can broadly be taken to mean that providers of training are not close enough to employers and their needs, and that not enough employers are actually involved in providing training themselves, then it is an issue which is at the forefront of the design of training credits. In the first place many pilot schemes will only contract with employers as providers of training and others will only issue a training credit if a work placement has been organised by the training provider. Secondly, the extension of the entitlement to training to all full-time education leavers whether or not in employment should lead to the involvement of more employers as they take on young employees able to 'spend' their training credit.

The second critique of YT comes from Youthaid (1992) and is based on a collection of evidence from a variety of published sources including Government statistics and those of TECs presented to the House of Commons Select Committee on Employment in 1991. Their critique is that there are not sufficient YT places actually to meet the Government's guarantee, and that much of what there is, is of low quality. The second of these is being addressed by a number of the pilot schemes which are taking the opportunity to introduce new quality assurance processes for providers of training. It is also being addressed by the point already made that all training credits must lead to a recognised vocational qualification. That there are insufficient places is almost certainly the case and an issue which cannot be addressed by the introduction of training credits, unless the training turns out to be miraculously cheaper than YT. That is a matter for government.

Training credits: The concept

It is clear that the Government's concept is very closely modelled on the proposals of the CBI outlined above. Essentially training credits are the replacement for Youth Training (YT) which, as we have seen above, has not achieved the quality, credibility and uptake necessary to deliver the skills needed to equip the future workforce of this country. It is important, therefore, to identify the ways in which training credits are different from YT. These are as follows:

- An entitlement to training for 16 and 17 year olds who have left full-time education (or those who have not completed two years full-time post-16) whether or not they are in employment. This is a significant extension from the YT guarantee which only applies to those young people not in employment.
- It includes those 16 and 17 year olds currently released not as part of YT by their employers to attend part-time further education at a local college.
- All the training provided through training credits funding has to lead to a NVQ level II qualification or equivalent except in the case of those with special training needs.
- An individual training plan must be drawn up with and for the young person which can be monitored and reviewed on a regular basis.
- The proposals in each area have been drawn up by the individual TEC or lec, in close consultation with local education authorities, education establishments, training providers and employers enabling the design to reflect local priorities and conditions unlike the total central design of YT.

The use of the word 'pilot' is potentially misleading in the sense that a 'pilot' TEC or lec is piloting training credits

nationally because not all TECs or lecs are using them. In its own
area, however, it is not a pilot because after the commencement of
operations there are no more YT starts; they are all training credits.

How training credits work and have been developed

The following description is drawn in the main from the
developments at South Thames Training and Enterprise Council
(STTEC) which is a second round pilot. It is not atypical but may
well place a different emphasis on certain features than other pilots.
The developments are grouped around three main themes; careers
education and guidance, marketing and funding/administration.

Careers education/guidance

The key principles of training credits are that of choice and
empowerment of the individual in the selection and process of their
training route.
    To achieve these principles it is vital that the individual:

- has access to up to date and accurate information on the
  opportunities available;
- is a good decision maker, able to interrogate and select
  career routes.

It is, therefore, essential that all young people go through a
process at school which equips them with the above skills. This can
be achieved through an enhancement of the provision of careers
education, guidance and counselling which is an important
dimension of the development of training credits. It is envisaged
that this process will result in the provision of individual action
plans (IAPs) for pupils which will record in tangible form the
process they have been through.
    Most of the training credit pilots have, therefore, sought ways
of working with both schools and careers services to bring about
the above. This has had to vary from area to area and school to
school as schools are at very different stages of development in
relation to individual action planning. In the case of STTEC this has
been undertaken in conjunction with the TVE(E) co-ordinators in
the four LEAs in its area (TVEI being a recent part of the scene for

these new LEAs) as the TVE(E) schemes have a common interest in IAPs.

Before a young person is issued with a credit they should, therefore, have an IAP, and enhanced advice and guidance delivered by the careers service after the decision has been taken to leave full-time education. This is recorded on the IAP or a separate document, the objective of this process being to:

- ensure that each young person is following a negotiated and agreed vocational path;
- ensure that there is sufficient information on the young person's needs and abilities to construct a realistic training plan.

In order to resource the above, agreement has been reached with the four local careers services on the funding for their role in the development of training credits including the promotion of credits to schools and the development of their part in the action planning process. The final part of the guidance process, the production of a detailed training plan which will build on the IAP, is seen as the responsibility of the provider of the training. No training will be able to take place without the existence of an agreed training plan.

Marketing

Marketing is a vital and essential part of the development and launch of any new product and, in the context of training credits, essential in order to get the message across to young people and the adults who influence them, and to the employers who will employ and/or train them.

The extensive evaluation of the first-round pilots indicated that their weakness in marketing terms was the lack of time which they had for market research. Following a tendering process, therefore, STTEC chose a company to oversee the marketing of training credits which had experience of a qualitative market research approach.

Their primary objective was to understand the various players in the training credits initiative in order to develop a targeted package and more specifically to:

- define exact package requirements;
- recommend design guidelines;

- identify briefs for advertising and promotions;
- assess relevant media;
- clarify the human effort required for a successful launch.

A qualitative group discussion and depth interview approach was utilised. A thorough research programme was conducted with the key target groups (young people and their influencers: peers, parents, careers officers, careers teachers and the media). Their orientations, attitudes, hopes, fears and beliefs about training were explored and they were exposed to a variety of stimulus material, including existing training credits literature, videos, strategic propositions, words and pictures and advertising ideas. Interviews were also held with groups of employers and training providers.

The product of the above market research was used to brief a graphic design company to produce a design for a brochure and flysheet aimed at school leavers capable of being adapted for other purposes such as a video, cinema and poster advertising, and a brochure for employers.

STTEC's marketing strategy will, therefore, consist of the following elements:

- brochure and accompanying video aimed at young people for use in schools by teachers and careers officers;
- cinema and poster advertising aimed mainly at young people but also aimed at raising awareness among employers and the general population;
- a brochure aimed at employers;
- launch events in the form of local low-key gatherings for groups of secondary headteachers, college principals, employers and training providers;
- local press editorial coverage through the identification and development of newsworthy case stories.

In addition to the above STTEC staff have been visiting individual schools, colleges and private training providers, and taking advantage of opportunities to address groups of staff and employers. The council also had the benefit of a secondee from Sainsbury one day a week for six months whose brief was to visit large companies in the council's area in an effort both to discover how to minimise the bureaucratic implications of training credits for them (their particular problem being that they may take training credit holders from, and therefore have to deal with, a number of different TECs each with a potentially different administrative system) and to raise their awareness of training credits.

Funding and administration

The following are the issues which needed to be addressed:

- costing current training provision across the range of providers both public and private;
- devising a pricing system for future training;
- trainee eligibility, 'spending' rules and their administrative implications;
- designing an administrative system which served the needs of the trainees, the training providers and the council;
- drafting a user specification for an information technology package to serve the needs of training credits, and evaluating systems already in use.

Costing provision

For the first round pilots the Department of Employment commissioned a study by KPMG Management Consulting of 'Cost banding issues'. The report of that study concluded 'we had originally hoped to construct a viable costings framework. . .but the quality of the data available has meant this was not possible'. The main reason was that training providers used such a variety of methods of recording cost that comparable data was not available.

STTEC had already commissioned its own study of the cost of youth training and employment training in its area from Ernst & Young. The conclusions were, *inter alia*, that youth training excluding allowances) cost an average of £63 per week with a range from £49 to £86. It also concluded that the council contributed on average only 45 per cent of that cost. Little was known however about what that cost 'bought', i.e. what qualification outcomes with what trainee/learner support are provided for that cost and how that cost varies for different training areas. This has had to be researched specifically in order to price training credits.

Also, STTEC knew little about the cost of part-time released further education in colleges and therefore commissioned research into this in order to try to produce a price structure for training credits which would encompass both this and YT. As for the research with private training providers, this would include the cost of trainee support needs such as literacy and numeracy provision and English for speakers of other languages.

Pricing provision

It is generally recognised that vocational education and training has differential costs by occupational area. This emerged in the studies undertaken by both KPMG and Ernst & Young referred to above. It is also recognised by the Government in relation to further education in that the legal basis of payments between local education authorities for students who live in one authority but are educated in another (known as recoupment payments) have differential rates for different subject areas.

The KPMG report recommended that for the purpose of pricing training provision for training credits purposes the Department for Education Recoupment Groups provided a reasonable guideline on cost rankings in the different occupational sectors. However, the issue is not so much the grouping of training provision into price bands for administrative convenience but the actual value attached to the bands. The evaluation of the first-round pilots indicated that the more researched and robust these values were, the more likely they were to be generally accepted. Hence the research work indicated in the section above.

The issues are, therefore, (a) how the price should be built up and (b) what payment system should be used. With regard to the former, the 'cost' of the training, and therefore the price paid for it, must take into account the current contribution made by employers under YT. Not to do so would actually reduce employers' contributions to training which is not one of the Government's objectives! The process would, therefore, seem to be:

identify price band for training area
or alternative outcome for STN

↓

identify any trainee support requirements

↓

minus any expected employer contribution

↓

produce costed training plan

With regard to the payment system, current YT practice is a mixture of output related funding (ORF) for the achievement of the target qualification and payment monthly in arrears for the attendance of trainees. Although the former provides some incentive for training providers to maximise the achievement of trainees the latter does not and neither provides much opportunity for the involvement of trainees. Given that one of the objectives of training credits is to strengthen the motivation of young people some variation of current practice seemed to be desirable.

Given that it is expected that training plans will detail not only the target qualifications but also the units or components which make them up, STTEC proposes that for training credits the payment for attendance will be replaced with a system of payment for trainee progress, i.e. for the achievement of units or components towards the target qualification. The trainees would be expected to 'endorse' that they have in fact covered that unit by means of completing a voucher or cheque as part of the process of 'spending' their training credit and would, therefore, be more involved in their own training. The training provider would then use the voucher or cheque to claim payment from the council. This represents an exciting move to achievement or progress related funding and has, not surprisingly, led to some anxieties both on the part of training providers and council staff. ORF payments will continue but will not constitute more than 50 per cent of the total value of any individual's training plan. The reason is that STTEC does not want a funding regime which encourages training providers to be over-selective in the choice of trainees or to drop trainees whose progress is not going to 'earn' the output funding.

Eligibility and spending rules

STTEC's original application to the Department of Employment to pilot training credits indicated that its preferred eligibility criterion was the full time education leaving cohort from educational establishments within the council's area. It acknowledged, however, that without inter-TEC agreement this would be impractical. As there is no inter-TEC agreement yet, the eligibility criterion of residence irrespective of place of full time education is the only practicable one.

In terms of 'spending' the training credit, it would be counter to the whole spirit of the scheme for choice to be restricted and there will, therefore, be a fair proportion of training credits spent with training providers outside the council's area. The general principle is that the money is tied to the individual and their training needs and can be 'spent' anywhere.

Administrative system

The administrative system for training credits must:

- be based on the process through which a young person passes from school into employment with training either during or prior to that employment;
- be simple to understand and operate while at the same time being sufficiently sophisticated to provide accurate and comprehensive information about the young person, the training they are receiving and the provider of that training;
- provide the basis of the contract, for the provision of training, both between the training provider and the TEC and between the training provider and the trainee.

Figure 11.1 sets out the contextual process. The stages which it has been attempted to illustrate in the diagram are as follows:

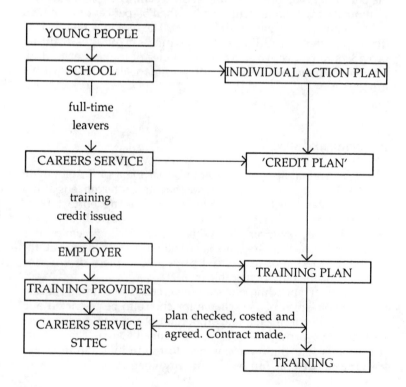

Stage1   All pupils in year 11 undergo a process of careers education and guidance enabling them to be in possession of an individual action plan.

Stage 2   For those who opt to leave full-time education, a visit to the careers service equips them with a serial-numbered training credit which also provides them with further careers advice based on the IAP.

Stage 3   Young people will either enter employment bearing a training credit to spend or buy a training place from a provider. The provider (whether employer, private training provider or college) will produce a training plan, based on the IAP which identifies the target qualification, the units which go to make it up, any extra support which will be provided (e.g. ESOL, literacy, childcare etc.) and any access to ongoing careers advice/guidance.

Stage 4   The training plan is submitted to the careers service/STTEC personnel for two purposes; (a) to ensure that the plan genuinely builds on the IAP (careers service role) and (b) is costed (STTEC role).

Stage 5   The agreed training plan forms the basis of the contract between the training provider and the council, i.e. the training provider is contracted to provide that which is detailed in the plan, and between the training provider and the trainee. The trainee's obligation under the contract will be 'compact style' i.e. related to attendance, punctuality, completion of assignments. A small bonus could be paid for the achievement of the obligations which would be designed not simply to reward ability, i.e. achieving a qualification, but also effort and perseverance. The training provider would be obliged to provide the training stipulated and adhere to a 'trainees' charter' which is currently under development.

Stage 6   Payment for training provided under the contract(s) would be made as and when an identified part of the training plan has been delivered and endorsed by the trainee, thus empowering the latter. (The total cost of the plan would need to be sub-divided for payment purposes between the elements which make up the plan.)

Figure 11.1 does, of course, represent an 'ideal' route for a school/college leaver and it has been necessary to address the issue of those young people who go direct from school/college either into employment or to join a training provider. How do they obtain their training credit and what process should they go through? Clearly there would be little point in requiring a young person entering employment with training who has obviously already made an informed career choice to go through a further round of careers advice/guidance. It would alienate young people and employers alike. For this group a streamlined training credit issue system will be available allowing for the rapid approval of a training plan.

On the other hand there must be further advice/guidance available for those young people who do need it, and some means of checking that the vocational training on training plans matches the career aspirations on IAPs. At the very least, a high incidence of mismatch would serve as a flag which staff could investigate.

Information technology

The major implication for the STTEC and most of the other pilots, is that training records will relate to individual trainees and not just training providers, and these training records will include detailed training plans. That will increase substantially the volume of data held by TECs. In STTEC's case it will also be necessary to provide an interface between the training records and the council's financial accounting system so that payments can be related to the individual training credit holders and the training plans for which the payments will be made.

Evaluation

Although it is early days in the operation of training credits, there has been very extensive evaluation of the first round pilots. Evaluation of each individual first round pilot was funded by the Department of Employment using a total of eight different evaluating organisations. These individual evaluations were then brought together by Coopers & Lybrand Deloitte (which also undertook three of the individual evaluations) in a five part evaluation of the national initiative. Other evaluations were undertaken by HMI, the Careers Service Inspectorate of the Department of Employment and the Policy Research Centre of Sheffield Business School commissioned by the Department. The results of each of these evaluations are dealt with below.

Coopers & Lybrand Deloitte

This is an extremely thorough evaluation produced in five volumes but, like the other evaluations referred to below, was undertaken very early in the life of the pilots. The fieldwork was undertaken between March and December 1991 and consisted of structured samples of employers and young people and interviews with key individuals. Despite the use of sampling the nature of the material produced was more qualitative than quantitative.

The evaluation concluded that the major areas of confusion surrounding the introduction of training credits related to the cross-boundary movement of young people, the age criteria for the use of the credit and the type of courses eligible for training credits purposes. The study concluded that it was too early to evaluate the relative merits of the different forms which the credit took, e.g. credit card, voucher, cheque, etc., but it did conclude that the future proliferation of different models and approaches by different TECs would be of concern to employers and training providers which had to deal with a number of different TECs.

The study concluded that a lack of flexibility in the contract between the Department of Employment and TECs was inhibiting the ability of the latter to be innovative in the design and operation of training credits schemes. Equally it was found that some pilots were developing procedures to run training credits which were overly bureaucratic and that this was inhibiting attempts to involve employers more in training, which was one of the objects of the exercise. It was acknowledged that the administration of training credits was not made simpler by the need to continue to operate YT for those in their second year.

In the key area of guidance, the evaluation found that young people were generally satisfied with the quality of the guidance they had received but that employers were not, feeling that many young people were not prepared adequately for the world of work. The study also found that guidance specifically about training credits was poor and that there was confusion about the proliferation of guidance-related documentation. A significant finding was that the careers guidance process was insufficiently integrated into the whole school curriculum, and did not start early enough. It was generally felt that the process would be more effective if introduced in years nine and ten.

In terms of the impact of training credits, there was little evidence that their introduction had had any impact on the training market which was one of its key objectives. There was also little evidence that the introduction of training credits had resulted in an attitudinal change on the part of young people who still regarded training as a bonus rather than an entitlement and were unable to use their possession of a training credit as a bargaining tool with employers. The study does not find that surprising in a recession and one wonders if it is ever a realistic scenario.

Finally the evaluation found that, despite the efforts put into designing training credits models which would take account of the needs of disadvantaged groups, there were very few examples of young people with special training needs using them.

Her Majesty's Inspectorate

HMI monitored the first-round pilot schemes in two stages. The first was an inspection of institutions in all the pilot areas in England and Wales but not Scotland during the academic year 1990/91. The second was a series of 52 inspection visits to schools and colleges in the pilot areas during the autumn and spring terms 1991/92. This therefore covered a period up to one term later than the Coopers & Lybrand Deloitte evaluation referred to above.

Unfortunately, as with so many thematic HMI reports, the findings are so general as to be of little practical value. The report found that about 60 per cent of the target group, i.e. those 16 and 17 year olds leaving full-time education, were taking up training credits but that a high proportion did not have employed status. It found that the use of action planning in schools varied considerably and was often not linked to other similar initiatives, such as records of achievement (the implication being that it is axiomatically good so to do) and, more interestingly, that the value of action plans was seldom recognised by the young people themselves.

The Inspector's report queried the extent to which students with special training needs are best served by training related to NVQ outcomes but did find that small businesses had been encouraged by schemes to give priority to training which they might not otherwise have done.

Careers Service Branch Inspectorate

Inspectors from the Careers Service Branch of the Department of Employment carried out survey work in all eleven first round pilot areas during October and November 1991. Although a good deal of this evaluation is in fact a description of how the first round pilots operate, it does contain some telling findings.

It considered the position of those from ethnic minority groups, those requiring special mental or physical consideration, or those wishing to cross stereotypical boundaries. For the first and last of the above the evaluation found no evidence that the introduction of training credits had made any impact on their level of opportunity. For the second group, only four out of eleven pilots had made extra effort to provide appropriate opportunities and in one of those it had had limited success.

In terms of enhanced careers guidance, although there was much evidence of additional training credits funding to support this, there was also evidence that the use of the funding was not being adequately monitored or evaluated. There was also evidence that access to ongoing careers guidance during training was largely by self-referral without systems to trigger it. The significance of this is compounded by the findings that, although young people had a general awareness of training credits, there was ignorance and confusion about the detail.

Policy Research Centre of Sheffield Business School

This evaluation took the form of a postal questionnaire sent to a selected sample of 4,371 young people to whom training credits had been issued in all eleven first round pilot areas in early December 1991. 2,529 responses were received, a response rate of 58 per cent. With a sample of that size it would seem to be worthwhile to summarise the findings:

- 91 per cent were happy with the quality of careers advice that they were receiving with 77 per cent agreeing on careers choices with advisers.
- 89 per cent were aware of training credits and 56 per cent reported that the scheme had had a positive effect on their training and career decision making.
- 51 per cent of those surveyed were receiving training paid for by training credits.
- 58 per cent received training at work and 29 per cent in colleges, 13 per cent were training elsewhere or did not know where they were training.
- The two most sought qualifications were City and Guilds (32 per cent) and NVQs (28 per cent)
- 80 per cent reported that training credits were easy to use.
- Young people of non-white origin were much more likely than whites to be receiving training through colleges.

Most of the above should be encouraging to pilot schemes except the last finding if the reason is that non-whites were more likely to be at college because they were unable to find employment. There is evidence from YT that leads to the conclusion that the development of training credits has much to do if it is to overcome racial discrimination in employment practice.

Conclusion

Although it is still very early to draw any definite conclusions from a development which is still so new, there are encouraging signs. It can be argued that at least some of the shortcomings associated with YT are being addressed by the pilot schemes, if not actually overcome. However, there is also evidence from the evaluations cited above that there is still much to be done to provide high quality training opportunities for young people which also maximise their employability.

Part of the responsibility for this lies with the TECs in the way in which they design and implement the schemes. Part of it lies with the LEAs and schools and colleges which need to work constructively with the introduction of training credits to ensure that young people make the best possible choice of route at the age of 16 or 17. Part of it lies with the providers of training of whatever kind to ensure that high quality training exists for young people to spend their credit on. Part of it lies with employers who need to take training seriously and to be serious about giving young people opportunities to prove themselves. Most importantly, part of it lies with government which must also prove that it takes training seriously and sees it as an important part of the solution to the economic ills of this country, and that it takes seriously the need to meet the aspirations of the young people of this country.

References

Careers Service Inspectorate (1991) *Stage Two Careers Service Inspectorate Survey of Training Credits.*
Coopers & Lybrand Deloitte (1992) *Training Credits Evaluation.*
DES (1991) *Education and Training for the 21st Century* (CM1536).
Evans B. (1992) *The Politics of the Training Market*, Routledge.

Her Majesty's Inspectorate (1992) *The Implementation of the Pilot Training Credits Scheme in England and Wales.*

KPMG Management Consulting *Employment Department: Designing & Training Credits Scheme: Cost Banding Issues.*

Raffe, D. (1990) 'The context of the youth training scheme: an analysis of its strategy and development' in Gleeson D. *Training and its Alternatives* Open University Press.

Sheffield Business School (1992) *Postal Survey of Training Credit Holders.*

Youthaid (1992) *A Broken Promise: The Failure of Youth Training Policy.*

12 TVEI and the curriculum 14–18

Angus Taylor

TVEI, the Technical and Vocational Education Initiative, was announced on 12 November 1982 by the then Prime Minister, Margaret Thatcher. It was to be a small pilot scheme starting in September 1983 involving projects in the education authorities in England and Wales for a limited number of schools and colleges, each lasting five years. The last handful of education authorities entered TVEI extension in September 1992, with funding lasting until 1997. During the fourteen years between 1983 and 1997, all education authorities in England, Wales and Scotland will have taken part, first in five years of TVEI pilot (or a three year preparatory phase for LEAs late to respond) followed by five years of TVEI extension, first announced in the White Paper *Working Together — Education and Training* (DES and DE 1982). While TVEI pilot was for a limited number of schools and colleges, and a limited number of students from each institution, by the end of TVEI extension, all school and colleges within each education authority, and all students in those schools and colleges will have experienced an education influenced by TVEI.

In 1976 the Prime Minister, James Callaghan, had criticised schools for failing to prepare young people for working life. During the so called 'great debate' on the role and content of education that followed, HMI contributed some working papers in 1977 (DES 1977). In addition to arguing the case for a common curriculum, they explored the role of the curriculum in preparing young people for work. Schools should accept the responsibility to organise the 'curriculum to equip. . .leavers with competence in appropriate skills. . .Skills can be taught without the introduction of a narrow or specialised vocational training. Every subject to be found in the curriculum of a school can and should make some contribution'

DES 1977). The paper asks that pupils be given some notion of what it is like to be at work, argues the case for closer co-operation between schools and industry, suggests that for teachers there are implications for teaching methods and that, 'A greater knowledge of local conditions can provide teachers of all subjects with immediate and appropriate source material from which to illustrate general ideas. . .' (DES 1977). Such comments provide a useful background to an exploration of TVEI and what it has been aiming to achieve. In launching TVEI pilot in 1983, Lord Young, the Chairman of the Manpower Services Commission, said, '. . .Our general objective is to widen and enrich the curriculum in a way that will help young people prepare for the world of work, and to develop skills and interests, including creative abilities, that will help them to lead a fuller life and to be able to contribute more to the life of the community'.

Any study of the nature of TVEI and its contribution to curriculum development needs to recognise the flexibility of the project. Following Margaret Thatcher's announcement of TVEI, the Secretary of State for Employment wrote to the Chairman of the Manpower Services Commission inviting the MSC to establish TVEI Pilot. The Commission set out five principles which included:

1 the Commission would work through local education authorities;
2 individual projects would adopt different forms according to local circumstances;
3 the precise curriculum should be a matter for local determination within certain general criteria/guidelines applying nationally. (DES/DE 1982)

Thus TVEI projects differ in organisation and emphasis from education authority to education authority while demonstrating common features consistent with national guidelines.

Furthermore TVEI has changed over time, reflecting the move from Pilot to Extension and the need to respond to a rapidly changing education environment. As HMI have commented, 'The guidelines issued to LEAs from the TVEI unit were revised each year in the light of experience, which sometimes led to the accusation of "moving the goal posts". There was, however, considerable strength in this flexible and sensitive strategy because LEA schemes could change their emphasis over time' (DES 1991).

As HMI continued in their review of TVEI 1983–90, 'TVEI was a unique educational project. . . It was the first centrally managed National Curriculum project' and 'It was managed outside the DES' (DES 1991). Initially this was by the independent government agency, the Manpower Services Commission. This became the Training Commission in 1987 and the Training Agency in 1988, within the Employment Department. Since responsibility for training passed to the new Training and Enterprise Councils in England and Wales and to Local Enterprise Councils in Scotland, national responsibility for TVEI has passed to the Training, Enterprise and Education Directorate within the Employment Department (TEED) in England, the Welsh Office and the Industry Department for Scotland.

These institutional changes and the Education Reform Act 1988 have led to a clarification of the Employment Department's stake in education, and a new focus for TVEI. Thus, TEED's immediate predecessor was the Education Programme Directorate of the Training Agency within the Employment Department. The Employment Department's role in education is 'to ensure that the workforce is equipped with the competence needed in a high productivity, high skill and high technology economy'. 'The Education Programme Directorate therefore seeks to ensure that the education system operates in a way which supports the Department's main role. It does this by helping Education to be:

- relevant to the world of work;
- responsive to the needs of employers;
- accessible to adults at any age or stage;
- practical and enterprising as well as academic;
- more flexible in delivery;
- responsive in raising standards of attainment;
- accredited by qualification or records of achievement. (Employment Department 1991)

The statement identified a number of elements common to Employment Department initiatives in education including the involvement of students directly in the world of work, the development of teaching and learning strategies which develop enterprise, initiative and capability in students, involving employers in learning (to make it more real, relevant, motivating and work related) and a guidance and counselling strategy. These elements are delivered through a range of programmes which, besides TVEI Extension, include Compact, Education Business Partnerships, Careers Service initiatives, Work Related Further Education and Enterprise in Higher Education.

TVEI Extension started in the year that the consultative paper on the National Curriculum was published, 1987. The TVEI national guidelines for extension reflected the 1985 White Paper *Better Schools* and the Munn Report in Scotland. They also anticipated the

Education Reform Act and the enactment of the National Curriculum. Thus the curriculum was to be broad, balanced, relevant and differentiated. There was for example an early stress on broad and balanced science, as well as a traditional TVEI commitment to technology and information technology. With the ERA enacted, the TVEI Focus Statement was developed in 1989 stating what TVEI was to contribute now that there was a statutory National Curriculum. The Focus Statement has had various formulations, all amounting to the same thing. Anne Jones, then head of the Education Programme Directorate at the Training Agency, wrote, (Jones 1989):

> TVEI aims to ensure that the education of 14–18 year olds provides young people with learning opportunities which will equip them for the demands of working life in a rapidly changing society. It does this:
>
> - by making sure the curriculum uses every opportunity to relate education to the world of work, by using concrete/real examples if possible;
> - by making sure that young people get the knowledge, competencies and qualifications they need in a highly technological society which is itself part of Europe and the world economy;
> - by making sure that young people themselves get direct opportunities to learn about the nature of the economy and the world of work — through experience, work shadowing, projects in the community and so on;
> - by making sure that young people learn how to be effective people, solve problems, work in teams, be enterprising and creative through the way they are taught;
> - by making sure that young people have access to initial guidance and counselling, and then continuing education and training, and opportunities for progression throughout their lives.

TVEI is then a curriculum initiative for 14–18 year olds. It is concerned with the effectiveness of the curriculum in the final years of compulsory education and its success in preparing young people to make the best use of the right choice at sixteen, be that:

- continued education, preferably through a course of study that breaks down the academic/vocational divide;
- high quality training leading to National Vocational Qualifications overseen by TECs and LECs;

- employment *with* training, the latter one of the objectives of the Compact approach.

TVEI aims to break down the curriculum divide at sixteen created by GCSE and the school leaving age by stressing the importance of progression. However, because the curriculum 14–16 is determined by GCSE courses and the National Curriculum extended core 14–16, and by different curriculum frameworks post-16, TVEI Extension plans for schools are required initially for 14–16, with more detailed plans for TVEI 16–18 submitted a year into the five year project. Thus the essential curricular features of TVEI for years 10 and 11 will be explored, the same exercise will follow for the 16–18 TVEI entitlement, before the return to progression 14–18, and the assimilation of the key features of TVEI and life after TVEI examined.

Applying the Focus Statement to the curriculum for 14–16 year olds can be organised through headings, under which can be grouped the key features, the heartlands of TVEI. Young people will be better prepared for the experiences post-16 and ultimately for adult and working life if curriculum managers plan:

- for the work related curriculum;
- effective learning, through a range of teaching and learning styles;
- to address all aspects of progression.

The work related curriculum is to do with the processes and contexts for learnings. It seeks to use all appropriate opportunities for real world applications; it seeks appropriate opportunities for placing learning, whatever the subject, in 'real world' contexts; and it seeks to enable young people to test their learning against the demands of the community outside of school and against adult and work situations. 'Real Life' means, of course, no more than 'representative of the community and society in which young people live now and will live as adults' (Taylor 1991a).

The feature of the work related curriculum which is most easily established and recognised in the curriculum of Year 10 and 11 students is work experience. In most education authority projects, all young people have at least one week's work experience in Year 10 or Year 11. The work is co-ordinated by a variety of agencies (Project Trident, the local Careers Service or TVEI funded work experience co-ordinators) so as to spread these weeks through the academic year, ensuring an adequate number of placements. Health and safety clearance is provided though the Careers Service. Quality work experience is now sought, with students briefed beforehand, employers prepared so that best use can be made of this time, diaries developed for students to record their experience, and debriefing designed to inform careers guidance and feedback to the curriculum, for example in GCSE course work. Work experience is important, but it is just one small aspect of the work related curriculum.

Implementing the work related curriculum involves bringing examples, case studies and problems into classroom practice from the outside community and the work environment. Teachers are experienced in quickly absorbing or gathering such material, and TVEI has been concerned with formalising these opportunities in association with other initiatives. Three examples illustrate the range of possibilities. The Teacher Placement Scheme was introduced by the Department of Trade and Industry to place 10 per cent of all teachers each year for a week in a business. The scheme is now funded by the Employment Department through Training and Enterprise Councils. Secondly, schools have used one or more training days to place all teaching staff in local businesses from which to feed experiences into classroom learning contexts and materials. A third exercise which could be made more of is the visits made by teachers to students on work experience.

An important feature of TVEI which becomes relevant in converting these potentially fragmented teacher experiences into an effective work related curriculum is the expectation of curriculum policy statements, planning, management and review. Before the contract is signed between the local education authority and the Employment Department, schools and colleges have to submit five year plans which will be the basis for any allocation of money from the education authority's TVEI project to the school or college. The school's TVEI spending will be reviewed against that plan each year, as part of the TVEI Annual Review procedures with the Employment Department.

Thus, over time, a school should be developing a policy on the work related curriculum, driven by an aim eventually to permeate all classroom practice. TVEI encourages the development of performance indicators so that a school can identify the steps required to help implement the policy, the processes that are being put in place and an assessment of the impact of the policy and the processes on student outcomes (Taylor 1991b). Thus, using the example above, a school policy on the work related curriculum might, in say the second year of the TVEI project, include among the enabling steps or indicators:

- 3 teachers to have one week placements in industry (5 per cent of the staff of 60, a step towards the 10 per cent aimed

for by the Teacher Placement Service); the subject areas
would be chosen according to readiness, need, and as part
of a rolling programme;

● all 60 teachers spend 2 teacher training days in a local
business placement, with the afternoon of the second day
back in school, perhaps with their business partners, in
curriculum development workshops;

● perhaps 20 staff are involved in visiting Year 10 students
on work experience, armed with a checklist that partly
supports the student visited and partly prompts curriculum
resource ideas.

All of this experience should feed into schemes of work and so
influence classroom practice, and in turn student outcomes.
Students should recognise the relevance of their learning and so it
should better prepare them for life ahead.

All these contribute to the second heartland of TVEI, the range
of teaching and learning approaches that contribute to effective
learning. Effective learning is represented as going beyond straight
mastery of the content of the curriculum, to applying, to problem
solving, to working with others. Few, if any, of the approaches
encouraged by TVEI are new. The emphasis is very much on giving
the students greater responsibility for their own learning, to ease
differentiation and enhance motivation, to increase the current
effectiveness of the learning process while encouraging a
commitment to lifelong learning.

TVEI has been much helped in effecting a review of teaching and
learning approaches by the introduction, in 1986, of the new GCSE
syllabuses. In most subjects learning outcomes were extended, often
to include a range of practical skills. Examinations were designed
to assess what students know, understand and can do. Coursework
enabled students to demonstrate a wider range of skills of the sort
TVEI seeks to encourage. The partnership between TVEI and GCSE
has done much to generate greater varieties of teaching and
learning, and raising standards. There must be concern that the
implementation of National Curriculum key stage 4 and constraints
on GCSE, including coursework, will together frustrate a less
didactic approach to teaching and learning.

While earlier government initiatives had begun the move to
introduce computers into schools, in many schools TVEI funding
has greatly extended the number and range of computers available,
in suites and stand-alone. The range of software has also increased
thus offering a range of facilities to support a variety of teaching
and learning approaches. Thus spreadsheets in mathematics, word
processing in English, control in technology, databases in history,

all contribute to effective learning. As the technology continues to develop so new facilities become available to schools. CD ROM is the most recent. Here the concern for the future must be funding, with TVEI spending on equipment limited (to about 20 per cent of the budgets) and with many LEA TVEI projects reaching the end of their 5 year life in 1992, 1993 and 1994. Computers require maintenance, and eventually replacement and upgrading. School budgets can go some way, but it is unlikely they can meet the full need.

Another TVEI initiative that has done much to support effective learning is the Record of Achievement. The processes of recording achievement, which eventually feed through into a summative record, are themselves all to do with supporting the learning process. Subject teachers review the progress of an individual student with the student, and agree areas of learning that need further emphasis. Tutorial reviews enable the students to consider their progress across subjects, and in areas of learning and experience outside of individual subjects — including the acquisition of interpersonal skills and involvement in extracurricular activity. This combination of review, recording and action planning has been encouraged by TVEI and is a powerful support to teaching and learning.

The whole school management of a more flexible approach to teaching and learning in the cause of effectiveness is a challenge. For this reason, TVEI supports a number of national Flexible Learning Projects which have funded schools to explore whole school approaches. The lessons from these projects are beginning to become available. As with most aspects of TVEI intent on affecting the whole curriculum, the first step must be for all staff to develop an understanding of what is intended and why. A curriculum policy cannot effectively be handed down from on high, although, without the commitment of senior management, progress to implementation and staff commitment will be limited.

The third heartland of TVEI, running through the 14–18 curriculum is all aspects of progression — building on prior learning, being on the right course, experiencing equality of opportunity (in the courses chosen and the learning process), obtaining qualifications, keeping a record of achievement as a guide to future progress, careers education and guidance and the development of an individual action plan. Many of these have been supported by other initiatives, but the TVEI project has aimed to tackle them together in order to prepare young people for adult and working life.

TVEI is concerned that there are a number of constraints to achievement which frustrate the education and training of large sections of the future workforce. These inequalities of opportunity lead to wrong choices being made by some students and a lack of aspiration and ambition from others. This means both a personal and an economic waste of talents otherwise available to the community. TVEI is thus committed to positive steps to achieve equality of opportunity. Concerns have included the imbalance in subject choice between boys and girls, special education needs, ethnic minorities and low educational aspirations among certain social groups.

Progress on equality of opportunity has been slow with awareness raising the initial priority. Nevertheless, progress has been made. The rapid development of broad and balanced dual award science has reduced if not removed sex stereotyping between the physical and biological sciences. In many TVEI projects, special schools have been drawn into the main school community resulting in substantial learning benefits for young people attending the special schools. Many secondary schools now have equal opportunity policies with a group of teachers taking positive steps to implement them. Inner city Compacts have supported TVEI in setting basic targets with under-performing groups of students to raise standards for their future.

Some very good careers education and guidance, involving both teachers and LEA careers officers, was in place before TVEI. But TVEI has stressed the importance of this work, if students are going to make informed decisions at every step. The student's interest must be at the heart of the decision, guided by his or her aptitudes and the opportunities that lie ahead. Neutral guidance during year 11 remains an often unresolved issue, with the Local Management of Schools and the incorporation of colleges intensifying competition for students for post-16 courses.

TVEI has been committed to the development of a summative record of achievement. The DES has also been a supporter and the RANSC report (1989) was consistent with TVEI developments. Most LEA TVEI projects had developed substantial local records of achievement when the DES and the Employment Department launched the National Record of Achievement in 1991. Now administered by the National Council for Vocational Qualifications (and thus replacing NROVA) it is free for all year 11 students (and youth trainees post-16). By 1992 the majority of students were receiving a National Record at 16. The next steps include preparing students to make better use of the NRoA, at interviews for example, raising awareness among users (employers and higher education) and developing the NRoA as a record to be updated through life, in education, training and employment.

While individual action planning has been supported by the Employment Department as part of training, it was adopted relatively late by TVEI. It is seen as part of the same process as recording achievement, but with a plan developed in year 11 as part of careers guidance informing decisions and progression. Where TECs have introduced or intend soon to introduce training credits for 16–18 year olds, careers guidance and effective action planning are important factors in preparing 16 year olds to make decisions, and where the decision involves a training route, to make good use of the training credits. Youth Development Projects in some parts of the country concentrated on IAPs, and in many cases TECs are supporting the continuation of this work.

It has been mentioned that TVEI is a 14–18 project, but because the 16–18 curriculum has a different structure and much of it is provided in further education, sixth form and tertiary colleges, LEAs are asked to submit separate 16–18 plans for TVEI. The Employment Department issues separate TVEI 16–18 guidance to assist LEAs, and their schools and colleges. The 16–18 guidance seeks the following curriculum components from schools and colleges for full time students.

TVEI is proposed as 'an opportunity to identify those key experiences and opportunities to which *all* students are entitled, regardless of their programme of study' (Employment Department 1990). This entitlement consists of a list of Common Learning Outcomes together with five themes which build on the TVEI curriculum 14–16 qualifications, records of achievement, work related activities, teaching and learning styles, and guidance and counselling.

The Common Learning Outcomes are listed (Education Department 1990) as follows.

All students should be able to:

- communicate effectively (where possible in more than one language);
- compile and use numerical information;
- use science and technology appropriately;
- understand the world of work;
- develop effective personal and interpersonal skills;
- work independently or in teams;
- solve problems;
- cope positively with change.

These are attributes TVEI seeks to develop pre-16 and it would seem entirely consistent that progression in these areas should be sought post-16. Those following pre-vocational (CPVE) and vocational (e.g. BTEC) courses are expected to continue to develop a range of core skills but those following programmes of study built up almost exclusively of GCE A level courses have no such entitlement. The National Curriculum Council reported to the Secretary of State during 1990 on 'the core skills which all young people need for adult working life'. However little progress has been made since then, and TVEI 16–18 projects have had to seek progress within the whole programme of study of each student.

Four of the thematic areas nominated as part of the post-16 entitlement involve progression from student experiences 14–16 and can be seen as features of 14–16 curriculum. Thus records of achievement will continue to 'record those elements which are not readily accreditable'. TVEI projects are asked to consider 'how continuity and progression of experience from the 14–16 progression phase will be secured and, especially, the machinery that will be established to facilitate transfer at 16+' (Employment Department 1990).

Work related activities create two challenges as far as progression is concerned. The division of routes into the academic, based on GCE A level, and the vocational, following courses leading to qualifications awarded by BTEC, City and Guilds and RSA are a challenge to maintaining a work related entitlement. Vocational courses offer natural opportunities for ensuring that courses of study are work related. GCE A level syllabuses and schemes of assessment offer little encouragement to relate learning to the world of work. Nevertheless, TVEI has encouraged schools and colleges to involve their students in projects which link A level study with the world of work and the community outside of school and to accredit such experience through the National Record of Achievement. The A level Enhancement Project based at Liverpool University is a good example of this.

The other issue of progression regarding work related activity is where work experience is organised for 16–18 year old students. Those on vocational courses can expect a very different experience from that in year 10 & 11. But A level students are in danger of having the experience repeated without issue of progression having been addressed. Linking 16–18 work experience with A level courses of study or providing a focus for making career decisions are ways in which this can be achieved. However many students in post-16 full time education are in part time employment, and these experiences may prove a more fruitful resource for relating full time learning to their part time world of work.

Progressing a range of teaching and learning styles across the 16+ 'barrier' has not been without difficulty. Many A level syllabuses appear to encourage a didactic approach, with examination papers emphasising the recall of knowledge. Many students transfer, for A level and vocational studies, to colleges, be those tertiary, further education or sixth form college. The amount of liaison necessary for effective progression varies considerably, although TVEI consortium working has done much to improve matters (and TVEI annual reviews often seek action). Furthermore there is evidence that in large colleges TVEI co-ordinators 'are generally at middle management level and do not have the same status or influence in policy making' as their counterpart in schools where the TVEI co-ordinators are at deputy head or senior teachers level' (Sanders *et al.*). Progress in colleges depends therefore on the commitment of senior management. Thus there are examples of colleges which have re-organised around resource based learning areas where students joining from 11–16 schools require training in the use of the facilities and different approaches to learning. These and other initiatives 'emphasise supported self study, providing students with learning resources and tutorial support that would enable them to work, both independently and in groups, through study assignments and tutorial support' (Sanders *et al.* 1992).

Careers education and guidance is regarded by TVEI as continuing to be of paramount importance post-16 as it is pre-16. For obvious reasons, careers education and interviews with careers officers have an important position in pre-vocational courses such as the CPVE, and is also part of vocational courses such as BTEC. However, for many A level students, the assumption is that they are bound for higher education and guidance is centred on UCCA and PCAS procedures, with many students using A level study to defer career decisions. With a high failure rate in the examination, this remains a weak area for progression post-16 and one that TVEI needs to continue to address.

It has already been intimated that the biggest barrier to progression in England and Wales is the existence of two separate frameworks for qualifications at 16+ and 18+, and the sharp division of the latter into two routes, one described as 'academic' assessed by GCE A level, the other described as 'vocational' and assessed by a range of qualifications and a number of competing awarding bodies. TVEI has in a number of LEA areas sought to influence the structure of the post-16 curriculum and qualifications. Initiatives such as the Wessex A level scheme are piloting modular A level and exploring the interface with BTEC National. The hope was to find a form of progression based on credit banking and credit transfer that would help, for example, the student embarking on an A level course who discovers he or she is not coping. The current choice is between dropping out and starting a new route, in education or outside, or carrying on and becoming one of the 20 per cent plus who fail to get a grade E or above.

The White Paper *Education and Training for the 21st Century* reaffirms the role and standing of GCE A level, encourages schools to introduce vocational courses (BTEC and the revamped CPVE — the diploma in vocational education), and introduced the GNVQ. The latter would seek parity of esteem with A level. At this stage, it is difficult to judge how these changes will help progression post-16. The following scenario might be a possibility for the mid-1990s.

Government see GNVQ as the basis for all full-time vocational qualifications 16–18. It is overseen by NCVQ and awarded by BTEC, City and Guilds and RSA, and perhaps by the GCE boards. By September 1993 GNVQ will be awarded at three levels 1, 2 and 3. GNVQ level 1 will offer progression for students in the lowest 20 per cent of the ability range, GNVQ level 3 is intended to be on a par with two A levels. GNVQ is organised in units with GNVQ level 3 built up from 8 compulsory units and 4 optional units appropriate to the GNVQ vocational area — business for example. The new principles for A and AS levels permit modular structures. Parity of esteem would be more likely if GNVQ units and A level modules were on a par. There is evidence in this first year of GNVQ of students following combined A level and GNVQ 3 programmes. TVEI's commitment to more effective progression would then become that much more achievable.

To conclude, TVEI is a curriculum project, centrally funded and involving all education authorities in England, Wales and Scotland. Its aim is to prepare young people in full-time education between the ages of 14–18 for working life by certain curriculum processes. These are the same in principle for 14–16 year olds and 16–18 year olds, but qualification structures and institutional breaks at 16 create a challenge for TVEI progression at 16+ which is met with varying degrees of success.

As for the future, note should be taken of the implications for TVEI related change of the imminence of the end of LEA projects and of a new agenda of Employment Department education policy. Education authorities that were first into TVEI Extension in 1987 and 1988 cease to have TVEI funding in part (where there has been phasing) or in total in 1992 and 1993. Others follow in 1994 and this continues until the national project finishes in 1997. The focus now in LEAs and their schools and colleges is on the assimilation of TVEI practice in day to day activity through their development plans. TVEI annual reviews of projects entering into this final year of funding seek this in the targets agreed. TVEI co-ordinators for

LEAs are working with colleagues in schools and colleges to identify three categories of TVEI related practice. First there are those TVEI practices that are essentially to do with hearts and minds rather than resources. Some aspects of teaching and learning styles, recording achievement and equal opportunities come into this category, and would be seen as important to school practice even without TVEI funding. The second category is of important TVEI practice that does depend on combined funding. Survival depends on recognition of its value. Effective co-ordination of work experience is an example and it is hoped that schools will, for example, pay towards LEA or consortium co-ordination out of their own budgets. Finally there is TVEI related activity which was particularly funding related. Information technology and its dependence on maintaining, updating and expanding computer provision is the most obvious case, and the one most under threat once TVEI funds end.

As for the new agenda, the government, Employment Department and TVEI, support the CBI promoted National Education and Training Targets. The targets for foundation learning have targets for achievement through education *and* training at NVQ 2 and NVQ 3 by the end of this decade. Foundation learning target 4 requires 'education and training provision to develop self reliance, flexibility and breadth'. These targets become part of the aims and objectives for the final years of TVEI. Will we achieve the effective progression, through education and training that will get us there? At this moment, Training and Enterprise Councils are striking up strategic fora with their partners in education and training to help make the National Targets attainable. The relevance of TVEI related activity within the curriculum 14–18 continues.

References

Curtis, J. (1991) 'A Summary of the TVEI initiative' *Technical and Vocational Education Review* January, Employment Department.

Department of Education and Science (1977) 'Curriculum 11–16' Working Paper by HM Inspectorate *A Contribution to Current Debate* December.

Department of Education and Science (1989) *Records of Achievement* National Steering Committee Report.

Department of Education and Science (1991) *Education and Training for the 21st Century* HMSO.

Department of Education and Science (1991) *Technical and Vocational Education Initiative (TVEI) England and Wales 1983–90* A Report by HM Inspectorate.

Department of Education and Science and Employment Department (1982) *Working Together — Education and Training* HMSO Command 9823.

Employment Department (1990) *TVEI 16–18 Guidance.*

Employment Department (1991) Memorandum.

Jones, A. (1989) 'The real aims of TVEI' *Education* 14 April.

Sanders, L. *et al.* (1992) *TVEI and the Management of Change: An Overview* NFER Evaluation of the Management of the TVEI Extension.

Taylor, A. (1991a) 'Curriculum matters' *Headlines* Secondary Heads Association, June.

Taylor, A. (1991b) 'Performance indicators and the work related curriculum' *TVEI Developments* 14.

13 Higher education and the 16–19 curriculum

Malcolm Deere

One can no longer consider the 16–19 curriculum in isolation from the provision being made in higher education. Both of these sectors are changing, at an accelerated pace. While some will argue that these changes amount to increased proliferation and confusion, one can equally make a case for saying that the sectors individually are beginning to converge within themselves. If that is the case we need to harmonise the changes towards an even greater convergence, where we consider the curriculum as running from at least age 14 to, let us say, age 23.

Even A level is steadily evolving, and it has been doing so for a considerable time. There is no reasons for supposing that this process is going to be halted. The Government's response to the Advisory Council for Science and Technology (ACOST 1991) Report:

> the Government recognises that there may be subjects and syllabuses, particularly the sciences, where many years of adding new factual content without discarding any has led to syllabuses attempting to cover far too much. This does not mean that a wholesale shift to an emphasis on understanding and skills at the expense of knowledge is justified. The issue is not which knowledge, understanding or skills to emphasise but how to maximise the development of each through a balance appropriate to individual subjects. The Government would not dispute that some science syllabuses are lacking in that balance. However, a number of syllabuses are already being pruned of excessive and outdated content and the slight shift towards greater emphasis on understanding and skills and less on factual content is evident in new and revised syllabuses. ...Any move to remove content should be taken only after careful consideration.

Higher education will probably not take issue with that comment, because this is precisely what it itself is attempting to do, but to a much greater extent. This is important, because my concern is the curricular junction between the two sectors, and progression between them. This is why I am never inclined to consider the 16–19 or the higher education curricula in isolation.

Higher education has now to accommodate two incoming routes: A level, and what (up to now) has been BTEC. There are also other routes, particularly those from Access Courses and/or direct entry of adult students claiming prior experiential learning. While these latter are not strictly part of the 16–19 discussion, they, quite rightly, have an influence on the same HE curriculum that younger students will also enter. Nevertheless, the first two routes mentioned have their own strengths and their own weaknesses. A level has certain qualities, but it would be unwise to brush aside its deficiencies. It does well, but only across a limited span. Areas in which A level provision could be improved would include:

- improving consistency, with clear criteria for quality — at present there is no real guarantee about the ground that is covered;
- A level is not a programme and there is no explicit coherence within it; there are no connections between the 'elements';
- in spite of the Government commentary noted above, content still tends to submerge skill;
- A level does not credit accumulate over time — it is 'all or nothing' at the end of the course;
- breadth and balance is not guaranteed, and the qualification suffers from early, narrow specialisation;
- there is an ambiguous relationship between A and AS (see later);
- there are too many syllabuses.

By contrast, BTEC is a programme. This has to be a strength, as does — from many points of view — the fact that it puts an emphasis on the application of knowledge. Nevertheless, while HE increasingly understands BTEC, rightly or wrongly it retains certain suspicions about the consistency of its quality assurance. Set against that, BTEC provides a range of assessment and therefore a range of learning styles. It is modular, but that modularity is positively structured, and above all it sets out to be integrative. This is pursued through features such as cross-modular assignments.

It has always been tempting to regard these various routes in terms of an 'academic/vocational divide'. There are two problems with this: firstly, it is probably not so much a divide as a set of different mixes of assessment and learning styles. Secondly, divide or not, both of these routes, together with others, have broadly to feed into the same HE curricular provision.

This brings us to our first contemporary interface problem. If you have two kinds of students they bring with them two kinds of experiential evidence. HE sees much more of the one than the other, feels it understands it — although that may be open to question — and understands far less the 'language' of the other. Accommodating several streams into the one programme requires equal understanding of all the antecedent experiences that will be met.

We must now turn to the second interface problem, that of breadth. The first feature of the problem is that while everyone supports the concept of breadth, there is not necessarily a common definition. There are various kinds of breadth: it can be achieved through a range of subjects; through a range of core skills; through a range of 'contexts' (well described in the report of the National Curriculum Working Group on Technology); or through a range of teaching, learning, and assessment styles. As Sir Gordon Higginson pointed out in his Report of 1988, breadth can be vested in programmes, but it can also be vested in individual subjects. Also, we are not considering breadth alone, but the concept of breadth and balance. This emphatically does not imply that the elements of a curriculum need to be of equal weight; breadth and balance relates to the interaction between elements, or connectiveness, as well as range.

None of the features so far described are necessarily at odds with Government policy, although many interested parties may fall out with Government over matters such as extent, emphasis, etc. The present Government policy is clear: in the 16–19 range it wishes to see two separate, but well-articulated kinds of programme on offer. It wishes to see quality in both of them, and equality of value from the point of view of the student, the providing institution, and the end-user (which includes HE but also employment). A Government of a different persuasion might have taken a different curriculum view. It might well have adopted a single post-16 system which, put over-simply, would have dismantled what we have and reassembled them into a single system. My own belief is that the Government is correct in principle: it would have been very difficult and even dangerous to scrap and start again. However, with what we now have we certainly need to continue to work to converge the routes towards a single system; better that way, than changing boats in midstream. The question of articulation leads to a recognition of two features, credit accumulation, and credit transfer, both in their own right and linked together. HE and virtually all of the organisations concerned with curriculum in the 16–19 sector will agree that those two features are critical to improving the quality of our provision.

As an example of 16–19/HE co-operation, in 1992 a joint statement on *Principles for a 16–19 Curriculum* was published by the GSA, HMC, SHA, APVIC, and SCUE. The statement argued that the 16–19 curriculum should conform to a set of essential principles:

- it should achieve a coherent system which converges and articulates separate pathways, with genuine parity in respect of value and utility;
- it should emphasise success, with accreditation of positive achievements at each stage of the course — within the framework of a National Record of Achievement and using processes of credit accumulation;
- it should encourage a variety of appropriate assessment methods;
- it should provide flexibility of provision and participation without endangering coherence, by recognising prior learning and by using credit accumulation and credit transfer.
- it should recognise that students learn and develop intellectually at different rates;
- it should secure the appropriate balance in programmes of study to encourage both breadth and depth of learning;
- it should incorporate core skills into individual students' programmes of study.

Of course, whether agreement will be maintained through the working out of detail to realise these principles is not yet determined, but it does look hopeful. Certainly, it cannot be emphasised too strongly that HE sees itself as having a stake in developing its antecedent curriculum. Above all, it is interested in the quality of that provision.

The basic A/AS quality initiative lies within the SEAC principles, to operate from 1994. Put briefly these address: the provision of clear assessment objectives, the coherence of modular programmes, the position of coursework (or, as I would rather describe it, centre-based assessment) and the provision of subject cores. In broad terms HE would probably support the SEAC proposals. What does remain contentious is the question of percentages of coursework assessment. HE would join with the post-16 providers in agreeing that a sensible balance needs to be struck, but would also point out that the balance can vary across different subjects and disciplines. What is crucially important is that there is an appropriate range of assessment styles. There is also the curious anomaly that equal value is sought for two kinds of qualification, yet the one contains a much higher proportion of centre-based assessment than does the other.

I turn now to look at some further specific initiatives, from an HE point of view. The Government's alternative to the Higginson approach was the introduction of the AS examination. This is not necessarily bad in principle, because, as noted above, individual elements do not mean equal weight, and even if it does not go far enough a range of subject areas does assist the achievement of breadth. Our problems have been:

- the relationship between A and AS has been vague, and we feel very strongly that the establishment of subject cores is vital to rectifying that deficiency;
- where AS examinations have taken off, they have been far too much in the 'complementary' mode than in the intended 'contrasting' mode;
- because it is half the weight, some providers have assumed that the AS is intermediate in level — it is not, and to that extent has been abused by being assumed to be a one-year course;
- schools and colleges see resourcing problems in providing AS alongside A examinations;
- if an AS examination simply follows on the title from its 'parent' A level syllabus then opportunities for contrast are lost because subjects like 'science' (as opposed to individual subjects) could provide useful contrast and yet are not available.

Nevertheless, AS remains very much on the agenda, it has positive features, and in spite of much comment to the contrary the evidence suggests that HE is increasingly supporting it.

As it has emerged, HE takes a different view about the Advanced Diploma. This is another proposal that was good in principle, given that its intentions were to promote academic/vocational mixing and the achievement of curricular breadth. The position was well described — even before the Government's proposals emerged — by the Royal Society in its extremely significant report *Beyond GCSE*. The report advocates securing breadth through three domains which it described as: social, economic and industrial; mathematical, scientific and technological; creative, language and aesthetic. It also advocated the introduction of an Advanced Diploma.

As it has now emerged, the AD is rather a weak creature. It requires three passes at A or AS (of which up to two can be at AS), or a GNVQ (see later), or an NVQ. In addition it requires performance in the areas of English, mathematics, and a modern foreign language, with the provenance being provided through different kinds of evidence. The weakness of these proposals derives from the fact that there is no real encouragement for breadth, the approach to core skills is confused compared with other parallel initiatives, and there is no cohering element. When the consultation document for the AD was first published Government made clear its view that breadth should come, not from a range of subjects, but from a range of core skills.

Curiously, as it has turned out, there is now common ground between the AD and some of the Government proposals with regard to vocational qualifications. The clear intention through the NVQ has been to provide coherence of provision through a single structure. So, each NVQ (and there are many) is made up of units, it credit accumulates, and therefore affords credit transfer. Provision is at one of five different levels, covering the full range of ability to the point where level 5 equates to a degree and professional qualification. The principles of NVQs are that they shall be accessible, based on outcomes of competence, measured in the workplace, be independent of the route or time taken to pass the competence requirements, and that they shall be not graded. The competence specifications are drawn up by Industry Lead Bodies representing the employers' point of view. The Government, from the very beginning, made it clear that it wished HE to recognise NVQs at level 3 and above as an appropriate avenue into HE.

The General NVQ is a later development. It is designed to fill a marked gap, and it probably does. It is intended to fit into the broad principles of the NVQ structure, but there are significant differences. Vitally, it is not intended to be taken in the workplace, and therefore bases its performance on achievement rather than competence. This point cannot be overstated, because the NVQ probably always would have been an unsatisfactory qualification within full-time education simply because of its workplace-relatedness. So, the GNVQ is: unitary, like the NVQ; but, unlike the NVQ, the units carry equal weight; the GNVQ is structured to a formal pattern; it contains core skills; very significantly; it is graded and in its initial introduction it operates in five occupational areas.

It is too early to be firm about it, but it could be argued that the five occupational areas first proposed are too specialist, and it could even be argued that too rigid a delineation within occupational areas inhibits the use of the GNVQ for progression into HE. What is very clear is that now that the GNVQ is with us, it has a much more important role in progression from 16–19 into higher education than ever the NVQ will have.

The structure of the basic GNVQ is 12 units. 8 of these units are mandatory, and the remaining 4 are optional, chosen from a fairly limited menu which includes GNVQ units from other occupational areas, or other NVQ units. In addition there are a further 3 core skill units (communication, application of number, information technology). The intention is that these 3 assessment units shall be applied within and across the basic 12 units. However, it is also assumed that more able candidates would take up to a further 6 units, drawn from a wider menu. These could include more GNVQ units, NVQ units, one or two AS examinations, a mixture of these, or a single A level. From this it will be seen that the very broad equivalence is that the GNVQ represents the same kind of challenge as does 2 A levels taken together. There are two clear schools of thought about the additional 6 units: some argue that it is a good opportunity to mix GNVQ units with A and AS, and to that extent it may be a better vehicle to do that than the AD; the other school of thought argues that the GNVQ is different and that it is in some way selling the pass to mix into it A level components. In any event, the idea of mixing is not new. The 'Wessex' scheme has already made two important contributions: firstly, it has sought to structure a flexible modular scheme on a core-and-options basis; secondly, it has pursued the inclusion of academic and vocational elements within the same qualification.

Although we have considerable reservations about the GNVQ, because it fills a genuine gap it needs our support, and on balance HE is likely to remain with it and assist in refining it. However, the reservations should not be under-emphasised. The relationship between the GNVQ and the NVQ remains ambiguous. Equally, the relationship between the core skills elements of the qualification and its main body strike us as being also ambiguous. A cardinal feature of the whole GNVQ/NVQ philosophy is that it is outcomes-based. There is no immediate quarrel with that, because it must be conceded that many of our existing qualifications, including those in HE, would be greatly improved if they also paid more attention to their intended outcomes.

The issue arises because most of HE would dispute that a qualification can be wholly outcomes-based, since there must always be a necessity to apply judgement. Indeed, some of the early standards that attach to NVQ and GNVQ are themselves ambiguous and shed little light on how you differentiate performance. Again, there is little doubt that HE welcomes the grading of the GNVQ. However, the nature of that grading and the way that it is going to be applied, remains too unclear for comfort.

Indeed, if one is not careful some of the quality assurance suspicions that at times attach to BTEC could also attach to the GNVQ itself. Finally, probably our biggest problem is of our own making and does not derive from NCVQ. It also extends more widely than the vocational qualifications. It is that GNVQ units are assessment units — they are in no sense necessarily teaching units. Until we can all develop a better understanding about the difference between these two concepts we are unlikely to realise the full potential of this new qualification. An extremely positive thing about GNVQ is the way that it is being introduced in a limited initial phase with the clear intention to investigate and explore. This means that the first fruits of its introduction are available to be ploughed back into its further development. HE is already a part of that process, and since the GNVQ does fill a gap there are grounds for optimism.

To summarise the HE position with regard to post-16 provision, there are clearly two paths, with a potential linkage, and there is a clear intention to address the quality assurance issue on the part of Government. This is welcomed, and the expected result is that all post-16 qualifications will be better specified as to their outcomes. There is clearly a long way yet to travel, although in one contentious respect — that of centre-based assessment — we could well have travelled too far already. There has been some movement, although not really fast enough, towards encouraging whole programmes of study, rather than, say, sets of A levels. In one pathway, and just a little in the other, we have seen the establishment of a unitary syllabus, with credit accumulation, and, as we shall see, within HE itself these two features together with credit transfer characterise what is now happening. There is also the dawning recognition of the necessity for structured and positively designed progression linking the post-16 sector with Key Stage 4 at one end and HE at the other. Finally, there is now visible movement towards establishing breadth in the curriculum encompassing the inclusion of core skills.

The original core skills were six in number, and were proposed by the National Curriculum Council during 1990. They comprised three (communication, problem solving, and personal skills) which they felt should be present in all syllabuses, together with a further three (numeracy, modern foreign language, and information technology) which should be present in whole programmes. It is probable that this list of six has been over-exploited, to a point beyond that intended by the original architects. Nevertheless, albeit in rather unsatisfactory form, we are seeing communication and application of number included in the academic route (Advanced Diploma) and the vocational route (GNVQ). The AD also includes the foreign language skill, and the GNVQ includes the IT skill.

Government has conceded that the personal skills element, and the problem solving element, are also vitally important, but has delayed their introduction pending proper development. This decision has surely got to be correct, but no-one outside HE has mentioned a further skill which is also necessary, and that is the ability to obtain, organise, and reflect upon, information. However, we are not starting from scratch.

These core skills, sometimes under other names, are, firstly, present in the National Curriculum. To take a small selection from the original Attainment Targets in Design and Technology, we see:

- to analyse information of several kinds and draw conclusions about the needs and opportunities for a design and technological activity, recognising and resolving conflicting considerations about what is worth doing;
- to identify and draw upon sources of expert advice relevant to the identification of needs and opportunities. . .;
- to convey, using presentation techniques matched to their audience, that their identification of needs and opportunities are justified and worth developing;
- to develop ideas by drawing on information and understanding from a broad knowledge of sources, and to show judgements about the detail required.

Similarly, existing BTEC programmes require the inclusion of common skills as follows:

- managing and developing self;
- working with and relating to others;
- communicating;
- managing tasks and solving problems;
- applying numeracy;
- applying technology;
- applying design and creativity.

Similar core skills are emerging within HE, for example in the Enterprise in Higher Education programme and are claimed by employers to be essential within graduate recruitment.

It is the concept of core skills that more than anything else offers the opportunity to thread together the various stages.

It is now time to relate these changes, in which HE is having increasing involvement, to the accelerating changes within HE itself. Firstly, Government has created a single sector for HE in a remarkably short time, bringing together the separate sub-sectors of universities and polytechnics. Within this movement, there are now clear strands of Government policy, some of which intersect those already mentioned for the post-16 sector.

Firstly, there is quality, evidenced by the setting up of a Higher Education Quality Council which among other things subsumes the operations of the Academic Audit Unit. This operates alongside a single HE Funding Council which will have its own quality assessment unit. Secondly, and most significantly, HEFC funds will be directly related to the quality of teaching and research within the institution. Next, it is Government's clear intention to increase participation in HE. The target is 1 in 3 of all young people participating by 1999. (This needs to be set against the figures of 1 in 500 in 1937, rising to 1 in 5 in 1990.) A further target is that the present participation overall should increase by 50 per cent within the same timespan. Moreover, alongside that increase in numbers is a clear intention to reduce unit costs. Further, as numbers increase, the diversity of entrant will inevitably and significantly broaden. Coupled with this is another clear element of Government policy, which is that HE should recognise VQs, and the GNVQ in particular. What it amounts to is an increase in recruitment numerically, a continually broadening spectrum of entrant, and significantly less funding. It is these two features — the post-16 developments already discussed, and the new fiscal and policy dimensions just discussed — that have informed the remarkable changes in the HE sector.

At this stage we need to consider the size of the situation. The figures relating to the 1991 entry are these:

- there were 208,000 applicants to HE with A and AS qualifications;
- there were 33,800 applicants with BTEC or SCOTVEC;
- there were 68,000 applicants with 'other' qualifications. This represented a total of 310,000 applicants compared with 271,000 the year before.

The success rate is described as follows:

- 142,000 students were accepted or admitted with A and AS qualifications;
- 20,000 students were admitted with BTEC or SCOTVEC;
- 39,000 students with other qualifications were accepted or admitted. This represents a total of 201,000 students accepted or admitted compared with 177,000 the year before.

These figures tell us quite a lot, in particular that we are clearly on course for meeting the stated targets by the end of the decade, although evidence suggests that the admitting rate will slow down. The issue that now needs to be addressed is rather more fundamental. The Government target represents 35 per cent of 'young people' entering HE. The same Government has repeatedly stressed that it sees A level as not appropriate to the whole cohort. The significant balance clearly will have to be taking other qualifications, perhaps approaching a more or less equal relationship between the 'two routes'; whereas up to now by far the dominant route has been represented by A level, the alternative routes are going to be much more prominent. There is, of course, another scenario: it is that the present proportion of A level based candidates holds up, but if that is the case we are going to see an increasing number of students pursuing an inappropriate qualification. Certainly one of the strongest sentiments that has emerged from a range of discussions with headteachers in the summer of 1992, over the introduction of the GNVQ, has been their total conviction that they have within their sixth forms a significant number of students who can succeed very well in HE but would fail to get there if present criteria were applied. This is a collective viewpoint that HE can no longer ignore.

Having established that HE will receive more students and students of increasingly different kinds, there is another numerical feature to be considered: the number of places available in the HE sector in different disciplines varies, and the number of applicants chasing those places varies even more. Thus there are some disciplines which are heavily over-subscribed, and others that are under-subscribed to the point where their future must be in doubt. This generates a number of real concerns, not least the fact that there are apparently well-qualified students who do not get what they want or sometimes anything like it. There is also the disturbing doubt as to whether these applicants make their decision on any kind of informed basis, and it must be true that whatever the decision it is taken too early. In the case of the sciences it may well be taken at the beginning of Key Stage 4.

The urgent imperative for HE to change its curriculum stems from all of these factors taken together, and points in the direction of two key features, namely flexibility and economy. There are several reasons why flexibility is necessary, some of which have already been discussed. Firstly, there is the need to accommodate a range of differently-experienced students; secondly there is the need to allow those students to change their minds subsequently once they have arrived and thirdly there is the need for this change of mind to extend, if appropriate, to a change of institution. The fact that we are now on the brink of one sector, one funding council, one admissions system, and one set of admissions documentation, must take this process easier to achieve.

The forces just discussed are external, but there are also very important internal influences as well. Whole disciplines are finding the need to reconsider the purpose and the nature and structure of their degree programmes. One of the first of these was the physics discipline, and in a report published in 1991 one finds the following extract:

> we try to teach too much, and in consequence teach it ineffectively. We crowd into the syllabus far more material than most students can absorb. If we aimed to teach less, we could teach it far better. . .students would then have time to learn how to find out things for themselves, from a variety of sources and we should have time to give them some training in communication skills and in the problem solving skills needed in industry. . .in doing so, we shall be giving them a far better education than we do at present. (Institute of Physics 1991)

As a result, the report proposes a reduction of at least a third in the factual content of a three year honours physics course. The report asserts that this does not imply a reduction in the intellectual content since students would gain a substantially deeper understanding and a greater range of skills resulting in a challenge at least as intellectually demanding as other honours degree courses.

Very similar sentiments were offered, slightly later, by engineering in their report: *The Future Pattern of 1st Degree Courses in Engineering*, (Engineering Professors' Conference 1991):

> We aim to decrease the content of engineering courses but to increase their challenge.
> (It is necessary for) departments (to) draw up, and agree to, a specification of educational goals. . .only then (can they) identify the fundamental concepts and relevant knowledge and skills to include in degree courses. . .
> factual material. . .should be reduced so that students will not need to spend so much time simply absorbing knowledge. . .degree courses should come instead to emphasise the 'understanding of fundamental principles' and the development of 'key engineering skills' more strongly. . .students should be helped to become lifelong independent learners.
> the removal of student overload is not intended to lower standards: on the contrary the proposed change in emphasis should raise the standard and quality of engineering degrees.

This report notes that many senior industrialists feel that the abilities of engineering graduates do not match the needs of today.

The real need is for broad-based, flexible graduates who can 'think' and solve problems, requiring skills such as design, modelling and simulation and decision-taking skills as well as various communication and decision-taking skills.

These sentiments are reinforced by, among others, the Council for Industry and Higher Education, which has represented employers as seeking general intellectual skills and particular personal qualities as well as academic abilities. The reasoning has been that students need to use a mix of disciplines, in order to become effective.

Again, the Royal Society Report already noted reported that A level courses were not welcome for many, causing them to reject such courses either before, or shortly after joining them. On the other hand, TVEI, BTEC and work experience courses evoked more positive actions from students, encouraging them to take responsibility for their own actions and learning.

The report went on to quote employers as increasingly looking for graduates with transferable skills that equip them to be flexible to the needs of a changing world, warning HE of the need to make more radical revision to its courses, adopting a more skills-and-process-based approach so as to equip students with flexible problem-solving skills; breadth of study, with communication skills and science and mathematics should be pursued by all.

We then have a very significant statement indeed from the Cabinet Office's Advisory Council on Science and Technology (1991):

> Our proposals are aimed at shifting the emphasis in education from processes that dissuade, sift out and exclude to those that attract, encourage and support.

The report went on to note the importance of understanding principles and method, and the acquisition of skills rather than factual content.

The burden of all this is that some disciplines within HE are reconsidering the context and the purpose of their degree courses. There is a tendency to reduce content and give a new emphasis to 'skills'. This does not mean that appropriate knowledge and content is thrown overboard, but rather the wish to restrike an appropriate balance. It does mean that the atmosphere of learning is being redefined, and perhaps most importantly of all the degree course is being repositioned both in relationship to higher degrees, and in relationship to subsequent continuous education and training.

It is likely that these discipline-based developments would have taken place even if there had been no suggestion of modularity and flexibility. What has happened is that these internal developments have operated alongside the responses to the external pressures previously discussed. What we are now seeing emerging most strongly is institutionally-based developments to provide the flexibility to cope with the diversity of entry and to enable mobility, both within the institution and between institutions and — now — between countries. It is now necessary to examine the more detailed nature of that curriculum development.

The process involves some ingredients that are not particularly new. For example, credit accumulation within HE has been operating for a very long time, and many, if not most, degree courses operate in that way. Credit transfer is altogether newer, and probably less widespread. It has been given a remarkable impetus over the last five years by the CNAA, and this is something that we will return to later. Finally, we have modularity itself, and even if the concept has not been recognised it has certainly existed. It would not be an exaggeration to say that, just below the surface, almost all degree courses have been modular by nature. Any one of these three features can exist on its own, and some of the most successful development has rested on a strategy that has sought to put in place one of the features, and then further to build on that by exploiting their inter-connections.

There are those who argue that establishing the modular curriculum is simply taking existing programmes and cutting them up into pieces, with the consequence that they look little different at the end, but more fragmented. This would be offered as a criticism, but one could argue with equal strength that even if a programme looks the same at the end of the exercise, those who offer it understand it much better and therefore its quality has improved. In any event, it is doubtful if it does look the same at the end of the exercise. So what is emerging is a curriculum that operates with credit accumulation, credit transfer, and modularity. It would be claimed on its behalf that its quality has improved, the relationship of assessment to intended learning is better identified, and, perhaps paradoxically in the context of modularity, the coherence of programmes is improved. This is probably because fear of fragmentation on the part of academics has made them doubly careful to try to ensure coherence.

I believe that we are seeing an improved quality assurance, within what some regard as a potentially vulnerable modular array. In fact, what we have is far from being 'pick and mix', and at first sight may well look little different from a listing of traditional single honours courses. Modules are often grouped together under seemingly traditional headings. Such module groupings might, further, identify modules that are essential, together with others that are recommended and still more that are truly optional. Within an institution sets of modules are submitted for quality assurance as a group, so that it is not only the individual unit that is 'authorised', but also the way that units are put together to make a pathway.

It is within those groupings that the initial flexibility is provided. An entrant can be deemed already to have satisfied some of the essential modules by virtue of past experience or qualification offered. Since the diversity of entrant (already mentioned a number of times) means that different students receive different exemptions, the idea of parallel tracks through a single broad pathway begins to emerge. In any of these tracks, the idea of optionality still remains, with the result that institutions can claim that within a familiar discipline pattern every single student might be pursuing a different combination of modules. It is also easy to see the added ability of a student to reconsider which pathway to follow at, say, the end of an academic year. The next stage of the 'new' pathway is clearly identified, and the accumulated experience of the student so far is compared with that to see what exemptions can be offered, what degree of option remains available, and what additional units have to be covered in order to effect the transfer. It is worth pointing out that, albeit on a more complex scale, the process of switching institutions is not so very different from that of switching pathways within the same institution.

There are also additional features which look likely to change the way in which students participate in higher education. The modular curriculum, as so described, enables students to enter a programme (pathway) downstream of its starting point, using precisely the same credit transfer processes. By the same token, it is possible for students to follow the programme part-time, over a longer envelope of time. It is also possible for a student to take time out at some point during the programme, either for personal reasons or to fit in placements within experience of work etc.

Modular programmes are in practice evidencing credit accumulation. The process of changing from one pathway to another at some mid-point is essentially credit transfer. This relationship between credit accumulation and credit transfer is absolutely crucial, and it is hoped that enough has been said about both features to indicate, first that they are not the same, but second that they offer considerable opportunity when taken together. Neither is credit transfer just about switching pathways; a student who wishes to proceed along the same pathway after a round of assessment is really being considered as part of a credit transfer process, except that in this case it is 'forwards', rather than 'sideways and forwards'. The process is, in principle, no different to that applied to an in-coming student who wishes to join the course downstream, by virtue of the prior learning that he or she then offers for consideration. Because of that, it is probably going to be helpful in the future if we regard the whole admissions process to HE as being itself a credit transfer operation, including the traditional A level student entering a traditional course at the age of 18.

While it is not the only system operating, the CNAA Credit Accumulation and Transfer System has over the last 5 years become well established. It has a numerical aspect, in that it assigns 120 points to one year's study at degree level. The size of unit can vary from institution to institution, but a module is normally recognised as being 'an agreed fraction of one-year's study load'. These 120 points per annum are initially described as general credit. Such credit can be contained within formal qualifications, including all those that have been noted so far in this chapter, but it can also represent prior experiential learning. When a student seeks to transfer credit, either to enter a programme or to transfer between programmes, the process amounts to converting general credit to specific credit; it is important to add that this is done with respect to an 'agreed programme of study, leading to a named award'. This is important because it emphasises first that credit transfer is not a random process, but is into a programme whose quality has already been assured and identified in terms of a specific outcome (say, the degree), secondly, such transfer is not automatic but is always at the discretion of the 'receiving' 'department'. In cases where the natures of the two pathways concerned are similar, the conversion from general to specific credit is probably total; in cases where they are unlike (in an extreme case, from archaeology to electronic engineering) the conversion factor (general to specific) may be low.

Up to now, the whole matter of modularising existing and new programmes has been an institutional responsibility. But, by its very nature, institutions have been working more corporately — in association with the CNAA — when it has come to credit transfer. What we are now seeing is a bringing together of these two kinds of task, with institutions forming consortia or federations, both to share the task of modular curriculum development, and to increase the power of credit transfer between them. The parallel development covering whole disciplines has already been a corporate activity involving many institutions.

One of the features that has increasingly encouraged such corporate development has been the question of semesters. The pattern that is strongly emerging is of a semester that occupies 15 weeks. 12 of those weeks are allocated to 'learning', and the remaining three to 'assessment'. Varying reasons are offered as to why the semester is seen to be a useful feature. They include establishing a better relationship between learning and assessment. Indeed, the whole process of considering modules and semesters has led to considerable rethinking about the whole process of assessment. While annual assessment is increasingly thought to be too 'long', assessment after a single term is also thought to be too frequent.

Others argue that the momentum of learning is better maintained if the academic year is divided into two sections rather than three. Be that as it may, the indications are that by mid-decade a majority of the original universities will be offering a modular system, and of those a very significant fraction will be operating it in a two-semester mode. However, it may not be possible to squeeze three full semesters into a single calendar year. One formula being considered is of a first semester that finishes before Christmas, followed by the second that commences around three to four weeks after that. The time left in the summer amounts to something like a half semester, and this could be used for a variety of teaching purposes. For example, it could be used as a 'bridging' period for particular students entering HE for the first time with unusual qualifications, or for existing students who either wish to remedy deficiency, or wish to make a pathway change which represents a significant leap.

In the end, a newcomer initially studying a university's modular programme may not see anything so different from a traditional presentation. They could note that the modular presentation looks remarkably like a two-dimensional grid indicating joint honours courses, and within individual disciplines they might be conscious that the content described is more clearly sectionalised. Indeed, for many students entering the modular curriculum the experience may not be so very different. However, what is important is what the underlying structure enables, which goes much beyond what the traditional curriculum has given us in the past.

We are entering a period of mass HE with many more students entering at an additional number of interfaces, and — as a form of safety net — some of them possibly seeking to exit with credit short of the award of a full degree. The enabling flexibility just described, is an essential part of that very new process. It requires a number of things from HE that HE has not been accustomed to provide thus far. It needs to define its study programme in more detail, and in a step-by-step way. It needs to be clear about the intended outcomes from each step, and what is required to enter the next step. The outcome from one unit matches to the input to the next. Because students will offer themselves for entry with a wider range of qualifications, some of which might be more informal, HE needs to be clear about the evidence that those qualifications can convey. Just as HE is increasingly sharing its curriculum development process between itself in order to maximise use of resource, it will almost certainly need corporately to analyse the full range of qualifications in order to identify the sources of its necessary evidence. No matter what formal qualification is offered, it seems likely that the record of achievement will, in the future, also be a necessary and additional source of such evidence.

It has already become a truism that the more flexible the curriculum, the more the student's need for guidance and counselling; this is both in terms of the process of entering a programme, and of the process of navigating a way through it. The record of achievement, mentioned in the last paragraph, may — in its individual action planning form — be a part of that recording, tracking, and planning activity that will become very necessary. The debate within HE is increasingly concentrating on the role of the transcript, broadly in the form that it is used in, for example, North America. This is accompanied by reconsidering the continuing need to classify degrees; the transcript may be the student's currency rather than the level of performance. Perhaps one can ask too much of a credit accumulation and credit transfer system; the tariff of 120 points a year, or any other tariff, simply indicates the extent of the student's study in the period involved; it does not immediately indicate the quality or grade of student performance.

The discussion so far has dwelt largely on curriculum structure and philosophy. The formal qualification, often in modified form, has been a form of transfer used by the student from one sector to another. The fact that increasingly this kind of 'qualification' may be more informal does not diminish that concept. Interestingly, however, we are beginning to see a rapid growth of another form of transfer, namely the institutional linkage. This is sometimes known as 'franchising', which may in time be seen to be an unsatisfactory term. In urging HE, using partly fiscal levers, to increase participation and width of provision. Government has made it clear that it sees no case for increasing the average length of courses. This is to say that there will be no 4th years, but institutional linkages recognise the need, for some students, to provide some transitional or foundation year, sometimes known as a 'year O'. Thus instead of adding an extra year at the end of the course, an additional one slots in at the beginning. One form of this is the '2+2' programme, whereby two years are studied in a college of FE, the student then transferring to the 2nd and 3rd years of an existing degree course on campus. Often, and desirably, the first two years are part of a BTEC course. The two institutions agree modifications to the BTEC course, and to the degree programme, to enable the linkage to operate, and if the student achieves pre-identified hurdles in the college of FE after two years then the student transfers, as of right, to the university course. A variant of this is where the university commissions a 'year O' from the college of FE, which is tailor-made to the needs of the university degree course as it stands. These arrangements, particularly the first, offer a valuable safety net to the student who is unable, or unwilling, to make the transfer to the degree course when the time comes. In the BTEC case the student simply completes the BTEC course and has lost nothing. Additionally, as credit transfer begins to take hold that same student could enter a degree course with advanced standing at some point in the future. Such arrangements also have the advantage of 'localness': the student can begin at home the sometimes daunting task of a degree programme, moving onto campus at a later time when confidence has begun to be built.

Similar, but less formal connections are inherent in 'educational compacts', although this is another term that we may wish to change before long. This is built on a school and university connection whereby the possessing of a formal qualification at a certain level of performance is in part replaced by the evidence that can be conveyed through mutual trust between the institutions. Such arrangements are often directed at attracting the kind of student who traditionally so far has not participated in HE. All such linkage arrangements rely on inter-institutional trust, and admission operates on the basis of a different kind of evidence, often more in tune to the 'ability to learn and to benefit from the course' criterion that Government is likely to emphasise in the future. Whichever way one looks at it, linkages do extend the interfaces between universities and their various feeder routes. And, in all these cases, admission really is the process of converting general to specific credit.

I said at the beginning of this chapter that it is necessary now to take the post-16 sector and the university sector together as a linked whole. They are becoming more closely bound together through a number of vehicles: both their curricula are unitary, giving the chance for some modules to be 'shared' so that they may be taught on either side of the interface; the need for greater specificity in assessment and qualifications, both sides of the interface, makes the use of qualifications for transfer purposes more valid and more reliable; mutual trust between institutions widens the kind of evidence, and the criteria applied to it, that can be used for transfer purposes; finally, aspects such as core skills form strands that intersect the compulsory, the post-16 and the HE curricula, and employers' needs alike, and offer commonality which we must be careful to retain.

The Students' Charter, that we are likely to see emerge during the next year or so, could prove to be a significant influence on the relationship between universities and those who provide their students. The Charter could require that students are given more information about the programme of study in higher education that they might want to pursue. This includes what will be required of them to enter those programmes, and the criteria by which they will be selected. This tunes very well with what the HE curriculum is becoming anyway, because it has already been emphasised more than once that if a modular curriculum needs anything it needs a clear definition of inputs and outcomes. One outcome is that students are likely to assist themselves in the admissions process by operating an element of self-selection; but they can only do this if it is made very clear to them what is required of them.

I, finish with some references from Sir Peter Swynnerton-Dyer, formerly Chief Executive of the UFC, in his Rede Lecture at the University of Cambridge in 1991. Interestingly, this is nearly 40 years after the C.P.Snow 'two cultures' contribution within the same lecture.

> (Science and technology are subjects) which, at least at the more elementary levels, deal in certainties: and they are also cumulative subjects. This means that they include courses which must be given in much the same way in every university. Nothing would be lost if the first courses in abstract algebra or thermo dynamics were everywhere identical.

This describes more or less exactly what the disciplines of engineering and physics are already seeking to do. But Sir Peter goes on further:

> A front-rank engineer needs a solid foundation of mathematics; a run-of-the-mill engineer does not. Virtually all engineering courses in higher education are designed to be capable of producing front-rank engineers so they demand qualifications in mathematics which are a formidable obstacle to entry. In this they are encouraged — even coerced — by the engineering institutions. This is a major reason for the notorious national shortage of engineers.

I would disagree with some of the inferences, but the broad thrust of the argument must be correct. But finally, there are references which are applicable to HE as a whole:

. . .and this will lead to pressure for longer first-degree courses. The rationale of this is that if students start further away from the frontiers of knowledge, they will take longer to reach them. There is an unspoken assumption here, that a first-degree course must take students to the frontiers of knowledge: except in professional subjects, it will be hard to persuade any Government of this — and especially so if we reject a longer teaching year as the means of achieving it. . .

The courses offered were not a response to student demand; they were those which academics wanted to teach. . .

but when the big increase in post-18 education comes, educators will have to ask themselves what kind of courses will best meet the needs of the new students. Institutions have a duty to teach courses appropriate to the students whom they actually have, rather than to those whom they wish they had.

References

Advisory Council on Science and Technology (1991) *Science and Technology, Education and Employment* Cabinet Office.

Engineering Professors' Conference (1991) *The Future Pattern of 1st Degree Courses in Engineering* Engineering Professors' Conference.

Institute of Physics/SCPP/CNPP Higher Education Working Party (1991) *The Future Pattern of Degree Courses in Physics* IOP/SCPP/CNPP.

Swynnerton-Dyer, Sir Peter (1991) *Policy in Higher Education and Research* Rede Lecture, University of Cambridge.

The Royal Society (1991) *Beyond GCSE*.

PART IV: ON TO THE NEXT MILLENNIUM?

14   The problems of choice and diversity

Harry Tomlinson

National Curriculum

The achievement of an approach to a National Curriculum should, even now, not be underestimated, despite the damage that the Government is continually inflicting on this, the most important part of its first Education Reform Act. The potential for enhancing the quality of education for all pupils was, and still remains, enormous, though this capability is gradually being eroded. The establishment of genuine curriculum continuity at the primary–secondary transfer stage alone should raise standards substantially. The Oracle Project in the early 1980s demonstrated that for many pupils their academic performance deteriorated, most clearly in mathematics, in the first year of secondary education. This was a direct result of a failure of schools to build on where each pupil was. When the National Curriculum is attacked for the many inadequacies it is important not to forget the even greater weaknesses of the system it replaced. There is precisely the same continuity problem at 16.

The complementary, and unresolved, problem at 16, even for the small proportion for whom A levels are allegedly appropriate, was demonstrated when the attempt to build core skills into all A level syllabuses proved impossible. The form originally proposed would inevitably have imposed excessive and irrelevant repetition. What is disturbing, and indeed becoming increasingly and deeply damaging, is the inability of those who had something approaching a vision to ensure this is sustained amidst the ever changing practicalities of attainment targets, programmes of study and key stage assessment. It is not unreasonable in retrospect to characterise Kenneth Baker and Duncan Graham as reaching out, albeit belatedly, to impose coherence. An obsessional political and bureaucratic interference is now hacking away at the whole which had begun to emerge, even though there had been no clear framework established initially.

In 1986 the School Curriculum Development Committee asked Eric Lord, formerly Chief Inspector in the DES, to produce a statement on 'the style, content and organisation of the whole curriculum 5–16'. He concluded that 'using our perspectives on the past and the future we can endeavour to shape a contemporary curriculum which, in the teaching and learning to which it leads, mirrors and prepares for those calls upon the mind, the heart, the imagination and the will which human life represents' (Lord 1986). There is a quality of vision here which was never achieved in the National Curriculum. Even in this document, however, there was no attempt to consider progression beyond 16, though the four curricular virtues of breadth, balance, relevance and differentiation which were recognised, would be even more applicable and necessary post-16. The ERA curriculum was rather less about the mind, the heart, the imagination and the will, than the packing in of content, assumed to be the same as knowledge. A significant and increasingly substantial part of that knowledge reflecting a conservative ideology.

Curriculum development in the 1970s

When the author was working in the Excepted District of Basildon in the early 1970s as a head of humanities, without exception the schools in Basildon had heads of humanities. This meant in practice that in all the schools, particularly in Years 7 to 9, there was a different planned and co-ordinated, but nevertheless highly idiosyncratic, curriculum which included in this particular case English, history, geography, religious education and social studies. All the schools, more or less independently, were attempting to produce a coherent humanities curriculum. Indeed the joy of curriculum development was that all were unique, allegedly appropriate to the special circumstances of each school. In practice this meant the individual interests of the teachers in the school since the pupils in groups had largely common needs. The schools which are now developing new curriculum emphases post ERA, in the age of choice and diversity, may similarly be doing so for political reasons rather than to meet the needs of their pupils.

In the first term of secondary education at this school the pupils studied Nigerian history, geography and literature. Tribal religions were not studied as the religious education content, since in

Billericay parents might have reacted adversely to such unwonted excitement. The unfortunate contribution of Christian missionaries to the economic and cultural development of Nigeria was given some emphasis. The humanities curriculum was seen as beginning to raise the issues associated with multiculturalism, then becoming significant in the more imaginative, though possibly more accurately, trend setting institutions. For the 14–16 age group an appropriate curriculum meant having the widest possible choice of O level and CSE courses. Choice and diversity regardless of coherence was the aim. It is easy to look back and recognise the weaknesses of such a system now, but the Schools Council itself was working in a not dissimilar way.

There were simply too many interesting and innovative curriculum developments which schools could dip into and use. Stenhouse's Humanities Curriculum Project was challenging schools to reconsider teaching styles, in some ways anticipating the methodological emphases of TVEI. This particular school was involved in parallel Mode 3 O level and CSE English schemes. In practice every school in the excepted district, in common with many schools in the country, was experimenting in what can now be recognised as an entirely incoherent way, meeting the needs of the innovatory curriculum developers rather than the pupils, many of whom, when they moved schools suffered quite disastrous consequences in terms of progression.

The Schools Council never seriously considered a National Curriculum, an ideal which actually belongs much more appropriately to the idealism associated with comprehensive schools and mixed ability teaching than the harsher Gradgrind ideology of the New Right. There was a consideration of the whole curriculum, but this was never pursued vigorously. The frittering away of the energy and resources of the Schools Council might have been avoided. The curriculum vision and commitment of all those involved might have been focused purposefully.

The recent study of curriculum and educational change has tended to assume that the Callaghan Ruskin speech was the start of an entirely new period of curriculum history. Though it was perhaps the most clear turning point in the post-war period, there have been some very significant missed opportunities. Perhaps the teachers, particularly through their professional associations, might have reacted much more constructively to aspects of the Plowden Report and the opportunities made possible by the Schools Council, embedding them in the culture of the education service.

After the Education Reform Act the whole curriculum somehow emerged as being subject based. The three core subjects, the seven foundation subjects, religious education and subsequently the cross curricular dimensions, themes and skills were not planned as a whole curriculum. Programmes of study, attainment targets and indeed assessment at the end of the key stages were generally accepted in principle. The rush to implement all of these without even the most elementary consultation has frankly caused chaos. This has already resulted in substantial changes in the number of attainment targets for science and mathematics, almost incessant changes to the English curriculum, very different interpretations of the nature of the subject of technology, changed emphases in attainment targets for music unacceptable to almost all those with any knowledge of music, and an apparently unquestioned assumption, in the era of Maastricht, that foreign language learning should start at 11.

When it was appreciated, much too late, that ten subjects would be an excessive GCSE workload attempts to create half subjects for history and geography, and in the end a devaluing of arts education solved the technical if not the educational problem. The reasons for these and other frenzied changes are not only a result of the Government having to face the reality of their own curriculum mistakes, often blamed on educational professionals, but also due to a further ratcheting in of New Right ideology.

In many of the groups preparing the separate subject reports there was political interference. Those preparing the history curriculum had to concentrate excessively on British history and even the aspects of British history the Government considered more appropriate, those which represented issues which perhaps supported its interpretation of history. It was the least difficult of the Secretaries of State who was involved in this particular damaging narrowing to a regrettably parochial nationalism. The National Curriculum has become increasingly unacceptable, as it has become a Government curriculum.

It is not possible here to examine in detail the massive interference in the teaching of English, by politicians, which has led to obsessional changes and which John Patten now wishes to change radically. The clearer thinking of Kingman and Cox led to the first attainment targets, statutory orders, and programmes of study, then we had 5 per cent off for bad spelling, and now for everyone *Julius Caesar*, *Romeo and Juliet* or *A Midsummer Night's Dream*. *Julius Caesar* is a play about stabbing the party leader in the back and treacherous politicians whose internecine struggles suggest they are almost all entirely self-serving. *Romeo and Juliet* is about underage sex, drugs, teenage gang warfare and a challenge to parenting which could undermine the whole rationale to the Education Reform Act. *A Midsummer Night's Dream* is about fairies. The English programmes of study has suffered most because everyone is an expert in English. The curriculum is to be changed again before it has even started at Key Stage 4. It is regrettable that it is no longer surprising that these changes to policy are based on the prejudices of a vociferous and disturbed Right wing clique out of touch with classroom reality. It would have been rational to evaluate the strengths and weaknesses of the English curriculum rather than changing it before it has been implemented.

When this book was being conceived it was thought that there was an emerging consensus about the National Curriculum 5–16, and that though there had been very little thinking about the whole at an early stage, a coherent curriculum might emerge. There was an expectation that it might be possible to explore, building on that breadth, balance, relevance and differentiation, the possibility of developing those same strengths beyond 16. TVEI provided a 14–18 complement to the National Curriculum 14–16, concentrating on skills and methodology, even though progression for the whole cohort beyond 16 within TVEI proved difficult. The strengths of the TVEI approach to learning, the relating of education to the world of work, learning in real life situations, the promotion of enterprise, creativity, teamwork and problem solving, and the encouragement of guidance and counselling, might similarly complement an improved 16–19 curriculum. The problem was that there was nothing to complement, just the jungle of qualifications on which an alleged parity was being imposed.

The curriculum and GCSE/A level

Those who have been involved in curriculum development are inevitably conscious that none of the many policy developments over the last twenty years have seriously addressed the issue of continuity at 16, particularly more recently, even for the group which has allegedly been well served by A levels. For the academically able there was some continuity at 16 from the O level to A level courses, mainly because they were organised by the same people within the same examination boards. In addition these students had almost always had a narrower education from 14–16 taking 7 academic subjects, 3 of which they subsequently took as their A Levels which they usually passed. Normally these would be within a narrow curriculum area, often mathematics and the sciences or the languages and humanities. The A level General studies was the most common means for providing breadth for all these students. In practice it was and is too much yet another content based examination. However if students did not take this examination, particularly up to the mid-1980s, then their education was excessively limited.

When the GCSE was established the new boards based on the CSE boards made possible a new and more challenging curriculum as a result of the improved assessment systems which broadened the aspects of work examined and explored a wider range of skills. However they became increasingly detached from the A level syllabuses where the form of the examination remained much more traditional and much less flexible, with regrettable implications for teaching methodology. The content gap emerged since A level syllabuses assumed a curriculum which no longer applied. Where flexibility has been developed to provide greater challenge in the newer A lever syllabuses there is constant Government and SEAC pressure to revert to more conformist and limiting final examinations. GCSE was to be about what students 'know, understand and can do'. A level remained too closely aligned to knowledge only and assessed particularly through testing memory, in two long examinations. This was despite some imaginative attempts in some of the newer syllabuses to incorporate increasing proportions of the very challenging coursework.

Education and training

There is very limited continuity and progression at 16 at present. To achieve this requires that parity of esteem is genuine, given the three obvious and approved tracks which are emerging post-16. A multitrack combination of these seems increasingly unlikely. In theory all three tracks will need to involve the acquisition of specialised knowledge, concepts and skills. At present one might argue that the three tracks, A levels, GNVQ and NVQ overemphasise each of these respectively. One problem with the skills based approach associated with NVQs is that it can reduce teaching, learning and assessment to a disconnected series of modular tasks that has no overall coherence. Indeed it might be argued that NVQs are about assessment and not a curriculum. Despite these real problems, SEAC is beginning to suggest that GNVQs and NVQs also should be established and recognised as gold standards. The apparent implication is that failure to agree to this unfounded assertion simply implies elitism. If all three tracks are to demand the intellectual capabilities of imagination and analysis, and both education and training are to require rigour and challenge then some of the proposals outlined below for a new coherent curriculum are preferable. Attempting to sustain the three alternatives whilst ensuring that they become more alike seems unnecessary. The imposition of parity of esteem, by *force majeure*, may have interesting repercussions. This is clearly the case when the Secretary of State suggests that those not capable of three A levels should take one A level and two BTECs.

Similarly an appropriate balance between formative and summative assessment, with the standards established accepted as comparable is a prerequisite for equal status. The multitrack model must ensure that the different routes can access the same professional career opportunities if there is to be parity. There is in Government policy perhaps an underlying and unquestioned assumption that training for enterprise will somehow facilitate a shift to tomorrow's occupations. These demand inventiveness, entrepreneurial skills and the possibility of self-employment for the small business person. However the GNVQ and particularly the NVQ curriculum may become a job creation process for yesterday's jobs. It is quite clear that the employment that will become available will be for those who have high level abilities, with one estimate suggesting that over 70 per cent of jobs will require managerial or professional, at least degree level, skills, though which skills are unclearly recognised at present.

Coursework

Coursework which tests different and perhaps more important skills than formal examinations is now being downgraded as a proportion of the marks at A level and GCSE. This proportion may become so small that it makes it difficult for teachers to persuade students to concentrate on what produces such an irrelevantly small proportion of the marks, particularly when there are examination only alternatives. However for the new GNVQs, which are to be of equal status coursework is central, even though there are end of topic tests. The exemplary unit in the original consultation document at GNVQ Level 3 in leisure and tourism related to 'providing customer care' may be of particular interest to teachers who work in a much more market oriented environment. That only one of the four parts of this unit involves 'planning a customer care strategy' suggests that there may be real difficulties about agreeing levels. The evidence required includes a customer care plan for a facility together with supplementary evidence to ensure coverage of all performance criteria.

For the NVQs assessment will be practical, indeed mainly on the job, and result in statements of competence. There is a danger with

NVQs that they will not be about improving skills but simply a means of assessing the skills which have been developed. The units of competence, elements of competence, performance criteria and range statements are to be established within the progressive levels of achievement. NVQ level 3, the equivalent of A levels requires competence in a broad range of varied work activities performed in a wide variety of contexts, most of which are complex and non-routine. It is therefore somewhat unclear what parity with A levels means. There is also the difficulty about what is meant by 'considerable responsibility and autonomy'. It is implied that the 'control and guidance of others' which is often required is comparable to A levels. The educational and academic value of work itself and its relation to other forms of learning is questionable.

Teaching to the syllabus and examination has become inevitable, possibly excessive, particularly at A level where each grade may be genuinely significant for the student. Grade boundaries are based on judgements which it is difficult to guarantee can be genuinely nationally comparable and validated. There is a similar technical problem with any teacher assessment which is now exaggerated at A level and ignored elsewhere.

Coursework could provide a means for assessing a much wider range of skills than is tested at A level by examination only, and indeed at GCSE. Those making policy appear to hold a belief that tests which are simple and conducted under examination conditions provide more genuinely valid evidence of achievement. This belief, which appears now to be unquestioned and unquestionable particularly for the more academic, betrays a particularly naive understanding of the nature of assessment and examinations. There appears to be an assumption that it is possible to state quite incontrovertibly at Key Stage 4 and A level exactly what a student has achieved in terms of a particular grade. Such ignorance of the technology of testing is almost absurd. Government thinking appears however to be based on a belief that it is possible to measure simply and absolutely spelling ability for example, and that measuring it improves it. These misconceptions about testing and examinations have already had a very damaging impact on the evolving National Curriculum because of the distortions that a misfocused emphasis on assessment has caused.

Flexible learning is somewhat similar to coursework in the skills it develops. It is about meeting the learning needs of students as individuals and in groups through the flexible management and use of learning activities, environments and resources. More particularly it gives the student increased responsibility for his or her own learning within a framework of appropriate support. This approach represents an educational way forward, as we move into the staffing ratios which increased efficiency is likely to mean in the new Further Education Funding Council (FEFC) world. The traditions of A level teaching, arguably imply more inflexible learning, and assessment with the emphasis on content recall. That the gold standard A level should be considered to provide an appropriate curriculum even for the academically able into the next millennium is somewhat surprising.

Modules

Those seeking to explore areas of comparability between A levels and BTEC Nationals in the past and with GNVQs in the future are finding the resistance of SEAC to modularisation within A level courses more than surprising. If credit accumulation and transfer are to occur then credits will need to be achieved within A level courses. At present ministerial fiat would appear to preclude this. As the process of modularisation in higher education accelerates, as Malcolm Deere demonstrates in Chapter 13 of this book, it still seems that the political determination to associate the 'gold standard' with simple straightforward examinations, insecurely founded in educational theory, remains inflexible.

The School Curriculum Development Committee (SCDC) produced its first curriculum issues document *Modular Approaches to the Secondary Curriculum* in 1985 when it suggested that the then current interest in the modular approach, which has certainly developed strongly since, stemmed from an increasingly wide application particularly in the 14–18 curriculum. The advantages and difficulties of modularisation were very clearly recognised. The educational implications of this, the first curriculum issue, recognised as crucial in 1985, remain without a satisfactory resolution. What is clear is that the surrounding assessment issues, admittedly complex and therefore requiring intelligent analysis, still have not been seriously addressed.

National Curriculum Assessment

The National Curriculum implies a largely common curriculum for all. Indeed attempts to pull back from this appear to give enhanced status to some subjects in a way which undermines the concept of a whole curriculum. A compulsory curriculum for all students in maintained schools only does not appear to align itself with a policy which is allegedly market orientated. However the White Paper *Choice and Diversity* (DES 1991a) appears to imply that the market orientation, with a rather less common curriculum up to sixteen, is becoming increasingly acceptable. There is of course the complementary, or contradictory, argument that the market cannot operate efficiently without appropriate comparable information and regulation which allows those using the market to make a soundly based judgement.

It cannot be assumed that the curriculum is a significant reason independent education is selected by many parents, though it may be the hidden curriculum. Indeed, a knowledge that such schools might possibly produce less good examination results, would undoubtedly have an impact on some decisions whatever the curriculum. Indeed the debate has been significantly and deliberately distorted to so change the emphasis from curriculum to assessment that curriculum is now almost irrelevant. All that matters is results. GCSE results are the issue of the moment with the Secretary of State attacking the examination boards whilst his junior minister congratulates the teachers and pupils on their achievements (1992). By 1993 there may be sound and fury signifying nothing about the publication of the results of Key Stage 3 tests. So inadequate are the preparations for Key Stage 3 that GSA schools might not take these particular tests to the apparent irritation of Baroness Blatch.

There is a widespread acceptance within the education and training services of the Confederation of British Industry (CBI) World Class Targets. If 80 per cent of young people are to obtain NVQ level 2 or the equivalent by 1997, and at least 50 per cent NVQ level 3 by the end of the century, then 54 per cent of sixteen year olds and 37 per cent of seventeen year olds in full time education is an unacceptably low base. This time wasted on valueless testing and the consequential distortions of the curriculum undermine achievement right through from Key Stage 1. Indeed the definition of the curriculum itself in terms of subjects may eventually need to be abandoned. The National Education and Training Targets do however provide an opportunity to identify the nature of the curriculum challenge as well as providing a focus for joint action.

The way forward would seem to be to attempt to secure the National Curriculum, now inchoate and in chaos in the 14–16 age group, and allow it to be clarified. There must be a tidying up of the Key Stage 4 and GCSE arrangements with as little further fragmentation as possible. At present Government policy initiatives are not intended to ensure that the more deeply flawed curriculum confusion post-16 will be resolved. It is dangerous to make assumptions about the future but there has been a stunning silence on the development of the advanced and ordinary diplomas throughout 1992 which it is assumed means that the Government recognises that, as almost everybody suggested in the consultation process, they serve no purpose at all.

Parity of esteem will not be imposed successfully by asserting that 4 GCSEs at National Curriculum level 7 is equivalent to GNVQ or NVQ level 2, or that 2 A levels (at grade E, after a preliminary skirmish at grade C) to GNVQ or NVQ level 3. The only evidence for this parity is that the Government asserts it. There is another interesting devaluation here, less public than the financial one. GCSE at National Curriculum level 7, equivalent to GNVQ and NVQ level 2, includes not only all the grade Cs but also half of the grade Ds in the GCSE. This makes the gap between GNVQ and NVQ level 2 and level 3 enormous, certainly greater than the progress achieved by most A level students. It is recognised that there are real problems of comparability even across NVQs for different occupations, though the insecurity of the comparability of BTEC Nationals even in the same subject area in different colleges will allegedly be phased out. The advanced diploma concept was entirely irrelevant to its original purposes — ensuring that high quality further education or training became the norm, that all round levels of attainment were improved, and increasing the proportion of young people acquiring higher levels of skill and expertise. Government policy appears to be to allow only the vocational route to be available for those unable to achieve A level success, thus devaluing the two alternative vocational routes before the issue of parity is even considered.

NEAB curriculum development

The JMB Examinations Council established a steering group which subsequently incorporated representatives from HMC, who had been making a case for an Intermediate Level examination, GSA, APVIC, SHA and NAHT, to explore the possibility of developing a new curriculum and examination. This would be for students for whom A level was too difficult academically and therefore inappropriate, including those who now fail the examination. Five subject groups devised outline two module one year courses. The five subjects which were worked on were English, history, French, mathematics and physics. There was initially some difficulty in deciding whether the emphasis should be on a one year course which could provide a bridging course to A level, as opposed to a two year course which could lead directly into higher education. It was agreed that the former was more important because that ensured progression more effectively. The alternative at present is a further year taking, sometimes repeating, GCSEs in preparation for attempting A levels. However since the GNVQ structure was being defined during the period of development, it was thought that this might provide an outline modular framework which it would be sensible to match.

SEAC and the Government might not accept such a proposal. There may therefore be no opportunity to take traditional academic subjects for those not capable of taking A levels. Students must concentrate on one of the five general vocational areas now available or others which become available in future. The mandatory units for the GNVQ in manufacturing were: design specification, product design, manufacturing systems, production costs and schedules, process operations, monitor and control, quality and safety, and environmental impact. The four optional units were to be selected from a list which includes: management techniques applied to manufacturing, customer care and computer-integrated manufacture. This 'curriculum' demonstrates that the GNVQ is not particularly general. Students must also reach a specified level in communication, application of number and information technology. There will be pass, merit and distinction grades based on a portfolio of evidence from assignments with supplementary tests. It is clear that such a programme could be as demanding as 2 A levels at grade E. It is not clear however how this will increase the quality of achievement through education or training of the whole cohort. The assumption appears to be that because the course is vocational it will motivate more students.

It would be possible to develop an educational equivalent to the GNVQ, on the assumption that the integrity of A levels is to remain unquestioned. The basic structure of the GNVQs for leisure and tourism, manufacturing, health and care, business and administration, and art and design require the basic twelve units. The twelve units in a general educational qualification might be from several different subjects, as might the possible extension to eighteen units for a full course equivalent to three A levels. The three core skill units, communication, application of number and information technology could similarly be applied within the twelve units. This could provide a basis for entry into higher education for students not capable of achieving academic success through the A level route, particularly if credit can be accumulated.

There seems to be no reason to deny these students the opportunity to study history and/or physics as opposed to manufacturing. Such a course would be no less coherent than the arbitrary choices of A level which are now normal. This argument is about breadth and complementarity, which is used as a reason for AS courses. It might be argued that with appropriate syllabuses the skills that are required in higher education and the world of work might be more successfully taught through this route. A planned coherent educational access route could be developed if we are to retain A levels. This argument would be logical since NVQs in particular are unlikely to be recognised as equivalent to A levels in academic rigour.

A levels actually are about preparation for the world of work, some of them more directly than others. Kenneth Clarke suggested that core skills were not necessary for A level students since they were part of the 16–19 curriculum. The relationship between the A levels and the course of study at university is often somewhat tangential, particularly since many students now are selecting more interesting and less narrowly focused combinations of A levels. At present admissions tutors for higher education are using A levels and BTEC Nationals for selection with little evidence that progression is built in by higher education as part of the induction process. Indeed the relationship between the degree studied and employment afterwards, if obtained, is very frequently even more indirect.

The question of progression after the first degree appears to be significantly less of an issue for these students except for those entering the traditional professions or scientific research. In the end it would seem that A levels, where there is still an excessive emphasis on content, and a degree in a subject not necessarily related either to the A levels or the subsequent employment area is a somewhat idiosyncratic way to explore the raising of standards through improved progression routes. Many graduates however appear to have the strengths of the mind, the heart, the imagination and the will discussed above which employers want. How much more would this be the case if there were any progression and coherence built in at 16 and 18 in particular, but also for lifelong learning and progression.

The Institute of Management is only the latest of many significant organisations in Britain which have called for an end to A level examinations, in order to improve standards, and to ensure there is a coherent 16–19 curriculum. It should be remembered that the gold standard was something we went back on to in 1925 and came off in 1931 when it was realised it was a serious mistake. If you make outmoded and evidently inappropriate assumptions about the value of something, let us say that the pound is worth 2.95 deutschmarks, then the foolishness of your insistence may eventually be revealed. There is usually an increasingly hysterical defence of the status quo until it has to change, as the departure from the Exchange Rate Mechanism demonstrated. In the end the market will not tolerate absurd anachronisms. The anomalous irrelevance will be adjusted. When however A levels are finally changed you may be assured that the Government will take the decision against the advice of the professionals!

The National Commission on Education is examining five key issues in an attempt to define, as part of its brief, educational goals and to assess the potential demand for education and training, in order to meet the economic and social requirements of the country and the needs and aspirations of people throughout their lives. The framework of effective schooling; schools, society and citizenship; the teaching profession and quality; higher and further education in the 21st century; and, preparing for work today and tomorrow, clearly have curriculum implications. The significance of the 14–18 curriculum in the considerations of the National Commission, particularly in terms of proposals for change, has as yet been relatively minor, but it underlies their thinking. Perhaps there does need to be a more direct statement than those in Briefings 3 and 5.

There have been a significant number of high quality proposals for developing the curriculum 16–19 all of which have a considerable amount in common. There would certainly be no significant problem in creating a consensus out of the different proposals of the Institute of Management (IM), the Royal Society (RS), and the Institute for Public Policy Research (IPPR), the Secondary Heads' Association and the Association of Principals of Sixth Form Colleges. The Confederation of British Industry, while recognising that the Government remains committed to A levels, asserts values which complement those proposals described briefly below. The Employment Department's common learning outcomes require all students to be able to solve problems, cope positively with change, communicate effectively and develop effective personal and interpersonal skills (Employment Department 1992). In the context of discussion about A levels and the education service these are skills which might be developed at Government level!

For the Institute of Management:

> The National Qualification should cover six subjects. Students would study at least one subject from four distinct areas and a further two optional subjects. . .The compulsory study areas would be: science and technology; social sciences; arts and creative sciences; and a foreign language. . .The curriculum should be relevant to the needs of people entering both higher education and work; this means combining academic rigour with work and life skills. (BIM, 1992)

The Royal Society's suggestions are somewhat similar:

> An appropriate framework could be based on three separate do-
> mains of study in which skills, competences, relevant knowledge
> and understanding, and common features are developed. The
> three domains are. . .social, economic and industrial domain;
> mathematical and technological domain; and a creative, language
> and aesthetic domain. . .with features including personal and ca-
> reers guidance, work experience and negotiated statement of
> achievement. . .foundations modules from each domain to ensure
> a breadth of background knowledge and skills. . .and advanced
> modules. (The Royal Society 1991)

The Institute for Public Policy Research, arguably from a
different political environment requires similarly:

> three domains of study, with each of three types of module avail-
> able within each domain. . .three types of module. . .core,
> specialist and work/community based. . .Domain A: social and
> human sciences. . .Domain B: natural sciences and
> technology. . .Domain C: arts. languages and literature. . .core
> content, core skills and core processes. (Finegold *et al.* 1990)

'Learning Pays' was the clear understanding reached by Sir
Christopher Ball in his first report for the Royal Society for Arts
(RSA). The reasons 16 year olds decided to abandon education and
training were our culture and attitudes, their confidence being
undermined by the experience of schooling, inappropriate options
and available opportunities, constrained resources, and defects in
the theory and practice of learning. This book suggests that the 14–
19 curriculum is a major contributor to four of these five
impediments to learning.

Conclusion

Britain remains undereducated, undertrained and underqualified.
There is a growing belief that the time has come to take the skills
revolution, lifetime learning and empowering the individual rather
more seriously. The evidence presented in this book demonstrates
that the crucial next step must be to create a curriculum for the 14–
19 age group which ensures that the whole cohort is better
educated and better trained. The haphazard erosion of what might
have become an acceptable curriculum for the 14–16 part of the
whole, and the failure of Government to even consider developing
a curriculum for the 16–19 group which would ensure that there was

coherence means that, despite the rhetoric of world class targets, the curriculum remains appropriate for a third rate nation in gentle decline, clinging on to the absurdities of the elitism and unregulated markets which are undermining the attempts of all those in the education service to raise standards. In the *Observer Second Opinion Column* (11 October 1992) it was suggested that 'It is starting to look as if only a collapse in the international banking system will shock gold out of its torpor'. It is therefore perhaps not too much to hope that, with the gold price gently falling as this book is concluded, the Government might be persuaded to get off the gold standard as an essential prerequisite for the raising of standards.

References

Ball, Sir Christopher *Learning Pays* Royal Society for Arts.

BIM Discussion Paper (1992) *A Level Reform — A Wider Choice.*

Department of Education and Science (1991a) *Choice and Diversity* White Paper, HMSO.

Department of Education and Science (1991b) *Education and Training for the 21st Century.*

Employment Department (1992) *Guidance for Authorities Preparing Proposals for the 16–18 Phase.*

Finegold, D., Keep, E., Miliband, D., Raffe, D., Spours, K., and Young, M. (1990) *A British Baccalaureat* Institute for Public Policy Research.

Lord, E. (1986) *The Whole Curriculum* School Curriculum Development Committee.

Observer (1992) *Second Opinion* 11 October.

The Royal Society (1991) *Beyond GCSE.*

Index